REINTERPRETING EMMET

Reinterpreting Emmet

Essays on the Life and Legacy of Robert Emmet

edited by

ANNE DOLAN
PATRICK M. GEOGHEGAN
and
DARRYL JONES

UNIVERSITY COLLEGE DUBLIN PRESS
PREAS CHOLÁISTE OLLSCOILE
BHAILE ÁTHA CLIATH

First published 2007
by University College Dublin Press
Newman House
86 St Stephen's Green
Dublin 2
Ireland
www.ucdpress.ie

ISBN 978-1-904558-63-7 pb

Cataloguing in Publication data available from the British Library

Typeset in Ireland in Plantin and Fournier
by Elaine Burberry, Bantry, Co. Cork

Text design by Lyn Davies

Printed on acid-free paper in England by
Antony Rowe Ltd, Chippenham, Wiltshire

PG: To my godchildren
Caitlin Geoghegan and Rowan Lawlor

DJ: To Margaret Robson
and Miss Morgan Elizabeth Hannah Jones, aged 11
with love

Contents

REINVENTING EMMET

REFLECTIONS ON EMMET

Contributors to this volume

THOMAS BARTLETT is Professor of Modern Irish History, University College Dublin. His numerous books and collections include *The Fall and Rise of the Irish Nation: The Catholic Question 1690–1830* (1992); *A Military History of Ireland* (1996), and an edition of *The Life of Theobald Wolfe Tone* (1998).

ANNE DOLAN is a lecturer in modern Irish history and deputy director of the Centre for Contemporary Irish History at Trinity College Dublin.

CHARLES FANNING is Professor of English, Southern Illinois University, Carbondale, where he directs the Program in Irish and Irish Immigration Studies. The author of numerous critical essays, he has also written, among other books, *The Irish Voice in America: 250 Years of Irish-American Fiction* (2nd edn, 2000) and *The Exiles of Erin: Nineteenth-Century Irish-American Fiction* (2nd edn, 1997).

PATRICK GEOGHEGAN is a lecturer in modern history at Trinity College Dublin, and author of *Robert Emmet: A Life* (2002).

ADRIAN HARDIMAN is a Justice of the Supreme Court of Ireland.

DARRYL JONES is Senior Lecturer in English and Fellow of Trinity College Dublin. His books include *Horror: A Thematic History in Fiction and Film* (2002), and *Jane Austen* (2004). He has also written numerous articles on eighteenth- and nineteenth-century literature.

SYLVIE KLEINMAN holds an Irish Research Council for the Humanities and Social Sciences Postdoctoral Fellowship in the Department of Modern History at Trinity College Dublin.

W. J. MC CORMACK is Librarian-in-Charge at the Edward Worth Library, Dr Steevens Hospital, Dublin. He was formerly Professor of English at Goldsmiths' College, University of London. Amongst his many books are *From*

Burke to Beckett: Ascendancy, Tradition and Betrayal in Literary History (1985, 1994), and *Blood Kindred: W. B. Yeats, the Life, the Death, the Politics* (2005).

SÉAMUS Ó BUACHALLA formerly taught in the Department of Education, Trinity College Dublin. He is currently working on a biography of Patrick Pearse.

JAMES QUINN is executive editor of the Royal Irish Academy's *Dictionary of Irish Biography*, and the author of *Soul on Fire: A Life of Thomas Russell* (2002).

MAEVE RYAN graduated from Trinity College Dublin in 2005 with a BA in History and English. She recently completed an MPhil in International Relations at the University of Cambridge.

NORMAN VANCE is Professor of English at the University of Sussex. His books include *The Sinews of the Spirit: The Ideal of Christian Manliness in Victorian Literature and Religious Thought* (1985); *The Victorians and Ancient Rome* (1997); *Irish Literature, a Social History: Tradition, Identity and Difference* (1990), 2nd edn (1999); *Irish Literature since 1800* (2002). He is the author of numerous articles and essays, mainly on Victorian and Irish literature and classical and biblical influences on British writing.

PATRICK WALSH is an Irish Research Council for the Humanities and Social Sciences postgraduate scholar at Trinity College Dublin, where he is completing a PhD thesis on the career of Speaker William Conolly (1662–1729).

TIMOTHY WEBB is Winterstoke Professor of English, University of Bristol. His books include *The Violet in the Crucible: Shelley and Translation* (1976); *Shelley: A Voice Not Understood* (1977); *English Romantic Hellenism, 1700–1824* (1982). He has also edited editions of Shelley and Yeats, and published numerous articles on Romanticism and on Irish literature.

Abbreviations

Add. MSS	Additional Manuscripts
AAE	Archives des Affaires Étrangères
BL	British Library
CPA	Corr. Politique, Angleterre
DCU	Dublin City University
DF	Department of Finance
DFA	Department of Foreign Affairs
DNB	*Dictionary of National Biography*
DT	Department of the Taoiseach
EU	European Union
fo.	folio
HO	Home Office (London)
NAI	National Archives of Ireland
NLI	National Library of Ireland
PRONI	Public Records Office Northern Ireland
RIA	Royal Irish Academy
SHA	Service historique de l'Armée
TCD	Trinity College Dublin
TNA	The National Archives, Kew
UCD	University College Dublin

CHAPTER I

Introduction

On 27 January 2004 the Taoiseach, Bertie Ahern, delivered the inaugural Robert Emmet memorial lecture to the College Historical Society in Trinity College Dublin. At the time Ireland held the presidency of the European Union and Ahern used the opportunity to discuss his presidency's theme of 'Europeans – Working Together'. Some protesters attempted to interrupt the proceedings, were quickly ejected by the large security contingent present, and Ahern delivered his address to a packed audience in the largest lecture theatre in the university. In his peroration Ahern connected his thoughts on the EU to his thoughts on Emmet:

> Robert Emmet had his hopes and aspirations two hundred years ago. These hopes were based on ideas of freedom and justice. The realisation of his dream was denied him. Looking around at the freedoms, opportunities and possibilities now available to Irish men and women perhaps, today, he would allow his epitaph to be written.

The speech was received enthusiastically by the students. Ahern brushed over any awkwardness in the relationship between Emmet and Trinity College, the university which had expelled him in 1798. He merely mentioned that some years after 'having abandoned his studies at Trinity, [Emmet] was tried for treason and subsequently hanged'. Trinity College had little to do with Emmet after 1798. But as part of the bicentenary commemoration of Robert Emmet's rebellion and death, a lecture theatre in the Arts Block was renamed the Robert Emmet Theatre. There was also a major exhibition on Emmet's life in the Old Library, and a major international symposium. Emmet's rehabilitation in Trinity was complete.

The story of Robert Emmet's life, death, and immediate elevation into the pantheon of Irish nationalist heroes probably needs no repeating here. He was born on 4 March 1778 at his parent's home on St Stephen's Green, beside what is now the Fitzwilliam Hotel. Educated locally, he entered Trinity College Dublin in 1793 and excelled at oratory, especially in the College Historical Society. Awaiting graduation in 1798, he was expelled as part of the infamous

Visitation to eradicate United Irishmen treason in the college. He was not involved directly in the 1798 rebellion, and afterwards was given a position of responsibility within the United Irishmen as it attempted to plan for a final, desperate effort against British rule. Travelling to the continent in 1800, he met with various French leaders, before returning to Ireland in the autumn of 1802 with some plans for a future insurrection. His rebellion, planned for 23 July 1803, proved to be an embarrassing failure. The men he had expected never arrived, the money he needed never materialised. Naïve, impetuous, and over-reliant on unreliable technology, Emmet abandoned the city as his rising degenerated into a vicious riot on the streets of Dublin. Captured soon afterwards he was tried for high treason on 19 September 1803. It was here that he won an unlikely victory of sorts with his powerful speech from the dock, a speech which held out the demand for his epitaph to remain unwritten until Ireland had taken its place among the nations of the earth. As Emmet insisted in his peroration:

> I have but one request to ask at my departure from this world: it is *the charity of its silence*. Let no man write my epitaph; for as no man who knows my motives dares now vindicate them, let not prejudice or ignorance asperse them. Let them rest in obscurity and peace: my memory be left in oblivion and my tomb remain uninscribed, until other times and other men can do justice to my character. When my country takes her place among the nations of the earth, then, and not till then, let my epitaph be written. I have done.

Found guilty and sentenced to death, Emmet was hanged and then beheaded at St Catherine's Church, Thomas Street, the next day. He showed no fear on the scaffold and seemed deliberately to be setting an heroic example for future generations. Ever since he has continued to inspire, infuriate, unite and divide.

As the bicentenary of Emmet's death approached, the meaning of his life and legacy was debated in Dáil Éireann. On Wednesday 12 March 2003 Joe Higgins, Socialist Party leader, asked the Taoiseach if commemoration was entirely appropriate given that 'Robert Emmet rose up prematurely and tragically against landlordism' and that now 'English landlordism had been replaced by almost as virulent a form of Irish landlordism which makes life extremely difficult for people trying to put a roof over their heads and trying to live a decent life'. The Taoiseach's response was uncompromising: 'I do not agree with anything Deputy Higgins says on this issue.' When pressed, he added, 'the deputy has asked me what I think of Robert Emmet. I think a great deal of him . . . I do not consider that Emmet rose up against landlordism because that was not his aim in the rebellion.'

Trevor Sargent, the leader of the Green Party, was also concerned with the problem of commemoration. He wondered if

> Robert Emmet might not be all that keen to have his life commemorated because it was not his life that he valued rather the objectives for which he stood and died? . . . The widening gap between rich and poor indicates to me that Robert Emmet would probably prefer not to be commemorated. This nation has not yet fulfilled his objectives for a fair republic where everybody is treated equally. I suggest that should be the focus of the commemoration rather than giving some kind of sentimental history lesson which will miss the point of why Robert Emmet died.

But again the Taoiseach was not convinced and dismissed the question. However, his final comments were interesting not only for what they revealed about his own views on Emmet but also for how he saw the planned commemorative events in 2003: 'People always remember the one line of Robert Emmet's speech but there is far more to the man than that one line about his epitaph.' The range of events which took place in 2003, the publications, the debates, the documentaries, the exhibitions, the parades, the criticisms and the tributes, would seem to have vindicated his confidence.

This collection of essays has its origins in the Robert Emmet Symposium which was held in Trinity College Dublin on 10–12 September 2003. But it also goes beyond it, bringing together some other perspectives and interpretations. The essays are divided into three sections. In the first, 'Revisiting Emmet', we offer a new perspective on some of the key events from 1803. Thomas Bartlett provides a new look at Dublin Castle intelligence in this period which has important implications for how we view the rebellion. James Quinn looks at the revolutionary ideology of Thomas Russell and builds upon his published biography to provide a new insight into one of the key figures of the rebellion. Patrick Walsh looks at the British politician Charles James Fox, whose brother was commander of the forces in Ireland in 1803, and reveals a startling new perspective on an aspect of the story which has previously been ignored by historians. Maeve Ryan looks at William Plunket, the friend of the Emmet family who assisted the prosecution at the trial of Robert Emmet. The Plunket papers, long ignored by historians, are used to reveal a nuanced portrayal of Plunket who has long been a victim of nationalist myth and hysteria.

Emmet's legacy, his long and continuing afterlife, is in some ways even more striking than his brief but eventful life. The second section, 'Reinventing Emmet', looks at some of the ways in which Emmet insinuated himself posthumously into the cultural imagination, in Ireland, in Britain, and in the USA. Timothy Webb's essay looks at Emmet's rebellion through the lens of English Jacobinism: his analysis of the Irish connections informing and paralleling the life and work of William Godwin provides, we believe, an extraordinarily detailed context in which to understand the interrelatedness of Anglo-Irish radicalism at this time. Perhaps most dramatically of all, Emmet's shade crossed the Atlantic, had his name recast as 'Robert Emmett', and became the most potent of all icons for Irish-American identity. It is this figure that is analysed in the essays by Charles Fanning and Patrick M. Geoghegan. Fanning concentrates on the endurance of Emmet in Irish-American popular cultural forms, where his presence becomes a kind of necessary signifier of cultural belonging, while Geoghegan looks at the ways in which Emmet's name and legacy were deployed and often 'hijacked by politicians attempting to make their own point'. Returning to Ireland, Norman Vance's essay considers the ways in which Irish Revival and Modernist writers engaged often critically with Emmet's ideological and cultural presence. Maintaining this sceptical attitude to the implications of Emmet's legacy, Anne Dolan concludes this section by arguing that the real significance of Emmet and his actions has been 'lost' as a consequence of generations of sentimental hagiography, in Ireland and America.

The third section, 'Reflections on Emmet', takes a rather different tone from the rest of the volume. Here, three distinguished commentators write, often personally and polemically, on what Emmet has come to mean to them. The first two essays in this section draw parallels and contrasts between Emmet and other major figures in the Irish national pantheon. Séamas Ó Buachalla draws on Emmet to offer a robust rebuttal of revisionist interpretations of the life and career of Patrick Pearse, while W. J. Mc Cormack examines the 'parallel roles' of Emmet and Roger Casement in 'the revolutionary period of 1798–1803 and the insurrectionary period of 1916–1923'. We conclude the volume by returning to the trial itself – Adrian Hardiman, a prominent contemporary jurist, provides the definitive answer to the question of whether or not Emmet received a fair trial.

* * *

Our thanks are due to all the people who contributed to the success of the Robert Emmet Symposium. We are particularly grateful to Professor David Dickson, the chair of the organising committee, for his enthusiasm and determination, and the other members who brought their own expertise to proceedings: Dr Kevin Rockett, Dr Jim Livesey, Dr Philip McEvanesoya, and Dr Charles Benson. We would also like to thank all the people who spoke at the symposium but who have not, for various reasons, been able to contribute to this volume: Professor Marianne Elliott, Tom Paulin, Dr Kevin Rockett, Dr Chris Morash, Ruth Ní Eidhin, Dr Ruan O'Donnell, Professor Fintan Cullen, Pat Murphy, Professor John Kelly, Dr Ronan Kelly, Dr Claire Connolly and Professor Luke Gibbons. We would also like to Mrs Justice Susan Denham who chaired one of the key sessions in the old House of Lords, College Green, and the members of the Supreme Court who attended the events. Tommy Graham and *History Ireland* also supported the symposium and the Robert Emmet issue which they published at the time made an excellent contribution to the debate. The Provost, Dr John Hegarty, was an enthusiastic supporter of the symposium and we are grateful to him and the College for the enormous contribution towards making it a success. We also benefited from a generous grant from Emmet 200, the commemoration group sponsored by the government, and we would like to thank Brian Ó Cleirigh for his consistent support. Two key sponsors were Robert Emmett's Bar and Restaurant, in New York City, and the Fitzwilliam Hotel, right beside Emmet's birthplace in Dublin, which provided accommodation for our speakers and a wonderful conference dinner. We would also like to thank Barry O'Kelly and Bank of Ireland for kindly providing the excellent venue of the old House of Lords for one of our key sessions. Finally, we would like to thank Barbara Mennell and the staff at UCD Press for their patience and support in guiding this publication along every stage.

The bicentenary commemoration of Robert Emmet's death produced a range of events, conferences and publications, which served to inspire, infuriate and inform. We hope this book will do the same.

ANNE DOLAN
PATRICK M. GEOGHEGAN
DARRYL JONES

REVISITING EMMET

CHAPTER I

'The cause of treason seems to have gone out of fashion in Ireland'

Dublin Castle and Robert Emmet

Thomas Bartlett

The roots of Emmet's rebellion of 1803 can be traced directly to the failed rebellion of 1798, and to the lessons that were learned from that failure. In early 1799, reports came into Dublin Castle that 'a new [United Irish] Directory is formed or forming and that the lower classes are kept in a constant state of readiness for insurrection'. Initially, government suspicion focussed on the so-called State Prisoners, those United Irish leaders currently incarcerated in Kilmainham gaol, for there were reports that despite their confinement they were 'actively employed in keeping up the rebellion'.[1] However, it soon became clear that Robert Emmet, younger brother to Thomas Addis Emmet, then in prison, was the chief person behind the new subversive organisation. Castlereagh gave orders for 'young Emmet' to be arrested in May 1799, but he eluded his pursuers and fled the country to France.[2] Emmet had concluded from the failure of the 1798 rebellion that any future organisation had to be structured on a much simpler, less elaborate footing; that only those who had proved their worth in that rebellion should be brought into it; and that all proceedings had to be conducted with the utmost secrecy. The oath-bound, mass-based, nationwide and complex organisation of the United Irishmen, which had shown itself to be both unwieldy and easily penetrated by informers, was to be eschewed in favour of a compact, tightly-knit, elite band of trusted rebels who would focus primarily on the city of Dublin.

In Paris, Emmet began discussions with the French authorities with a view to securing military assistance for another insurrection in Ireland. It seems clear that, despite signals to the contrary, Talleyrand, French foreign minister, had no serious interest in a military expedition to Ireland; and it is likely that he was playing a double game – encouraging Emmet with his plans for insurrection in order to put pressure on the British government to conclude a peace with France. With the Treaty of Amiens duly signed between Great Britain and France in March 1802, Emmet saw that there could be no prospect of French military assistance and he returned to Ireland, arriving there in October 1802.

In Ireland, Emmet made contact with, among others, Michael Quigley, the Kildare United Irish leader, James 'Jemmy' Hope, the northern revolutionary then domiciled in Dublin, Miles Byrne, the youthful veteran of the Wexford rising, and Michael Dwyer, the Wicklow insurgent who had been conducting a little war or *guerilla* in the Wicklow mountains since 1798. It says much for Emmet's strong personality, personal charisma and seriousness of purpose that these seasoned veterans of the 1798 rebellion were prepared to fit in with his plans to stage another rising and to yield the leadership to one who was much their junior in years and military experience.

Emmet's plan appears to have been devised over the winter months of 1802–3, and in March 1803 he set about implementing it. His plan was breathtakingly simple. Dublin Castle, poorly defended and with its gates always open, was to be seized in a surprise attack, and the contents of its arsenal, reputedly well stocked, distributed to his followers. Then, with the symbol of British power in Ireland in rebel hands, the adjacent counties of Kildare and Wicklow and, further afield, Antrim and Down under Thomas Russell, would rise out in rebellion. We may note that though war had been resumed between France and Great Britain in May 1803, Emmet had no expectation of, or reliance on, French military assistance.

Emmet had inherited some £2,000 on the death of his father in 1802 and he used this money to purchase weapons, gunpowder for his rockets, and to rent safe houses close to Dublin Castle wherein his clandestine preparations for rebellion could take place. The Castle was entirely ignorant of these activities, and all might have proceeded as planned but for an accidental explosion and fire on 16 July 1803 in one of Emmet's arms depots in Thomas Street. One man was killed and another seriously wounded. The incident alerted the authorities that something untoward was afoot, but they still did not realise the seriousness of the situation. Emmet, however, could take no chances and hastily brought forward his rising to Saturday 23 July. Hope and Russell were dispatched north to raise Antrim and Down; Michael Quigley's Kildare rebels were deputed to be in the vanguard of the assault on the Castle; while Michael Dwyer, more prudent, would only promise assistance when he should see the rebel flag flying over Dublin Castle. Emmet prepared himself for the great day by taking possession of a gorgeous green uniform, trimmed with gold braid.

The events of 23 July have been well described by Emmet's recent biographers and only a brief summary is required here.[3] Almost nothing went to plan, and as the day unfolded confusion, chaos and mayhem reigned. The Castle was not seized, and after some hours of milling about, the rebellion fizzled out in the Thomas Street area, though not before an unlucky Lord Kilwarden, lord chief justice, his nephew and a handful of army officers, were slain in the streets around the Castle. A dejected Emmet had already fled the scene before Kilwarden was killed. After a period in hiding, he was arrested on 25 August while visiting his sweetheart, Sarah Curran. He was tried on 19 September 1803, and executed the following day.

Many questions arise from this brief narrative of Emmet's rebellion. What were his ultimate objectives? Could he have succeeded? Given his inglorious failure, whence derived his reputation as pre-eminent in the Irish pantheon of republican martyr/heroes. These and other matters are addressed by other contributors in this volume. Here, the focus is on a single question: why was Dublin Castle so completely taken unawares by Emmet's rebellion? Even after the premature explosion and fire in the Thomas Street depot, the Castle was oblivious to what was being planned in the Liberties of Dublin, barely half a mile from its (wide-open) gates. In the years before the 1798 rebellion the Castle had an enviable (or sinister) reputation for running informers, infiltrating agents into subversive organisations, and general intelligence-gathering. Yet in July 1803, contrary to the heated denials of Lord Hardwicke, Lord Redesdale and William Wickham, respectively viceroy, lord chancellor and chief secretary, it was evident to well-placed observers that the Castle, 'lulled into a false sense of security' had been taken 'by surprise' by a rebellion that was 'certainly unexpected', and on which 'no intelligence' had been received beforehand.[4] How could this have happened?

I

One essential context within which to examine Dublin Castle's apparent intelligence failure in 1803 is that provided by the devastating defeat inflicted on the United Irish rebels in 1798. Many thousands had been slain in battle, and many hundreds more executed, imprisoned, exiled to the United States, transported to Australia or shipped off to the Prussian army. Even the most bloodthirsty loyalists, despite their loud protests at Lord Cornwallis's alleged 'leniency', derived some reassurance from the knowledge that a dreadful drubbing had been meted out to the rebels. 'The former lesson to rebels [i.e. the Williamite wars, 1688–91]', Sir John Hort remarked grimly to his friend Sir James Caldwell, 'held by my computation about 100 years . . . ; that to which you and the other gentlemen of Ireland have so nobly contributed will I trust serve them for the whole of the century which is to finish with AD 2000'.[5]

In addition to battlefield defeat, there was for the rebels the sickening realisation that their organisation had been from an early date beset by treachery and betrayal by those who were among the most trusted with its secrets. The Leinster directory had been betrayed by Francis Magan, Lord Edward FitzGerald's whereabouts had been divulged by Thomas Reynolds, the Down United Irishmen's organisation had been revealed by Nicholas Mageean, the United Irishmen's 'partnership' with the French had been detailed by Samuel Turner, and their legal defences and routine chit-chat had been assiduously passed on to Dublin Castle by one of the chief barristers who acted for them, Leonard MacNally. The publicity given to these betrayals – or to some of them, for others were to remain hidden for decades – was scarcely calculated to encourage among the rebels the desire for another rising. Moreover, the decision taken by the so-called State Prisoners, those leading United Irishmen in prison since before the rebellion, to reveal their plans to government in return for exile rather than execution had proved controversial and demoralising. True, the State Prisoners would not be released from the military prison in which they were held at Fort George in Scotland until peace had been settled with France in March 1802; but for the lesser fry facing execution, or imprisoned in the hulks or awaiting a prison ship to Australia, it must have seemed as if they had been betrayed by the leaders who had saved their own skins. Lord Cornwallis, the lord lieutenant, and Lord Clare, the lord chancellor (for once in agreement with each other), had calculated that if the State Prisoners, in return for their lives being spared, were to make a full statement of their subversive activities, such a disclosure would sow dissension and sap morale among their less elevated comrades, and so it had proved. After his capture in August 1803, Emmet was offered his life in return for a full statement of guilt along the lines of that agreed to by the State Prisoners of 1798, but he scorned the offer.

Two other developments since 1798 may also be noted as contributing to the initial context within which to view the Castle's 'intelligence failure' in 1803. The first of these was the dramatic turnaround in opinion among the Presbyterians in the north. Ulster, particularly east Ulster, had been the engine of disaffection in the 1790s, and there had been a creditable turnout in the summer of 1798, but thereinafter radicalism, let alone disaffection, had cooled appreciably. Whether produced by disillusion at Bonaparte's treatment of Switzerland or driven by the attractions of a pan-Protestant Orangeism, or dictated by the absence through death, imprisonment or exile of the old radical leadership cadre, or by a combination of all three, radical Presbyterians and radical Presbyterianism ceased to embrace disaffection in the aftermath of the 1798 rebellion. Reports of Catholic atrocities in Wexford and elsewhere, assiduously collected and published, also allegedly had a dramatic effect on Presbyterian opinion. Sir Richard Musgrave, prime exponent of the rebellion-as-Popish-Plot thesis, remarked to a correspondent that 'the sanguinary designs which they [Irish Catholics] schemed during the late rebellion against

Protestants of every description have completely detached the Presbyterians from them, and the latter are now loyal'.[6] In the north-east, noted one army officer in 1799, the old radical leadership is merely 'a rope of sand – here and there a particle, but without power'.[7] And from within what remained of the United Irish organisation in the north-east, an informer reported in July 1799: 'I consider rebellion so completely put down and communication so effectually cut off that the country [i.e. Antrim and Down] could not be brought to act' even if there were an invasion and 'not even then, except well assured of a considerable force'.[8]

Again, the fundamental weakness of the United Irish–French alliance had been revealed by the extremely poor French performance at the time of the rebellion and after. A number of small raiding parties, dispatched after the rebellion was over, only one of which managed to get ashore (at Killala, under General Humbert), scarcely seemed an adequate recompense for all the promises of extensive French military assistance. And, of course, the ensuing negotiations between the French and the British, concluded at Amiens in March 1802, had offered precisely nothing to the United Irishmen, indeed they had been fortunate not to be expelled by the French as part of the peace terms. To those in Dublin Castle charged with the defence of Ireland, the only conceivable danger after 1798 could come from a French expedition, and by 1802 there was almost no prospect of that.

2

The second context for understanding the Castle's apparent 'intelligence failure' in 1803 is that offered by the Act of Union and the new order which it promised to usher in. And here we must remember that apart from its legislative details, and its economic and religious provisions, union between Great Britain and Ireland was heralded as a major counter-revolutionary instrument. Just as the United Irishmen and their French allies had sought to prise Ireland and Great Britain apart, so union was perceived as the prefect riposte to the separatists. There would henceforth be one kingdom, not kingdoms, separation would be impossible, it would disappear from the political agenda, and with it, any prospect of Irish revolution.

Moreover, the arguments that had been advanced in favour of union, and the predictions made as to how Ireland would benefit from it, had been so categorical, so insistent and so optimistic, that that measure had, on the pro-Union side, become a panacea for all Irish ills. Those jealousies that had bedevilled Anglo-Irish relations would be removed at a stroke; English capital, English manners and English industry would flow into Ireland; talented Irishmen would find careers in the revitalised British empire; a new impartial legislature would convene in London and deal soberly and fairly with those knotty problems – of religion, education, tithes, even clerical salaries – that the old Irish parliament had been unable or unwilling to address. Above all, a mild government, resolutely embracing 'British standards' and acting on 'Union principles', a government that would be paternal, not repressive, acting in an even-handed, not one-sided way, would be instituted in post-Union Ireland.[9] In this way, the perceived evils of Ireland – endemic violence, sectarian divisions, chronic poverty, widespread disaffection, and bankrupt institutions run by failed politicians – all of which were inextricably linked with *ancien régime* Ireland, would quickly fade from view under the new dispensation ushered in by union.[10]

This new spirit infusing post-Union government in Ireland soon brought results. The draconian Insurrection Act of 1796, which had effectively abolished all rights at common law, was allowed to lapse, and so too was the act putting on hold *habeas corpus*: such legislation belonged to the repressive past, and was now out of place in that new country, post-Union Ireland. Charles Abbot, the first post-Union chief secretary, was determined to free Irish government from 'Irish animosities, prejudices and corruptions', and he grandly announced that the 'profligacy of Ireland before the Union', a condition he believed brought on by 'the looseness of Irish morals' was at an end.[11] What this meant in practice was that those who had formerly been key members of the viceroy's 'cabinet' at Dublin Castle – men such as John Beresford, Lord Clare and John Foster – now found themselves cold-shouldered. John Beresford's tenure as the long-term head of the Irish Revenue Board came under scrutiny, and an investigation into his handling of his office was got under way. Not surprisingly, an outraged Beresford denounced such scrutiny by a 'vain, silly man' [Abbot] as variously 'contemptible', 'offensive' and 'injudicious'.[12] John Foster, the former speaker of the Irish House of Commons, given his resolute opposition to union, could scarcely have expected to be welcomed back to the Castle with open arms. Still, the continued elevation of his rival, Isaac Corry, as chancellor of the Irish exchequer, was galling, and so too were cutbacks in the Yeomanry service, one of Foster's hobby-horses.[13] Foster was quickly put in his place and informed that while his support for administration was welcome, he would not be permitted to 'get up on the coachbox' much less allowed 'to govern Ireland'.[14] As for Lord Clare, 'mainspring of Union', he too was shunned: his legal recommendations were ignored,[15] and it was made clear that his customary advice, along the lines of 'the mass of the people are disaffected and ripe for revolt', was entirely unwelcome.[16] More forthright than Beresford and Foster, Clare denounced Hardwicke as entirely under the thumb of his chaplain, Dr Lindsay, described Charles Abbot as 'the most arrogant, presumptuous, empty-headed prig I ever met or heard of', and revealed that he was 'bitterly disappointed in [his] expectations of the consequences that ought naturally to have resulted from Union'.[17] When Clare died in January 1802, Hardwicke's immediate reaction was one of good riddance, and he agreed with his brother's characterisation of him as 'a man calculated for times of trouble, difficulty and danger', someone who, regrettably, was 'little adapted for quieter moments when *a vigour beyond the law* [*sic*] was become unnecessary and hurtful'.[18]

It was a similar story when Abbot was replaced as chief secretary by William Wickham in February 1802. Wickham immediately announced his intention of doing away 'with jobbery and the old system', and declared his conviction that no Irish politician, 'even the best', could be trusted, for they would 'one and all desert like rats in a sinking ship'.[19] He dismissed as exaggerated reports of agrarian disorder in counties Limerick and Tipperary by claiming that 'there is nothing of rebellion in them nor even anything of religion', and he steadfastly resisted calls for the deployment of the Yeomanry on 'permanent duty, meaning only that they should receive permanent pay', for such a demand was an essential part of that 'system of jobbing' by local vested interests that he was determined to end.[20]

With such men at the helm in Dublin Castle, there was no disposition to accept and act on reports of subversion in the country; nor indeed to seek out intelligence on the disaffected. The rebels had been crushed in 1798, Great Britain was now at peace with France, and those Irish politicians sending in reports of disturbances, and darkly hinting at a wider conspiracy, could not be other than discredited alarmists playing their old game for their own purposes. Alexander Marsden, under-secretary in Dublin Castle, had little patience with them. Initially, he purported to be amused by such alarmist reports. For example, in January 1803 he ridiculed Prendergast Smith's warning that Tipperary town might be soon sacked by insurgents, and he rolled his eyes at the predicted consequences – 'his china would be broken and his favourite ladies all Lord knows what'.[21] Two months later, however, he was less indulgent: further reports of imminent disturbances led him to conclude that 'it is a sad thing that we are forever to be duped in this vile country'.[22]

In any case, so far as Dublin Castle was concerned, matters appeared to be improving in Ireland in the few years after the Union. True, there had been a major food shortage in the years 1800–1, but the Castle had responded energetically to the crisis by offering a bounty on the importation of American corn, and in any case, dearth had pre-dated union.[23] Similarly, while the opening years of the new century had indeed witnessed agrarian disturbances in Galway, Tipperary, Waterford and Limerick, and elsewhere, such disturbances had begun before union and, as noted above, official opinion was adamant that wretchedness, not disaffection lay behind them.[24] Edward Cooke, soon to resign over the failure to grant Catholic emancipation, wrote: 'I do not believe [the disturbances] originate so much from disaffection as distress of the lower classes', while even the tough-minded General Sir James Duff, on duty in Limerick, attributed the unrest there to 'the wretched situations of the lower orders of the people'.[25]

In other areas, the high hopes held out by those most in favour of union seemed to be well on their way to being met within a short period. In August 1801, Castlereagh congratulated Hardwicke on 'the present tranquillity of Ireland' and cooed that 'the Union has already discharged the public mind of a greater portion of the political mischief which has incessantly disturbed it for the last twenty-five years than its most sanguine friend could have expected'.[26] Encouragingly, Irish revenue, stagnant before the Union, was 'beyond expectation flourishing' by August 1802, and British ministers were not slow to claim credit for the £800,000 surplus which had opened up.[27] Of course, union had not solved every problem: Castlereagh, in praising the good effects of union was careful to add that there still remained 'one great question which can hereafter produce any particular fermentation', but even here, he was satisfied that in the matter of their emancipation, the good sense of the Catholic leaders would prevail.[28]

In short, those in charge of government in post-Union Ireland were determined that there would be no going back to the bad old ways (as they saw them) of Ireland-before-the-Union. The principal features of that country – jobbery, corruption, sectarianism, repressive legislation, and alarmist reports stressing the ineradicable nature of Irish disaffection and religious hatred – would steadily be eliminated as 'British standards' were relentlessly applied. Allegations of subversion, insurrection, popish plots, French emissaries, imminent massacres and the like were to be treated with scepticism, if not incredulity, and regarded as a symptom of how much had yet to be done in healing the public mind in Ireland, rather than as evidence of a deep-laid conspiracy there. Given this mindset, and given their evident mistrust of all those who had been involved in pre-Union Irish politics, it was probably inevitable that the new men in Dublin Castle would miss some clues concerning the activities of Robert Emmet and his co-conspirators.

3

Emmet's rebellion constituted, in the final analysis, an intelligence failure on the part of Dublin Castle; and yet, on the face of it, this conclusion seems puzzling. Throughout the 1790s, the Castle's spy network, ably conducted by Edward Cooke, had won a reputation for ubiquity and omniscience. Such a reputation might not have been entirely merited – the French expedition to Bantry Bay caught the Castle by surprise, and so too did the rebellion in Wexford. None the less, the Castle, and its numerous and well-placed spies, informers and informants, did record major successes against the disaffected in the run-up to the rebellion, with the result that when the rebellion broke out most of the established leaders of the conspiracy were either in gaol or dead. In any discussion of the reasons for the rebellion's failure, the fact that most of the United Irishmen's secrets were, *or were believed to be*, in the hands of government should be given prominence. Moreover, William Wickham, the chief secretary at the time of Emmet's rebellion, was no mere bureaucrat. He had been Pitt's spymaster in the 1790s, at the very centre of British counter-intelligence in Europe, and he had been very well briefed on the continental plans of Irish subversives.[29] Surely he, of all men, would have been alert to the need for continued surveillance and intelligence-gathering.

In fact, the reality was quite different, for in the years after 1798, the Castle's spy-network had undergone a huge reduction. Partly this was a result of what we may call natural wastage: a number of its key agents had died (Francis Higgins, Edward Newell), left Ireland (Thomas Collins, William Bird, possibly Captain Andrew MacNevin) or had had their cover blown through testifying in open court or otherwise (Nicholas Mageean, Thomas Reynolds, John Hughes). Again, its prime agent on the continent, Samuel Turner, appears to have assumed that with the signing of the Peace of Amiens, his services were no longer required. Similarly, Samuel Sproule, a very effective spy in Dublin from 1798 to 1800, subsequently took himself off to London where he dabbled in currency reform. Of the remaining agents who had been active in the pre-Union period, only Francis Magan, Leonard MacNally ('JW'), and James McGucken continued to supply the Castle with intelligence. Magan, a Dublin barrister, became something of a recluse after the death of his handler, Francis Higgins, in January 1802, and largely confined his information to Catholic politics. MacNally, a barrister, continued to emphasise his connection with long-standing radical, James Napper Tandy, then in Paris, and to ply the Castle with information gathered while he was out on the Munster circuit. McGucken, a solicitor based in Belfast, kept the Castle informed of developments among the remnants of the United Irish in the north-east.[30]

Consideration will be given presently to the value of the information McGucken and MacNally sent in, but first it is clear that those agents from the 1790s who for one reason or another stopped gathering intelligence for Dublin Castle after 1800 were not replaced. Not only were substitutes not recruited, but there was a dramatic cutback in the amount of money paid out for information: a secret service bill that was running at around £13,000 p.a. between 1797 and 1801 was ruthlessly pared back to just over £3,000 p.a. (mostly for pre-Union commitments) between October 1801 and July 1803.[31] The inevitable result was that much of what passed for intelligence reports in the years before Emmet's rebellion was little more than angry, occasionally piteous, epistles from impoverished informers complaining of neglect, recalling past services and demanding adequate recompense.[32] In addition, just as the Castle apparently saw no need to recruit replacements, so too it seemed determined in the early years of the century to get rid of the agents that still remained on its books. The Boyle brothers, Thomas and Edward, had remained active after 1800, and two payments were made to them, one for 30 guineas in July 1800 and another for £200 in December 1802: but since the amounts were described in the ledger as 'in full discharge of services' and 'in full of all claims' respectively, we may surmise that these were seen as a final settling of their accounts.[33] It was a similar story with Samuel Turner, far and away the most valuable informer among the United Irishmen in France and Hamburg in the late 1790s. Seemingly no longer of use when the Peace of Amiens was being negotiated, he wrote to the Home Secretary (and former chief secretary in Ireland, 1795–8), Lord Pelham, complaining of neglect. On the back of his letter someone, possibly Pelham's clerk, has scribbled: 'to enquire who Mr Turner is and what was his connexion with government'.[34] Then, when the Peace of Amiens was breaking down, Turner made further contact with British diplomats in Paris, but he received a cool reception. James Talbot, the *chargé d'affaires* there, wrote to his former colleague, Wickham, that 'a Mr Turner – I think he says he comes from Newry and who subsequently lived in Hamburg where he says he was employed by the British government – offered his services as a spy shortly after our arrival, but he is such an impudent and suspicious-looking fellow that we would have nothing to do with him'.[35] It was a similar story with Sproule: on his return to Dublin from London in 1801, he appears to have been told that his services were no longer required.[36] The inescapable conclusion is that in post-Union Ireland, the Boyle brothers, Turner, Sproule and others like them, were viewed as more of an embarrassment than an asset by the Castle. Informers and spies were regarded as distasteful products of that inexhaustible Irish 'capacity for rapacity' held to have characterised pre-Union Ireland, and which, under the new dispensation, was no longer to be indulged but, rather, ruthlessly curtailed.

Moreover, if spies were in short supply after the Union, so too were spymasters. Edward Cooke had controlled the Castle's espionage network of the 1790s, but while he had been, as he modestly put it, 'not unsuccessful' in his efforts to gain intelligence on the United Irishmen, his sudden resignation and departure from Ireland in 1801 had thrown the entire information-gathering apparatus into disarray.[37] Agents felt abandoned by one to whom they had looked for reward, and because Cooke had kept so much intelligence in his head, rather than consign it to paper, there was to be no seamless transfer of office. Marsden, Cooke's successor, was criticised in the aftermath of Emmet's rebellion for being frankly 'incredulous' at reports of conspiracies. Admittedly, when war had resumed between Britain and France in March 1803, he had dismissed as bogus all 'reports of plots and meetings', explaining,

'I discover so many of these reports to be fabrications or upon insufficient surmises that it is impossible any evil of serious extent can be concealed'.[38] In addition, he had drawn further comfort from the fact that 'a separation has taken place between Catholics and Protestants which, however to be lamented in respect of the general welfare of this country, will work materially for us in case of Ireland becoming a seat of war'.[39] All in all, Marsden had concluded complacently, 'the cause of treason seems to have gone out of fashion in Ireland'.[40] And as we have seen, there had been little appetite on ideological grounds for continuing, much less expanding, the 'dirty war' of the 1790s.

Again, the appointment of Pitt's spymaster, William Wickham, as Abbot's successor, in reality had little impact on the Castle's intelligence-gathering capacity. Wickham had not sought a position in Ireland, and had only taken the chief secretaryship (for which he was almost entirely unqualified)[41] because his activities in the 1790s had made him unwelcome in the major courts of Europe (neither Vienna nor Berlin would touch him). With hindsight, it may be suggested that Wickham was suffering from 'burn-out' as a result of his espionage operations on the continent, and that Ireland was attractive to him precisely because it appeared to offer him a quiet berth and a modest recompense rather than a scene for yet more cloak-and-dagger work.

To this picture of an administration that viewed with some distaste the grubbier features of British rule in Ireland, and which apparently believed that subversion and disaffection were almost entirely features of pre-Union Ireland, we may add the significant detail of strained relations between the London and Dublin governments in the early years of the Union. To an extent, problems of jurisdiction were inevitable, given that the Union had been put through with very little thought accorded to the administrative arrangements that would follow it. But Pelham, the former Irish chief secretary, appointed Home Secretary in July 1801, made matters worse by his domineering manner and, it seems, by his inefficiency.[42] Pelham had immediately clashed with Charles Abbot over their respective areas of authority, and he had continued the quarrel when Wickham was selected as Abbot's successor. Pelham's dilatory ways compounded the problem. The result was a frosty silence between London and Dublin in the years before Emmet's rebellion. Hardwicke was moved to complain of the 'very remarkable . . . want of efficiency and indeed of common attention in Lord Pelham's office',[43] while, revealingly, Wickham himself protested to Lord Eldon, the lord chancellor, at the lack of secret information coming into Dublin from 'your side of the water'. He revealed to Eldon in November 1802 that he had received almost no information on 'what our banished traitors are about in France and Germany, of all of which we used formerly to keep this government [Dublin] so very well informed', and he recalled that when he was in charge of espionage in the 1790s 'I never sat down to my dinner without fully informing Lord Castlereagh of everything that had passed that could in any way affect the cause of the disaffected in Ireland or throw the remotest light on their proceedings.'[44] In short, even if the Home Office had uncovered intelligence of Emmet's intentions, given the strained relations between it and the Castle, there could be no guarantee that this information would have been speedily passed on (or heeded). And of course, as was pointed out later, in these matters of foreign intelligence, Dublin Castle had no option but to rely entirely on London because 'the Irish government has no foreign ministers or foreign agents of any description and [has] . . . no means of obtaining intelligence of anything happening abroad'.[45]

Nor did the domestic information that the Castle had coming in from its two prime agents, Leonard MacNally (JW) and James McGucken, give rise to any concern, much less alarm. MacNally, had acted as an informer for Dublin Castle since 1795, and as a leading barrister frequently called upon to defend subversives, he appeared very well placed to discover what, if any, plans were afoot.[46] His letters in the months and years before July 1803 were almost entirely reassuring. In May 1801, he reported that he, 'in the minutest manner, inquired from all whom I suppose to have knowledge of the business [i.e. subversion], and I am persuaded from their reports that the spirit of disaffection sleeps'.[47] A month later, he revealed that the 'principal subject of conversation among our friends [i.e. subversives]' was the likelihood of a French invasion of Ireland launched from Galicia in Spain, quite an impossible undertaking.[48] In April 1802, he remarked reassuringly that 'the spirit of rebellion is completely suppressed and that even a wish to renew it does not exist'. At the same time, he wrote that, again following the 'most minute enquiry', he could find no hint of a rebellious spirit and, encouragingly, he added that the Irish in Paris were fighting among themselves and complaining of French government neglect.[49] In November, MacNally reported a whisper that something was afoot among the rebels in Paris and that Thomas Addis Emmet (not Robert) was behind it: but this news was not followed up.[50] As late as 19 July 1803, i.e. after the initial explosion at the arms depot but before the rebellion 'proper' broke out, MacNally was able to reassure Dublin Castle that, while on circuit, he had been told by former rebels that nothing was going on, but that if the French invaded many would join them.[51]

It was a similar story with McGucken. He was a lawyer based in Belfast who acted for the Ulster United Irishmen, but had turned informer following his arrest at Liverpool in May 1798.[52] He claimed that he was regarded as one of the remaining rebel leaders in the north-east, and that this position gave him great authority over other subversives. In March 1800, he reported that 'there is no reason for alarm at present as I shall be at the bottom of the whole immediately', and in September 1802 he was still confident enough to report that since 'all look up to me as one of the [rebel] executive', little or nothing could go on without his knowledge.[53] In general, he reported that all was 'quiet, with no system', and he dismissed as insignificant, reports of sightings of former rebels such as Samuel Neilson, 'Hoope' [i.e. James 'Jemmy' Hope], and Samuel Turner.

Moreover, if the Castle's spies saw no cause for concern, neither did the self-appointed elite observers of the behaviour of the Irish peasant classes. In October 1801, Lord Clanricarde was delighted to report a resurgence of brawling and fighting at hurling matches between Galway and Clare for they 'seemed to denote a return to manners and conduct similar to what existed before rebellion prevailed'.[54] A view echoed, rather unluckily, by Lord Ashtown, a Galway peer, a matter of weeks before Emmet's rebellion when he was pleased to report that while 'the lower classes' were getting 'drunk and breaking heads now and then, as usual, at fairs and markets', this was in fact a cause for celebration. 'Unquestionably, . . . for some months previous to the late Rebellions', explained Ashtown 'drunkenness was almost unknown, and a private quarrel, extremely rare.'[55] Perhaps surprisingly, this scarcely scientific view found its way into the Castle's report on the rebellion: it explained that there was no warning of the Emmet rebellion because 'the people in Dublin continued to be drunken and idle – unlike in their conduct in every respect to what they were previous to the rebellion in 1798'.[56]

Lastly, Emmet conducted his affairs with the utmost secrecy. True, he was known to the authorities, but not nearly so well known as his brother, Thomas Addis Emmet, or James Napper Tandy, or Arthur O'Connor or the remaining leaders of the 1798 Rebellion, and it was to these former chiefs that the Castle's attention was directed.[57] In its account of Emmet's rebellion, the Castle brushed away its failure to be forewarned by claiming that the conspiracy had 'received its chief protection from the insignificancy [sic] of the parties engaged in it', and from the fact that no more than eight persons had known about Emmet's arms depot, on which his 'whole game was staked'.[58] Nor had any correspondence been uncovered with France which proved that the French authorities themselves had no idea what was going on.[59] Robert Emmet was, in the end, 'a general without an army', and, continued Redesdale,

> those with whom he principally concerted, dreaded discovery of their designs before they should be ripe for execution. They had the experience of 1798 to inform them that even the secrecy obtained by the extraordinary constitution of the United Irishmen[60] and the extraordinary fidelity of those bound together by that bond were not sufficient to preserve them from detection. They therefore determined that no man should know more than it was absolutely necessary for him to know – indeed not half so much – for he [Emmet] professed to know nothing of the country and to confine his knowledge to Dublin. . . . Their plan was that the right hand should not know what the left hand was doing and this extraordinary secrecy, whilst it tended to prevent discovery of their plan, tended

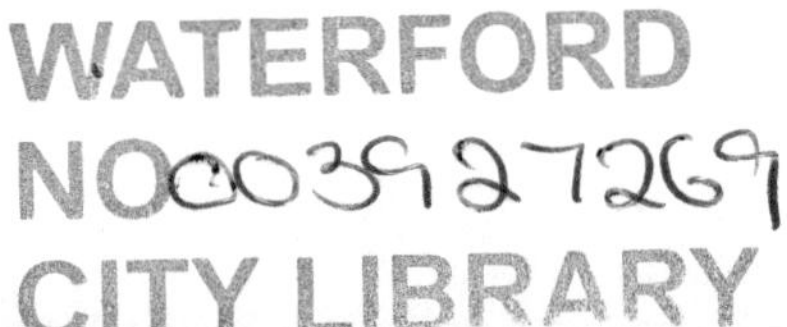

> also to render its execution impossible. . . . That under such circumstances government should not be *fully* informed is not surprising.[61]

If we put all of the foregoing together, the failure of Dublin Castle to discover in advance what Emmet had intended is readily understandable. The shattering defeat of the rebels in 1798 seemed to render inconceivable any resurgence, and divisions among the former rebels as to French objectives appeared to make this conclusion doubly secure. Post-Union government in its determination to put a distance between itself and the 'corrupt' pre-Union administration had wound down, or allowed to fall into disarray, its information-gathering network. New agents had not been recruited, and long-serving agents had not been adequately primed with fresh instructions: more often, they had been given their marching orders. Cooke's resignation had been a huge blow to the Castle's spy-network, and Marsden, his replacement, was temperamentally averse to the work: his major insight into the world of spies, informers and informants was hardly penetrating: 'To discriminate between the true and the false [reports] will not be an easy matter and it will be still more difficult to give a right understanding to others.'[62] Nor was the appointment of Wickham as chief secretary an adequate answer. He had arrived in Dublin in August 1802, but had then left for London early in February 1803, and had not returned to Dublin until August 1803. He was, in fairness, a reluctant chief secretary, but his strained relationship with the Home Office in London had made matters worse. Moreover, he had been suffering from stress on his arrival in Ireland. His encounter with Robert Emmet would push him over the edge: Emmet's eve-of-execution letter to him affected him deeply; he shortly after resigned his position; and though he lived until 1848, he was never again to hold public office.[63] Finally, Emmet's code of strict secrecy and his reliance only on tried and trusted men – no hint of mass participation here – effectively kept Dublin Castle in the dark concerning his plans.[64]

Notes

1 Castlereagh to Wickham, 2 April 1799, *Correspondence of Charles 1st Marquis Cornwallis*, Charles Ross (ed.), 3 vols (London, 1849), III, pp. 85–6.

2 Castlereagh to Wickham, 6 May 1799 (TNA, HO100/86/325).

3 Patrick M. Geoghegan, *Robert Emmet: A Life* (Dublin, 2002); Marianne Elliott, *Robert Emmet: The Making of a Legend* (London, 2003); Ruan O'Donnell, *Robert Emmet*, 2 vols (Dublin 2003).

4 Edward Cooke to Buckingham, 28 July 1803, Richard Plantagenet Temple Nugent Brydges Chandos Grenville Buckingham and Chandos, *Memoirs of the Court and Cabinets of George the Third*, 2 vols (London, 1853), III, pp. 316–17; Castlereagh to Melville, 1 Aug. 1803 (W. L. Clements

Library, Ann Arbor, Michigan, Melville MSS); Redesdale to Percival, 16 Aug. 1803 (PRONI, T3030/7/7; Yorke to Hardwicke, 29 July 1803 (BL Add. MSS 35702, fo. 281).

5 Hort to Caldwell, 21 Dec. 1798 (PRONI, D1634/2/94). We may note that other loyalists drew an opposing conclusion. Richard Griffith, formerly MP for Askeaton, had been active in suppressing the rebels in Kildare in 1798, and was eager for 'moral instruction' in Ireland. He bluntly warned Pelham that 'Paddy since the rebellion is an altered being. The bare possibility of a general open resistance did not before occur to him, but though foiled and beaten, he *now* thinks he *might* have succeeded and he now looks for another opportunity to try his strength with the assistance of France'. Griffith to Pelham, 19 Feb. 1803 (BL Add. MSS 33110, fos 447–50); Edith Mary Johnston-Liik, *History of the Irish Parliament, 1690–1800* 6 vols (Belfast, 2002), IV.

6 Musgrave to Portland, 19 June 1801 (TNA, HO100/66/289).

7 Col. David Leslie to Lord Balgorie, 2 June [1799] (Scottish Record Office, GD26/9/524/11).

8 James McGucken to Edward Cooke, 3 July 1799 (NAI, Rebellion papers, 620/47/77).

9 Charles Abbot to Charles Yorke, 28 Aug. 1801 (BL Add. MSS 35711/102).

10 For the classic statements of what union would mean for Ireland, see Pitt's speeches on union, especially those of 23 Jan. and 31 Jan. 1799, *The Parliamentary History of England from the earliest period to the year 1803*, 36 vols (London, 1806–20), XXXIV, pp. 242–9; *A Review of a Speech of the Rt. Hon. William Pitt* (Dublin, 1799).

11 Abbot to Yorke, 28 Aug. 1801 (BL Add. MSS 35711/102). We may note that Abbot, when seeking to oblige Lord Rossmore was flexible enough to accept the fishing village of Arklow as eligible for a grant under a scheme to promote 'internal navigation'. Abbot to Hardwicke, 13 July 1801 (BL Add. MSS 35711/81).

12 Beresford to Auckland, 5 Sept. 1801 (PRONI, T3229/2/63).

13 Hardwicke to Pelham, 31 Oct. 1801 (TNA, HO 100/107/151). For Foster on the Yeomanry see Foster to Sheffield, 3 Nov. 1803 (PRONI, T3465/138). As the only Irishman in the post-Union Irish government, Corry was suspected of seeking to be a leader of Irish MPs at Westminster, and also, with rather more reason, of being insatiable where patronage was concerned. See A. P. W. Malcomson, *Isaac Corry: An Adventurer in the Field of Politics* (Belfast, 1974), pp. 26–9.

14 Abbot to Hardwicke, 31 May, 29 June, 1801 (BL Add. MSS 35711/25, 61).

15 Clare to Hardwicke, 16 Sept. 1801 (PRONI, T3287/8/16).

16 Clare to Auckland, 22 Oct. [1801] (PRONI, T3229/1/39).

17 Clare to Auckland, 19 Sept., 22 Oct. [1801] (PRONI, T3229/1/38, 39).

18 Hardwicke to Yorke, and Yorke to Hardwicke, 18 Jan., 1 Feb. 1802 (PRONI, Hardwicke–Yorke transcripts, T3451).

19 Wickham to Abbot, 15 Dec. 1802 (PRONI, T2627/5/F/23); Wickham to Addington, 18 Dec. 1802 (PRONI, T2627/5/D/34).

20 Wickham to Liverpool, 13 Dec. 1802 (PRONI, T2627/5/O/36).

21 Marsden to Wickham, recvd. 10 Jan. 1803 (PRONI, T2627/5/K/3).

22 Marsden to Wickham, 4 Mar. 1803 (PRONI, T2627/5/K/58).

23 E.B. Littlehales to Marsden, 23 Aug. 1800 (TNA, HO100/97/128). For a full study see Roger Wells, 'The Irish famine of 1799–1801: market culture, moral economies, and social protest', in

Adrian Randall and Andrew Charlesworth (eds), *Markets, Market Culture and Popular Protest in Eighteenth-Century Britain and Ireland* (Liverpool, 1996), pp. 163–94.

24 Extract of letters, Mar. 1799 (TNA, HO100/86/246–9).

25 Cooke to King, 13 Oct. 1800 (TNA, HO100/94/177–8); General Duff to Dr Lindsay, 8 June 1801 (PRO HO100/102/242–3).

26 Castlereagh to Hardwicke, 18 Aug, 1801, quoted in Michael MacDonagh, *The Viceroy's Postbag* (London, 1904), p. 254.

27 Hardwicke to Pelham, 18 Aug. 1802 (TNA, HO100/110/261); Wickham to Castlereagh, 17 Aug. 1802 (PRONI, T2627/5/G/16).

28 Cooke to King, 13 Oct. 1800 (TNA, HO100/94/177–8); General Duff to Dr Lindsay, 8 June 1801 (TNA, HO100/102/242–3).

29 For Wickham's career in the 1790s, see Harvey Mitchell, *Underground War Against Revolutionary France: The Missions of W. Wickham, 1794–1800* (Manchester, 1965); see also R. G. Thorne, 'William Wickham', in R. G. Thorne (ed.), *History of Parliament: The Commons, 1790–1820*, 5 vols (London, 1986), v, pp. 549–53.

30 For details on Higgins, Magan, Sproule, Reynolds, Turner, McNevin and the others see my *Revolutionary Dublin: The Letters of Francis Higgins to Dublin Castle, 1795–1801* (Dublin, 2004), pp. 13–70.

31 Calculations based on the sums listed in, 'Account of the secret service money' in J. T. Gilbert (ed.), *Documents Relating to Ireland, 1795–1804* (Dublin, 1893), pp. 1–88.

32 See the lengthy letter from McGucken, entirely taken up with his pension: McGucken to [Marsden?], 2 Feb. 1802 (NAI, Rebellion papers, 620/10/121/3).

33 Gilbert, 'Account of the secret service money', pp. 44, 72.

34 Turner to Pelham, 8 Sept. 1801 (TNA, HO100/99/190).

35 Talbot, Paris, to Wickham, London, 29 Mar. 1803 (PRONI, T2627/5/Y/2).

36 Sproule to Abbot, 23 Nov. 1801 (NAI, Rebellion papers, 620/60/102).

37 Cooke's memorandum on his career [1801] (BL Add. MSS 33107, fo. 165).

38 Addington to Wickham, 15 Aug. 1803 (PRONI, T2627/5/D/17); Marsden to Wickham, 9 Apr. 1803 (PRONI, T2627/5/K/117).

39 Marsden to Wickham, 16 Mar. 1803 (PRONI, T2627/5/K/77).

40 Marsden to Wickham, 4 Apr. 1803 (PRONI, T2627/5/K/108). In fairness, John Pollock, a level-headed loyalist who had played an important role in Irish espionage in the late 1790s had written to Marsden shortly after he had succeeded Cooke, advising him 'be assured nothing can stir here without my knowing it instantly'. Pollock to Marsden, 25 Sept. 1801 (NAI, Rebellion papers, 620/49/55).

41 He had no parliamentary experience, and appears to have viewed the position (for which he was second choice and which he only obtained through his friendship with Abbot) as a recompense for his failure to get a diplomatic pension or posting. Thorne, 'William Wickham', *History of Parliament 1790–1820*, v.

42 D. R. Fisher, 'Thomas Pelham', in *History of Parliament 1790–1820*, iv. Much to everyone's amusement, a letter from Lord Redesdale highly critical of Pelham's conduct and efficiency was in error delivered to Pelham himself. Wickham to Marsden, 14 Feb. 1803 (PRONI, T2627/5/K/23).

43 Hardwicke to Wickham, 3 May 1802 (PRONI, T2627/5/E/35).

44 Wickham to Eldon, 23 Nov. 1802 (PRONI, T2627/5/O/33).

45 Redesdale to 'my dear Sir', 14 Dec. 1803 (PRONI, T3030/10/9).

46 On MacNally, see my 'The life and opinions of Leonard MacNally, playwright, barrister, United Irishman and informer', in Hiram Morgan (ed.), *Information, Media and Power Through the Ages* (Dublin, 2001), pp. 113–37.

47 JW to [Cooke?], 13 May 1801 (NAI, Rebellion papers, 620/10/118/12).

48 JW to [Cooke?], 3 June 1801 (NAI, Rebellion papers, 620/10/118/14).

49 JW to [Marsden?], 27 Apr. 1802 (NAI, Rebellion papers, 620/10/121/10).

50 JW to [Marsden?], 13 May 1801 (NAI, Rebellion papers, 620/10/121/19).

51 JW to Marsden, 19 July 1803 in MacDonagh, *Viceroy's Postbag*, pp. 279–80.

52 For McGucken, see my *Revolutionary Dublin*, pp. 58–60.

53 McGucken to Pollock, 22 Sept. 1802 (NAI, Rebellion papers, 620/10/131/16).

54 Clanricarde to —, 1 Oct. 1801 (TNA, HO100/104/185).

55 Ashtown to Hardwicke, 4 July 1803 in MacDonagh, *Viceroy's Postbag*, pp. 267–8.

56 Marsden, 'General statement . . . relating to the insurrection of 23 July 1803', in *Memoirs and Correspondence of Viscount Castlereagh, Second Marquess of Londonderry, edited by his brother, Charles Vane, 3rd Marquess of Londonderry*, 12 vols (London, 1848–54), IV, p. 333.

57 Both T. A. Emmet and Arthur O'Connor were reported in Ireland in March 1803, but the sightings were pronounced 'vague'. Marsden to Wickham, 11, 29 Mar. 1803 (PRONI, T2627/5/K/75, 96).

58 Marsden, 'General statement. . .relating to the insurrection of 23 July 1803' in *Castlereagh Correspondence*, IV, pp. 327–9.

59 Ibid., p. 330.

60 A reference to the requirement that members of the United Irishmen must swear two oaths, one to reveal nothing of what passed in the society and the second to abide by its declaration.

61 Redesdale to 'my dear sir', 14 Dec. 1803 (PRONI, T3030/10/9). See also Hardwicke's comments along the same lines: 'The plan of rising in Dublin . . . was a perfect secret among the leaders themselves . . . [which] . . . at the same time that it diminishes our chance of procuring good information, . . . must greatly diminish their chance of success at any point'. Hardwicke to Yorke, 11 Aug. 1803 (BL Add. MSS 35702, fos 300–5). I owe this reference to Dr Gillian O'Brien.

62 Marsden to Wickham, 16 Mar. 1803 (PRONI, T2627/5/K/77).

63 In later years, Wickham never tired of showing Emmet's letter to all and sundry, and he was a firm advocate of the disestablishment of the Church of Ireland as a remedy for Ireland's wrongs (PRONI, T2627/5/2/1–31).

64 My thanks to Dr Gillian O'Brien and Professor Kevin Whelan for their comments on this chapter.

CHAPTER 2

Revelation and Romanticism

The Revolutionary Ideology of Thomas Russell

James Quinn

Few historical events are so closely associated with one man as the insurrection of 1803 is with Robert Emmet. But 1803 was most certainly not a one-man show, and Emmet, who before the insurrection was not a particularly well-known figure, did his best to recruit as many experienced veterans of 1798 as he could. Among those who responded enthusiastically to Emmet's call was Thomas Russell, one of the most dedicated of all the United Irishmen.[1] Russell was the only leading United Irishman whose career spanned the founding of the society in 1791 and the insurrection of 1803, and throughout this career he was driven by a intriguing mix of political, religious and philosophical ideals.

Russell is perhaps best known as the 'P. P.' in the journals of Theobald Wolfe Tone, his close friend. Tone had dubbed Russell P. P. after a fictional character, an earnest young clergyman in Alexander Pope's *Memoirs of P. P., Clerk of this Parish,* who despite his intentions to live a virtuous life frequently succumbed to the temptations of women and alcohol.[2] The moral struggles of Pope's character were mirrored by Russell's own battle to reconcile his sincerely held Christian principles with his fondness for drinking and whoring. This was simply one of Russell's many contradictions: he often displayed an earnestness that approached solemnity, but could also be playful and witty; he denounced duelling as a vice of the rich, yet he himself would not back away from any challenge impugning his honour; he frequently criticised war as an abomination against the laws of God, yet he had served as a soldier in India for several years. Clearly we are dealing with a complex and contradictory man here – the Man from God Knows Where is elusive in more than geographical terms.

Russell was, in many ways, a figure standing at the cusp of the Enlightenment and the Romantic age, and like many men of his time, was torn by contradictory forces and values. He strove to reconcile reason and sentiment, science and religion, nature and society, liberty and social justice, the national and the cosmopolitan. Many of his beliefs strongly anticipate Romanticism: Russell had a strong emotional bond with nature, looked upon the poor and simple as the truly virtuous, and believed that a divinely ordered natural world had been corrupted by human contrivance. In comparison with the detached scepticism and restrained stoicism of Tone, Russell was a more passionate man, often carried away by the intensity of his beliefs. His remarkable journals reveal an introspective and troubled soul, often afflicted by doubts, misery and even self-loathing.[3]

Russell's greatest contribution to the United movement was the leading part he played in building up a popular revolutionary organisation in Ulster in the mid-1790s. He was one of the first to realise that in order to democratise Irish politics the United Irishmen would have to transform themselves into a mass movement open to men from all walks of life. During the growth of the movement in Ulster, he was a member of a small executive committee that took all the main policy decisions, supervised the creation of new societies and co-ordinated the activities of local clubs.[4] But Russell was much more than just a committee man. He was also active on the ground and for two years travelled widely throughout Ulster recruiting new members, founding new clubs, and preaching the gospel of revolution. He had considerable success in these efforts, and during the mid-1790s cropped up frequently in the reports of informers as one of the key leaders (probably the key leader) of the United Irishmen in the North. Many of these reports stressed his dangerously subversive views, a Belfast informer for example, described him as 'the most violent democrat on the face of the earth'.[5]

Russell was probably the most geographically and socially mobile of all the United Irishmen, regularly sharing the homes and food of peasants and artisans on his rambles through the countryside. His frequent contact with the poor convinced him of their intelligence and discernment, and he became a fervent advocate of their political rights. Realising that the United Irish programme of parliamentary reform and Catholic emancipation could seem distant to the poor, he attempted to make it as relevant as possible by linking it to everyday lives. He was prepared to challenge the sanctity of private property and advocated changes to the existing system of land holding, believing that tenant farmers deserved better security of tenure and perhaps even some form of co-ownership of land. He also strongly criticised the economic exploitation of factory workers, and encouraged tradesmen and labourers to form combinations to protect their livelihoods.[6] Russell may have had some influence on the measures proposed in the revolutionary proclamation of 1803: in addition to democratic parliamentary reform, the proclamation announced that tithes were to be abolished and church lands nationalised, although its social measures probably did not go as far as he would have wished.[7]

Russell believed that the social and political injustices he saw around him were an affront to God, the work of self-interested minorities who had used their powers and privileges to frustrate the divine plan of liberty and justice for all. He denounced injustices wherever they occurred and, in particular, condemned the slave trade as an abomination. It was, he wrote 'such a system of cruelty, torment, wickedness and infamy, that it is impossible for language adequately to express its horror and guilt, and which would appear rather to be the work of wicked demons than of men'.[8] Russell's social radicalism was largely a product of his religious beliefs. Born an Anglican, he took an ecumenical view of religion, believing that all forms of Christianity were valid and stressing those elements that united rather than divided Christians. His radical social views and absence of anti-Catholic prejudice meant that, along with his close friend Henry Joy McCracken, he was one of the most enthusiastic and effective United Irish leaders in forging the alliance with the Defenders, the radical Catholic secret society that thrived in the northern half of the country during the 1790s. An account written by Russell of a clash between militia and Defenders in County Leitrim in April 1795, in which as many as 100 Defenders were killed, gives a good indication of the depth of his engagement with the Defenders.[9]

> When I read those daily accounts in the papers which . . . advertise the cruelties committed by and upon this wretched race of people I feel all that is Irish within me melt with compassion. When will this social war cease? When will the heart whisper – these are my *countrymen* . . . How my heart beats when I think that all this bloodshed may be owing to the want of mutual explanation . . . Jesus wept – Were He to revisit this earth, where would he be found? Would it be at a visitation of the clergy? Would it be at the episcopal tables or with stall-fed theologians? . . . [No] He would be found in the cottier's cabin . . . His hand would pour balm on the mangled body of the expiring husband; and his eyes would spread the consolation of heaven upon the wretchedness of an Irish peasantry.[10]

Russell was not a detached bourgeois radical, but observed the hardships of the poor at first hand, and listened attentively to their political opinions. Over a glass of whiskey in the cabin of a mill-worker in County Antrim, he was told, 'I think liberty worth risquing life for. In a cause of that sort I think I should have courage enough . . . to brave death . . . it does not much signify now as to myself but it gri[e]ves me to breed up [my] children to be slaves. I would gladly risk all to prevent that.' Russell reflected, 'When will a man of fortune in Ireland reason thus? Our senators and great think of nothing but their own sordid interests. Here was a peasant interested for the freedom of mankind. Such I have frequen[t]ly met.'[11] In contrast to his admiration for the Christ-like simplicity and virtue of the poor, Russell regarded the rich as a corrupt and selfish class who had shamelessly abused their privileges. He believed that for their own interests they encouraged sectarian animosity, continuous warfare and the oppression of the poor and weak. Russell noted in his journal 'power and wealth corrupt and harden the heart . . . He who knew the recesses of the heart loved not the rich.'[12] He believed that they would pay a heavy price for their sins, observing that

> when I see the dreadful catastrophe of the kings, princes, nob[l]es and rich of France, I can't help calling to mind the passage where God says He will visit the sins of the father on the children. I think the same fate attends the great in all the European country[s] at no very remote period. They will persist in their oppressions till veng[e]ance comes.[13]

Like many of those whose frame of reference was set by the Bible, Russell believed that the explanation for the great upheavals of the day lay in scripture. He was convinced that the world was undergoing the troubled times that the Book of Revelation had foretold would precede the thousand years of Christ's reign on earth. Russell's years in Belfast were an important influence in this regard. In Ulster several well-known Presbyterian ministers such as Samuel Barber, Thomas Ledlie Birch and William Steel Dickson, who formed an important element in the leadership of the United Irishmen, fused their advanced politics with apocalyptic beliefs, and expounded an explicit millennialist theology throughout the 1790s.[14] They preached that history was unfolding according to a divinely ordained pattern, claiming that the reign of the antichrist had begun when Christianity had been corrupted by its adoption by the Roman empire. The Reformation had been the beginning of the sundering of this unholy alliance and the overthrow of the monarchy in France, Europe's most powerful Catholic nation, had weakened it still further.[15] Steel Dickson's *Scripture Politics*, for example, forecast a blissful future when 'the pure spirit of the gospel, unadulterated by the politics of the world, [will] warm us into mutual kindness, restore us to confidence, and soothe us into peace'. This time was now at hand since the French Republic 'has burst the chains of prejudice and slavery . . . [and] sent forth her arms, not to destroy, but restore the liberty of the world and extend her blessings to all'.[16]

Some believed that the millennium would be inaugurated by the actual physical coming of Christ who would act as the primary agent of sudden and apocalyptic change. Such a view, usually known as pre-millennialism, generally had a populist tone and predicted in lurid terms the coming of Armageddon and the bloody annihilation of the forces of the antichrist. Post-millennialists, who were often intellectual dissenters, took a less dramatic view, maintaining that the millennium would evolve gradually though progressive improvement. They believed that the second coming of Christ would only occur after humanity had prepared the way by creating a world worthy to receive him. They maintained that progress in science and technology, in economic development, in the spread of literacy and political awareness, and the decline in superstition and religious intolerance, all offered evidence of a world gradually evolving towards a state of perfection.[17]

To a great extent, Russell shared the post-millennialist views of leading intellectual dissenters such as Richard Price and Joseph Priestley, and believed that the millennium would be realised only when the laws of man were at one with the laws of God. Man-made laws that contributed to ignorance, intolerance and brutality, directly contravened the divine will and would have to be swept away. This explains his fervent opposition to the slave trade, to oligarchic government, and to the penal laws – the denial of liberty on religious grounds was particularly repugnant to him. His belief that the millennium was at hand, far from producing an attitude of political quietism in Russell, encouraged him to press ahead more forcefully to achieve it. He believed that although the progress towards a better world had been divinely ordained, it would be attained by human efforts, and it was the duty of all Christians to do their utmost to create the New Jerusalem. As he wrote to a friend: 'I trust that the error of supposing that the affairs of the world can be tranquillised in their present form, does not obtain amongst my friends – this is a most awful crisis – may they be found doing their duty, by exerting themselves to extend virtue and liberty.'[18]

In addition to the intellectually respectable millennialism of scholarly dissenters was a folk tradition of prophecy and apocalyptic expectation, which in Ireland, as elsewhere, came to the fore strongly during the troubled years of the 1790s. The oaths and catechisms of the Defenders were steeped in millenarian imagery of deliverance, playing on the very real prospect of French invasion.[19] Apocalyptic prophecies that strongly focused the inchoate resentments of the poor against the rich and powerful and prepared their minds for revolution were a powerful propaganda weapon for the United Irishmen. Russell, whose interest straddled both scholarly and popular forms of millennialism, appears to have put them to good use in his revolutionary proselytising. Just as his revolutionary views when couched in the language of Daniel or Revelation had a strong appeal to a Presbyterian audience for whom scripture was the ultimate sanction, so folk prophecies that carried the stamp of the Gaelic tradition enabled him to harness the apocalyptic expectations of the Defenders. Millennialism was a highly effective means of convincing people that great changes were at hand, and they had a part to play in bringing them about. Thus Russell's combination of radical politics and millenarianism enabled him to tap directly into the pervasive revolutionary spirit of Ulster of the 1790s.[20]

For Russell the rights of man were God-given natural rights, and he believed that it was his Christian duty to create a new political order where they could be freely enjoyed. The revolution he sought was an all-encompassing transformation in which the world would be purged of sin and corruption and restored to a state of prelapsarian simplicity. He believed that in the future

> gover[n]ments will be almost totally done away [with] [sic] and little more than society remain. I think in proportion as gover[n]ments grow more simple, men will be better. His duty to his god and his interest will clash less. As he has less to do with human laws he will have more inclination to respect divine ones.[21]

One of the works that greatly influenced Russell was William Godwin's *An Enquiry Concerning Political Justice* (1793), which he praised as 'masterly'. The central idea of *Political Justice* was that most evils stemmed from unnecessary coercion by the state. Instead man should simply ignore the oppressive apparatus of the state and trust his private judgement. This would allow free scope for the development of his natural benevolence which would enable him to live peaceably and usefully with other men without the restraints imposed by law and government.[22] Godwin's influence on the romantic poets – Blake, Wordsworth, Coleridge, Southey and Shelley – was considerable. William Hazlitt wrote of the attractiveness of Godwin's ideas to such passionate minds: 'there was nothing better calculated to at once feed and make steady the enthusiasm of youthful patriots than the high speculations in which he taught them to engage on the nature of social evils and the great destiny of his species'.[23]

Like the poets influenced by Godwin, Russell too had a special reverence for nature, and saw its unspoilt beauties as a haven from the corruptions of society. An inveterate rambler, he was at his happiest wandering alone through bogs and mountains. The consolations of nature were clearly of great therapeutic value to his often-troubled soul. Walking through the Fermanagh uplands he noted 'The way lonely and wild which I like. When in these sort of places I feel so tranquil that I almost doubt whether man was formed for society.'[24] At times he would sit alone for several hours and fall into a reverie contemplating the beauties of nature, and his journals are studded with vivid descriptions of mist-covered lakes, steep precipices and cascading waterfalls, the standard staples of Romantic rapture. The appreciation of nature was an emotional and deeply religious experience for him and occasionally when contemplating spectacular natural scenes he regretted his lack of poetic ability to express how strongly he was moved.[25]

Russell's literary tastes also provide evidence of his Romantic sensibilities: some short extracts from Rousseau's *La Nouvelle Héloïse*, one of the seminal works of Romanticism, are to be found copied out in his personal papers; and he had a strong passion for Gothic novels. The melodramatic works of Ann Radcliffe, crammed with isolated castles, dingy dungeons, ghostly spectres, fierce thunderstorms, pursued maidens and evil villains, were particular favourites.[26] His lively, enquiring mind ranged far and wide through the arts and sciences: he had a particular interest in geology, never missing an opportunity to record geological data or collect rock samples on his rambles. This fascination with geology, he admitted to a friend, stemmed mainly from a desire to find evidence in support of scriptural accounts of creation that would be useful in defending Christianity from the attacks of Deists and sceptics.[27] A strong interest in anthropology is also evident from his papers: he was fascinated by distant and savage cultures, and regularly contrasted the ingenuousness and simplicity of 'noble savages' with the artifice and greed of Europeans. In one of his regular denunciations of the slave trade he painted a vivid picture of innocent and benevolent Africans forcibly abducted from their West African Eden and brutalised by those who claimed to be civilised.[28]

Because he regarded man as a naturally benevolent creature, Russell, like Godwin, believed that he was capable of dramatic improvement, particularly once the oppressive shackles of the state were removed, and as he grew more virtuous, so society would become more just and equitable.[29] The concept of human perfectibility had strong personal resonances for Russell. He was often afflicted by bouts of deep anguish and remorse in the wake of his debauches, and cursed himself as an abject sinner. The chasm between his desire to live a pure Christian life and his frequent moral lapses usually left him bewildered and depressed, but he continued to hope that some day he would mend his ways. One of his main reasons for keeping a journal was that it might over time reveal an improvement in his morals. He regularly subjected himself to bouts of self-examination, in which he was invariably found wanting. After yet another fall from grace he concluded: 'such I am – so vicious, so imperfect, with wishes and desire for virtue and a firm belief in revelation, and yet lapsing into vice on the slightest temptation. I do not improve.'[30]

Clearly his personal difficulties contributed to his belief in another Romantic commonplace – the distrust of the omnipotence of reason, and for many years he planned to write a work in which he would examine 'the insufficiency of reason' as a philosophical creed.[31] He recognised the limits of Enlightenment rationality, and his restless mind sought inspiration elsewhere, in some of the more arcane parts of scripture and in the promptings of his own heart. He knew only too well the inadequacy of human reason when it clashed with powerful desires, and he often demonstrated a preoccupation with the irrational, writing of ghosts and the possibility that dreams might foretell the future.[32]

Russell's sympathy with budding Romantic beliefs was also evident in his interest in folk culture. He was appointed librarian of the Belfast Society for Promoting Knowledge in 1794, and was an enthusiastic participant in the society's efforts to promote the study of Irish antiquities. He was one of the main figures who encouraged the collection and publication of the old Irish airs that were eventually published by Edward Bunting as *A General Collection of the Ancient Irish Music* in November 1797. It seems that Russell himself tried his hand at playing these tunes on the harp, and throughout his life he maintained a strong interest in Bunting's work.[33] He also took an interest in the Irish language, and in 1794 he began to take Irish lessons from Patrick Lynch, a Gaelic scholar from Loughinisland, County Down; he may already have had some familiarity with Irish from his childhood in counties Cork and Kilkenny.[34] He was the likely author of a *Northern Star* article that encouraged its readers to learn the Irish language to allow them to 'more easily and effectually communicate our sentiments and instructions to all our countrymen'. In addition to its cultural significance, learning Irish would have been an invaluable aid to Russell in recruiting United Irishmen in Irish-speaking parts of Ulster.[35]

Russell was in the forefront of a group of Irish radicals, that included William Sampson, William James McNeven and Whitley Stokes, who sought to rediscover Ireland's Gaelic past and create a distinctive national culture untainted by political or sectarian animosities that would be the common inheritance of all Irishmen. Although United Irish moves in this regard were tentative, they did at least manage to point the way to a programme of cultural regeneration that would be more eagerly taken up by the Romantic nationalists of the Young Ireland group in the 1840s. The nationalism of the United Irishmen was strongly influenced by Enlightenment cosmopolitanism, but it also contained the seeds of the more particularist nationalism of the nineteenth century. Russell certainly balanced his universalist ideals with strong nationalistic feelings. In his speech from the dock in 1803 he noted 'I have travelled much and seen various parts of the world, and I think the Irish the most virtuous nation on the face of the earth – they are a good and brave people, and had I a thousand lives, I would yield them in their service.'[36]

This interest in folk culture can also be seen as an attempt to bridge class differences within the United Irishmen. Just as Russell respected the political understanding of the poor, so he respected their culture, and believed that it should be preserved and promoted. His respect and sympathy for working people made him a highly effective recruiter for the United Irishmen, and in June 1796 he was appointed commander-in-chief of United Irish forces in County Down. Russell looked the part of a leader: tall and well built, with Byronic good looks and a fascinating personality, he seemed a heroic and almost aristocratic figure. To a great extent Russell played a similar role to that of Lord Edward Fitzgerald in the Leinster United Irishmen, a charismatic leader with the common touch, who inspired fierce loyalty in his followers. Russell and colleagues such as Henry Joy McCracken and Fr James Coigly had considerable success in building up the United Irishmen in Ulster and the picture that emerges is of a fairly cohesive radical movement taking shape in the mid-1790s with a well-informed rank and file and a radical leadership cadre very much in sympathy with their aspirations.[37]

This largely explains the considerable anxiety of the authorities by the autumn of 1796 and their attempt to decapitate the Ulster United Irishmen by arresting its leaders. On 16 September 1796 Russell and several others were arrested in Belfast and taken to prisons in Dublin. Given Russell's love of nature and rambling through the countryside, his years of close confinement in Newgate's dank cells bore heavily on him. He wrote to his friend John Templeton, a Belfast botanist and walking companion, of how desperately he longed for their 'pleasant journeys, contemplating the works of nature and adoring its Divine Author'.[38] Increasingly he turned to his other great enthusiasm, scriptural prophecy, from which he drew solace that his sufferings and those of his colleagues would not be in vain. He had always had a predisposition for millennialist beliefs (noted by his close friend Dr James McDonnell),[39] but his years in prison appear to have turned an interest into an obsession. He brooded more and more on world events, and became convinced that they were evolving to a divinely ordained pattern. He chafed at his inaction during the insurrection of 1798 and emerged from prison in June 1802 more intent than ever on mounting a revolution in Ireland.[40]

He met Emmet soon after his release and they discussed the prospects of a rising. In March 1803 Emmet summoned him back to Ireland and gave him the task of raising Ulster, hoping that his reputation in the North would help rally support. In July 1803 he travelled to former United Irish strongholds throughout Antrim and Down calling on the people to rise, but almost everywhere he was greeted with apathy or even hostility. On the day set for the rising small groups of United Irishmen did gather in both counties, but they were too few to mount any effective action. Lacking either clear orders or determined leaders they became demoralised after a few hours and gradually melted away.[41]

The political situation in Ulster had changed dramatically in the seven years of Russell's absence. The high hopes of the 1790s had dwindled in the aftermath of the crushing defeats at Antrim and Ballynahinch; they had been further dampened by the lurid accounts of sectarian atrocities that had occurred in the south in 1798 and they were all but extinguished by the sight of France becoming yet another plundering imperial power, rather than the hope of humanity. For most people, by 1803 the millennialist map to a better future had too many wrong turnings for it to be taken seriously again.

But not so for Russell. Driven on by his millennialist zeal, he was completely confident in ultimate victory. He seems to have believed that he was stepping back into the Ulster of 1796, and that his very presence was enough to ignite a mass rebellion. But this very confidence led him to neglect the detailed planning and preparation required to mount an effective insurrection. His amateurish efforts to raise the North contrast unfavourably with the detailed planning and preparation that characterised Emmet's efforts in Dublin. Emmet had arms, men and a realistic plan of action; Russell had none of these. There were pockets of disaffection still remaining in Ulster in 1803 and had Russell made better preparations, he might possibly have mounted a useful diversionary rising to assist Emmet, but his efforts proved completely ineffectual.

Insurrection had become for Russell a kind of sacred mission, part of a Manichean struggle between the forces of light and darkness. The forces of light were those of the original French Revolution, seeking to establish the sacred values of liberty, equality and fraternity; those of darkness were the corrupt monarchies and wealthy aristocrats who opposed change. Russell saw his struggle as much more than establishing his country's independence, rather it was part of a universal crusade to create a better world for all. He described the current war as 'a contest between the two principles of despotism and liberty and can only terminate in the extinction of one or other. Reason and religion leave one no doubt which will triumph.'[42] As with most crusaders, adversity only served to steel his resolve. Although the people of Antrim and Down had failed to support him in large numbers, he was convinced that they could eventually be brought to their senses, and he made several attempts to do so.[43] Baffled and frustrated by their refusal to follow him, he remained blind to the underlying causes for their caution and concluded that 'courage alone was wanting here as far as I can see to render our success not only certain but easy'.[44] He remained convinced that the cause of justice and liberty had merely lost a battle in a war in which there could be only one ultimate victor.[45]

Intellectual dissenters such as Joseph Priestley and Richard Price had expounded a plausible form of millennial utopianism under which the world would gradually evolve towards a more perfect state in accordance with the design of providence. It was this rational vision that influenced Russell, rather than, for example, the deranged messianism of a Richard Brothers, an English contemporary who considered himself 'Prince of the Hebrews'. However, Russell took the rational millennialism of Priestley and Price to an extreme, substituting their faith in evolution with his commitment to revolution. While most of the Ulster Dissenters who had expounded millennialism in the 1790s had by 1803 either turned away from or toned down its revolutionary implications, Russell did the opposite, becoming ever more extreme in his millennialist outlook. Millennialism became for him a kind of monomania that blinded him to the changed political realities of Ulster in 1803, and led him to embark on his ill-fated attempt to raise the North. Arrested and charged with high treason, he, like Emmet made an eloquent and defiant speech from the dock, in which he expressed himself well pleased with his life's work.[46] After he had been found guilty and sentenced to death, he requested that the sentence be postponed for three days to give him time to complete a commentary on the

Book of Revelation.[47] His request was turned down and he was hanged and beheaded in Downpatrick on 21 October 1803, the last well known United Irishman to be executed in Ireland.

There was a sad inevitability about Russell's death on the scaffold. In the troubled times in which he lived, his millennialist zeal and Romanticism formed a dangerous concoction that was always likely to have fatal consequences for him. It brought him to a conviction that revolution was not simply sanctioned by scripture, it was *ordained* by it. This millennialist vision transformed his efforts to secure his country's independence into a sacred crusade, that required struggle, sacrifice and, if necessary, martyrdom.

Notes

1 Russell was born near Mallow, County Cork, in 1767, the son of a Protestant army officer. He served as an army officer in India (1783–7) and in Belfast (1790–91). A founder of the United Irishmen, he was librarian of the Belfast Society for Promoting Knowledge (1794–6), during the mid-1790s he was a leading United Irish organiser and a journalist with the Belfast *Northern Star* newspaper. Arrested on a charge of high treason in 1796, he was imprisoned in Newgate, Dublin (1796–99) and Fort George, near Inverness (1799–1802). He was hanged in Downpatrick in October 1803 for attempting to incite rebellion in County Down.

2 See *The Works of Alexander Pope, esq.* (London, 1769), III, pp. 217–26; cited in C. J. Woods (ed.), *Journals and Memoirs of Thomas Russell, 1791–5* (Dublin, 1991), p. 31n).

3 See especially the entry in Russell's journal for 21 Nov. 1797, his thirtieth birthday (TCD, Sirr papers, 868/1, f. 2).

4 Examination of John Mitchell, Ballynaslee, County Antrim, *c.* 1796 (NAI, Frazer MS II/16); see also Nancy J. Curtin, 'The United Irish organisation in Ulster', in David Dickson, Dáire Keogh and Kevin Whelan (eds), *The United Irishmen: Republicanism, Radicalism and Rebellion* (Dublin, 1993), p. 217.

5 Rowland J. O'Connor, Belfast, to Sackville Hamilton, Dublin Castle, 7 June 1795 (Kent County Record Office (Maidstone), Pratt (Camden) papers, U840/0147/4/1).

6 For proposals on land reform see Russell's statement, Downpatrick, 17 Oct. 1803 (Michael MacDonagh (ed.), *The Viceroy's Postbag* (London, 1904), pp. 424–6); for his article on combinations see *Northern Star*, 14 Nov. 1793; for authorship of the latter see Russell's journal, 14 Nov. 1793 (Woods (ed.), *Journals*, p. 135).

7 'The provisional government to the people of Ireland', printed proclamation found in the Thomas Street depot, July 1803 (NAI, Rebellion papers, 620/11/134).

8 Thomas Russell, *A Letter to the People of Ireland on the Present Situation of the Country* (Belfast, 1796), p. 22.

9 *Faulkner's Dublin Journal*, 5 May 1795; Liam Kelly, *'A flame now quenched': Rebels and Frenchmen in Leitrim 1793–1798* (Dublin, 1998), pp. 38–41.

10 *Northern Star*, 18 May 1795; on Russell and the Defenders see also L. M. Cullen, 'Political structures of the Defenders', in Hugh Gough and David Dickson (eds), *Ireland and the French*

Revolution (Dublin, 1990), p. 131; L. M. Cullen, 'The internal politics of the United Irishmen', in Dickson, Keogh and Whelan (eds), *United Irishmen*, p. 179.

11 Russell's journal, 9 July 1793 (Woods (ed.), *Journals*, p. 82).

12 Ibid., p. 83

13 Russell's journal, 7 May 1793, 19 Jan. 1794 (Woods (ed.), *Journals*, pp. 75, 142).

14 Pieter Tesch, 'Presbyterian radicalism', in Dickson, Keogh and Whelan (eds), *United Irishmen*, pp. 46–8; James S. Donnelly Jr, 'Propagating the cause of the United Irishmen', *Studies: An Irish Quarterly Review* 69 (1981), pp. 5–23, at pp. 16–17; I. R. McBride, *Scripture Politics: Ulster Presbyterians and Irish Radicalism in the Late Eighteenth Century* (Oxford, 1998), p. 199.

15 William Steel Dickson, *Three Sermons on the Subject of Scripture Politics* (Belfast, 1793), pp. 15–16, 55; foreword by William Stavely to Robert Fleming, *A Discourse on the Rise and Fall of the Antichrist Wherein the Revolution in France and the Downfall of the Monarchy in that Kingdom are Distinctly Pointed Out* (Belfast, 1795); Thomas Ledlie Birch, *The Obligations Upon Christians* (Belfast, 1794), pp. 26–7.

16 Steel Dickson, *Three Sermons*, pp. 16, 35.

17 Jack Fruchtman jr, 'The apocalyptic politics of Richard Price and Joseph Priestley: a study of late eighteenth-century millennialism', *Transactions of the American Philosophical Society* 73: 4 (1983); see also W. H. Oliver, *Prophets and Millennialists: The Uses of Biblical Prophecy in England from the 1790s to the 1840s* (Auckland, 1978), pp. 20–1.

18 Russell to Templeton, 5 June 1802 (TCD, Madden papers, 873/638).

19 Thomas Bartlett, 'Select documents XXXVIII: Defenders and Defenderism in 1795', *Irish Historical Studies* 24: 95 (May 1985), pp. 372–94, at p. 377.

20 John Gray, 'Millennial vision . . . Thomas Russell re-assessed', *Linen Hall Review* 6: 1 (Spring 1989), pp. 5–9, at p. 9; see also David W. Miller, *Queen's Rebels: Ulster Loyalism in Historical Perspective* (Dublin, 1978), p. 55, and David W. Miller, 'Presbyterianism and "modernisation" in Ulster', in C. H. E. Philpin (ed.), *Nationalism and Popular Protest in Pre-Famine Ireland* (Cambridge, 1987), p. 101.

21 Russell's journal, 9 July 1793 (Woods (ed.), *Journals*, p. 83).

22 William Godwin, 'Perusal of Dr Parr's Spital Sermon', p. 326, appendix to K. Codell Carter (ed.), *Enquiry Concerning Political Justice* (Oxford, 1971).

23 W. C. Hazlitt (ed), *Letters of Charles Lamb* (London, 1886), 1, p. 209; cited in Albert Goodwin, *The Friends of Liberty* (London, 1979), p. 475.

24 Russell's journal, 7 May 1793 (Woods (ed.), *Journals*, p. 74).

25 Russell's journal, 25 Nov. 1794 (Woods (ed.), *Journals*, p. 178).

26 For extracts from *La Nouvelle Héloïse* (TCD, Sirr papers, 868/1, f. 206); for Russell's interest in Radcliffe, see Martha McTier to Drennan, 17 Mar. 1797 (PRONI, Drennan papers, T765/652).

27 Russell's journal, 4 Sept. 1793 (Woods (ed.), *Journals*, p. 121); Russell to Templeton, 14 Feb. 1798 (TCD, Madden papers, 873/635).

28 [Russell] to *Northern Star*, 11 Feb. 1792; manuscript (NAI, Rebellion papers, 620/19/56).

29 Russell's journal, 9 July 1793 (Woods (ed.), *Journals*, p. 83).

30 Russell's journal, 3 Nov. 1794 (TCD, Sirr papers, 868/1, f. 15); Thomas Russell to Margaret Russell, 22 Nov. 1801 (TCD, Sirr papers, 868/1, ff 289–90); Russell's journal, 9 June 1794 (Woods (ed.), *Journals*, p. 151).

31 Russell's journal, 30 Sept. 1793, June 1792 (Woods (ed.), *Journals*, pp. 129, 62–3); 21 Nov. 1797 (TCD, Sirr papers, 868/1, f. 2).

32 Russell's journal, 30 Sept. 1793, June 1792 (Woods (ed.), *Journals*, pp. 129, 62–3); 21 Nov. 1797 (TCD, Sirr papers, 868/1, f. 2).

33 The Minute Books of the Society for Promoting Knowledge, 7 Mar., 19 Oct., 27 Dec. 1793, 13 Jan., 23 Oct., 4 Nov. 1794, 3 Sept. 1795 (Linen Hall library, Belfast); Russell's journal, 10 June, 5–6 Nov. 1794 (Woods (ed.), *Journals*, pp. 152, 174–6); see also William Simms to Russell, 22 Jan. 1798 (TCD, Sirr papers, 868/2, ff 258–9); Russell to Templeton, Fort George, 2 Sept. 1800, 5 June 1802 (TCD, Madden papers, 873/636, 638).

34 Séamas Ó Casaide, *The Irish Language in Belfast and Co. Down 1601–1850* (Dublin, 1930), pp. 32–3; *Bolg an tSolair* (Belfast, 1795); Mac Giolla Easpaig made a strong case for Russell's involvement in this work citing his interest in the Irish language, the similarity of some of his personal notes (TCD, Sirr papers, 868/1, f. 37) copied from *O'Brien's Irish-English Dictionary* (Paris, 1768) with the published preface of *Bolg* and the fact that, although future numbers of the work were intended, publication stopped in 1795 – at a time when Russell was busily engaged in political activities (Séamus N. Mac Giolla Easpaig, *Tomás Ruiséil* (Dublin, 1957), pp. 91–2).

35 *Northern Star*, 20 Apr. 1795; Mary Helen Thuente is of the opinion that Russell was 'probably' the author (Mary Helen Thuente, *The Harp Re-strung: The United Irishmen and the Rise of Irish Literary Nationalism* (New York, 1994), pp. 10, 95).

36 Russell's trial speech (TCD, Madden papers, 873/700).

37 Jim Smyth, *The Men of No Property: Irish Radicals and Popular Politics in the Late Eighteenth Century* (Dublin, 1992), p. 165.

38 Russell to Templeton, 2 Sept. 1800 (TCD, Madden papers, 873/636).

39 R. R. Madden, *Lives and Time of the United Irishmen*, 3rd series (Dublin, 1846), II, p. 280.

40 Russell to Templeton, 5 June 1802 (TCD, Madden papers, 873/638).

41 See James Quinn, *Soul on Fire: A Life of Thomas Russell* (Dublin, 2002), pp. 256–77.

42 Thomas Russell to John Russell, Fort George, 10 Dec. 1800 (copy) (TCD, Madden papers, 873/655).

43 Rev. Snowden Cupples to Rev. Forster Archer, 14 Sept. 1803 (NAI, Rebellion papers, 620/11/158).

44 Russell to Frank McCracken, c. Aug. 1803 [?] (copy) (TCD, Madden papers, 873/640). This letter is dated 15 July 1803 but from its content it appears to be written some time after the attempted rising.

45 Thomas Russell to John Russell, Fort George, 10 Dec. 1800 (copy) (TCD, Madden papers, 873/655, f. Iv).

46 Russell's trial speech (TCD, Madden papers, 873/700).

47 *Dublin Evening Post*, 22 Oct. 1803; Wickham to Pole Carew, 24 Oct. 1803 (MacDonagh, *Viceroy's Postbag*, pp. 426–7).

CHAPTER 3

'Permanent tranquillity will not be established while the present system is continued'

Charles James Fox and Ireland 1801–3

Patrick Walsh

Following the successful defeat of Emmet's rebellion in 1803, Henry Grattan wrote to the British opposition leader, Charles James Fox, saying that he was inclined to think that 'if Lord Hardwicke had been viceroy and Lord Redesdale lord chancellor in 1798 the former rebellion might never have happened'.[1] Conspicuous by his absence in this list was Fox's younger brother, General Henry Fox, the commander of the forces in Ireland at the time of the rebellion who had since been dismissed. He had been blamed by the Irish administration for his indecisive reaction to the events of 23 July and his unceremonious departure encouraged his brother to take an active interest in the events surrounding the rebellion. Charles James Fox had long been a supporter of Irish causes at Westminster and held close personal and political ties with members of the Irish opposition. Historians have long been divided over the extent and motivations of Fox's interest in Irish affairs. In his authoritative biography L. G. Mitchell has accused Fox of cynical political opportunism in relation to Ireland, commenting that 'Irish patriots were never sure of Fox and their doubt was entirely justified'.[2] This view has, however, been challenged in Martyn Powell's recent study of Fox's interest in Ireland.[3] He has argued that while Fox was foremost a British politician, his interest in Ireland was real and often motivated by his close connections with the Irish patriot opposition. Thus, he suggests that Fox was consistent in his support for a conciliatory policy for Ireland and in his opposition to the Dublin Castle administration. Powell's study concentrates on the events of the early 1780s and also briefly on the period following Fox's support of the Catholic petition in 1805. He makes scant reference to the years between the 1798 rebellion and Emmet's rebellion, a period in which Fox's actions bear out his thesis. The traditional interpretation of this period in Fox's career is that following his parliamentary secession in 1797, which was motivated by his opposition to the war with France, he abandoned politics for gardening and the study of history. However, this interpretation does not do justice to Fox's enduring interest in Irish affairs, an interest ignored by his biographers.[4] If the 1798 rebellion largely passed him by, according to his nephew this was partly because of the death in it of his cousin, Lord Edward Fitzgerald.[5] The Act of Union, the subsequent resignation of his old rival William Pitt, and the rebellion of 1803 did excite Fox's interest. This chapter will examine this interest in Ireland with particular reference to the period following Emmet's rebellion.

The Act of Union has been termed the matrix of modern Irish history.[6] The Union brought an end to two parliaments, the old Irish and British parliaments, and created another, the new Imperial parliament, which sat for the first time in 1801. So when Charles James Fox returned to the House of Commons in 1801 he was entering a different parliament from the one from which he had seceded in 1797. Despite their dramatic and far-reaching consequences, the Union debates did not persuade Fox to return to the Commons. If he interrupted his secession for this issue then he would have to abandon it completely, something he did not wish to do. Fox's lack of activity during the Union debates has been criticised by his biographers and by historians of the Union.[7] They argue that instead of articulating his opposition privately to friends, Fox should have done so in public in the House of Commons. One biographer of Fox has written that during the Union debates, 'Fox idled away his time keeping good Whig company and writing doggerel on the deaths of a friend's two dogs'.[8] He did, however, work behind the scenes to try and influence the debates in both Dublin and London. He advised speakers such as Richard Fitzpatrick, Charles Grey and Lord Holland on the conduct they should follow in London, while he also corresponded with Irish Whigs such as Grattan and Ponsonby on the matter. On a rare interruption of his secession for a debate on peace with France, he also made an attack on the government over the Union.

Fox was at first uncertain what stance to take on the Union, and writing to Richard Fitzpatrick he commented that 'whatever Foster opposed must have some good in it', a reference to the Irish speaker's opposition to the measure.[9] By early 1799 Fox was a definite opponent of the measure, and he wrote to Holland in London and Grattan in Dublin to advertise his 'decided disapprobation'.[10] Despite increasing pressure from his friends in London to attend the Union debates in parliament, Fox refused to break his secession, reasoning that it would do more harm than good. Instead, Fox urged Holland 'and others (including Grey and Fitzpatrick) to voice the objections he felt to its policy'.[11] They were, in effect, acting as Fox's proxies in the House of Commons and his correspondence, particularly with Lord Holland, is full of arguments against the Union, mostly related to his Lockean theory that parliament was incompetent to vote the Irish legislature out of existence.[12] Similar arguments were used by Henry Grattan in Dublin in a speech upon which Fox's influence can be detected, especially as it was somewhat different from Grattan's usual style.[13] Fox may not have entered parliament to oppose the Union, but his colleagues did manage to put forward his views without too much deviation. Perhaps this was the wisest course of action considering the degree of antipathy directed at Fox from the government benches since his secession. By voicing his arguments by proxy, Fox was able to avoid unnecessary opprobrium being cast upon them.

Fox, at the outset of his secession from parliament, had suggested that he would return to the House of Commons to debate any motion on peace proposals with France. In February 1800, the French consular government made some overtures for peace and the issue came before the House of Commons. Fox made his sole appearance in parliament during that year to urge acceptance of these overtures. He also used the opportunity to make a brief reference to events in Ireland. He suggested that the government was hypocritical in its attitude to the French: 'But how this house can be so violently indignant at the idea of military despotism is, I own a little singular when I see the composure with which they observe it nearer home.'[14] ('Nearer home' is a reference to Ireland and the imposition of martial law.) He went on to suggest that the imposition of martial law was influencing the discussion of that 'most interesting question of a legislative union',[15] and asked 'do we think it precisely the period and the circumstances under which she may best declare her free opinion'.[16] This stinging rebuke of the government's policy in Ireland was compounded by Fox's claim that 'Gentlemen who talk in this way about Ireland, can not with good grace rail at military despotism in France.'[17] The conduct of Pitt's government in Ireland, Fox claimed, was no better than that of Bonaparte. This attack on Pitt's policy towards Ireland during a debate on France, in this rare interruption of his secession, shows the level of Fox's opposition to the Union. It has been neglected by the historians of the Union but is important as it shows that Fox publicly opposed the Union and that he did not ignore its passage through parliament. This speech, while his only parliamentary contribution on the subject, was not Fox's only public denouncement of the Union. On 6 May 1800 he made a speech to the Whig Club, perhaps belatedly outlining his opposition to the Union, claiming that his position was the same as it had been in relation to America 25 years earlier: 'He who had opposed the enslaving of America must now be hostile to the enslaving of Ireland.'[18] He also argued that the Union contravened what he termed the fundamental principle of all well constituted states, 'The sovereignty of the people, that man should be his own government.'[19] The Whig Club speech certainly cleared up any ambiguity about Fox's stance on the Union but probably came too late to be of any practical benefit. It did, however, serve to answer contemporary critics as well as later historians who argued that he remained in retirement throughout the Union period. This simplistic analysis does not reflect his extra-parliamentary activity or the weight of his influence on those Whigs who did attend parliament. In reality Fox was constantly thinking and writing privately about Ireland and eventually he decided to make these views public in his brief reference in parliament and in his speech to the Whig Club.

If the Union debates did not entice Fox away from the pleasures of his garden at St Anne's Hill, the resignation of his great rival, William Pitt, in January 1801 drew him back into parliament. Pitt's resignation was greeted with scepticism and disbelief by many, but the circumstances of his resignation offered Fox and his followers new hopes of ending their long exile in opposition. Raising Irish affairs, in particular the Catholic question, was seen as the best way of attacking Addington's new ministry, which was founded on an anti-Catholic platform. The search for the real cause of William Pitt's resignation has puzzled historians for generations. Even Pitt's most authoritative biographer, John Ehrman, could not find a conclusive reason, and wrote that the 'occasion has remained one of the special mysteries of the age'.[20] The evidence, however, suggests that the reason for his resignation was the reason given, because of his failure to introduce Catholic emancipation as part of the Union with Ireland. Other extenuating circumstances connected with the war against France and Pitt's health also contributed, but this was the primary cause. Only one other prime minister apart from Pitt, W. E. Gladstone in 1886, would resign because of an Irish matter, and it is possible that the neglect of Irish affairs by British historians has led to the confusion over Pitt's resignation. The cause of the collapse of the government was so unlikely that Henry Dundas reputedly said that though the reason given was the real one, no historian would believe it, and so it has transpired.[21] However, recent research by Patrick Geoghegan has shown that Pitt's resignation was indeed linked to the Act of Union and specifically to the question of Catholic emancipation.[22] Even this interpretation has, though, ignored an analysis of Fox's reaction and his subsequent return to parliament. The amount of historical debate that Pitt's resignation has generated suggests that the reaction of Fox and his followers, initially disbelief then scepticism, was perfectly understandable.

Fox's reaction to Pitt's resignation has been criticised by later historians.[23] His comment in a letter to Richard Fitzpatrick that it 'looks as if there has been some strange juggle, but what is the nature of it can not be guessed', is always quoted by historians of the resignation and by biographers of Fox.[24] This excerpt suggests that the collapse of Pitt's government took Fox by surprise and that he did not understand it. This is partially true, but Fox was not as distant from events as has been suggested. The letter to Fitzpatrick was written on 3 February, the day Pitt resigned, showing that Fox was in touch with events. Pitt's resignation brought the issue of Fox's continued secession into question and he was writing to Fitzpatrick looking for advice regarding a possible return to parliament now that Pitt's ministry had fallen. Fox was aware that the Catholic question had brought down the government and he told Fitzpatrick that 'if the catholic question comes on I must attend', giving an indication of how important an issue this was to him.[25] He was also aware of the court machinations that had brought down Pitt, and wrote that 'Fitzgibbon and the bishops have pushed the king to resist Pitt in this instance'.[26] The acknowledgement by Fox of Fitzgibbon's role in the collapse of the government shows that he was aware of the Irish dimension to Pitt's resignation.[27] Fox does appear to have been flummoxed by the appointment of Addington as prime minister to replace Pitt, writing that it was 'totally incomprehensible'.[28] This was perhaps not surprising since Addington had not had the most impressive political career, and his family background was not especially distinguished. His father had been Lord Chatham's physician, something which earned his son the disparaging sobriquet 'the Doctor', and he had a close alliance with the younger Pitt, under whose patronage he had prospered. Fox was thus right to be sceptical when he replaced Pitt. He repeated his scepticism about Addington's ministry in a letter to Lord Holland writing: 'I cannot help admiring the ease which you talk of the new administration as if any such thing existed.'[29]

Within weeks of Addington's accession as prime minister, Fox was trying to get his colleagues to raise the Catholic question. He had perhaps realised that he had acted too late over the Act of Union and that the collapse of Pitt's ministry presented an opportunity to argue for this issue. He suggested in a letter to the Earl of Lauderdale that perhaps Charles Grey or George Ponsonby should raise the issue in parliament.[30] The choice of Ponsonby is interesting and shows that Fox wanted to involve the Irish Whigs who now sat in the House of Commons especially on an issue which concerned Ireland. Raising the Catholic question would serve to discredit Pitt and his associates. If Pitt refused to support a motion for Catholic emancipation as Fox suspected he would then 'it will tend more to disgrace him and show the abject state both of the late ministers and parliament in the strongest light'.[31] Fox was, however, motivated both by party political interest on this issue and by principle, and when support for bringing the question was not forthcoming he wrote that he was 'totally against using persuasion on the subject' even though he was the most ardent supporter of the issue.[32] His supporters would ultimately choose whether to raise the issue themselves and only a minority were interested in raising the question including figures such as Fitzwilliam, Fitzpatrick, Grey and Lauderdale. Fox himself was only prepared to return to parliament if 'the catholic question is brought on and upon that only'.[33] The Catholic issue in this period had thus superseded the war with France as the most important issue for Fox.

On 25 March 1801 Charles James Fox made his first appearance in the imperial parliament at Westminster. Pitt's resignation and the new opportunities that beckoned brought an end to his self-imposed exile from the House of Commons. He spoke on Grey's motion on the state of the nation and he used the opportunity to severely criticise both Pitt's outgoing government and Addington's incoming government. Much of the speech was taken up with an attack on the conduct of the war with France but he also made a stringent attack on Pitt's Irish policy and especially on the failure to introduce Catholic emancipation. He argued that a 'system of prescription on account of theological differences' was unjust and, furthermore, that the division of the country by the government only tempted invaders.[34] In a reference to the 1798 rebellion he suggested that 'rebellion is the fruit of bad policy'.[35] The implication was clear: there would be further trouble in Ireland unless there was a change in policy. He claimed that the failure to resolve the Catholic question had left both parties in Ireland discontented and disgusted, the Protestant zealot had no security and the Catholic claimant had no satisfaction.[36] According to Fox, such was Pitt's 'infelicity upon this question that the measure which was to be the remedy had become the source of all distempers'.[37] Pitt's failure to honour the pledge to the Catholics had served only to increase their sense of grievance.

Fox also attacked the reasons given for the refusal to grant emancipation using an almost Burkean argument that the Catholics were not disloyal and that they were not 'traitors' as some on the government side claimed. If they were traitors then Fox asked what was the benefit of the Union if it brought about the junction of four or five million traitors to the state. He then entered into an impassioned defence of the Irish people and the Irish nation saying, 'Sir I love the Irish nation, I know a good deal of that people. I know much of Ireland having seen it; I know more from private friendship with individuals.'[38] This defence of the Irish nation showed both Fox's concern for Irish affairs and also an implicit rejection of the government's attitude to Ireland and their lack of knowledge about Irish affairs. He had used this argument that he was better acquainted with Ireland before in debate, and certainly of the major British politicians of the era he was one of the few to visit Ireland, albeit in 1777. For instance, neither Pitt nor Addington ever crossed the Irish Sea. He also had extensive political and familial contacts in Ireland. He finished his argument regarding Ireland with an appeal to the government to change their policy: 'Let impartiality, justice and clemency take the place of prejudice, oppression and vengeance.'[39] It was an eloquent reiteration of the Whig principle of conciliation instead of coercion. Following the Whigs' expected defeat on the motion, Fox resumed his retirement as he had promised in a letter to Lauderdale a few weeks earlier: 'When we are beaten on the state of the nation, I mean to attend no more until the Catholic question is brought on, and in that case upon that only.'[40]

Fox was suspicious of Pitt's commitment to the Catholic question, and in May 1801 he suggested that 'the principle had not taken very deep root in his [Pitt's] mind',[41] a statement which was closer to the truth than Fox knew as Pitt had pledged in March not to raise the Catholic question again for fear of injuring the King's sensibilities. Fox, unlike Pitt, continued to maintain interest in the Catholic question. It did after all provide 'excellent grist to the Whig mill'.[42] It could be used as a means to drive Pitt and Lord Grenville apart since the latter was avowedly pro-Catholic. It could also be used to discredit Pitt if he refused to support emancipation considering his previous stance, and finally, if emancipation was passed by parliament, then it would mean a victory for parliament over royal prerogative. Despite all this, Fox continued to be reluctant to engage fully in political affairs. For instance, he spent much of 1802 in France researching his book on the 1688 revolution. His *History of the Early Part of the Reign of James II* was, however, written partly to vindicate his actions in the 1790s, and included a discussion of royal prerogative, perhaps influenced by the King's actions in January 1801, suggesting contemporary politics were never far from his thoughts.[43] The real reason for his lack of activity on the Catholic question could be linked to the lack of support for this issue within his own party. Through late 1801 and early 1802 Fox seems to have been becoming more frustrated at the lack of activity on the Catholic question. The Irish Whigs were lukewarm about raising it in parliament, while Fox felt that the opportunity was being lost. In late 1801 he wrote to Fitzpatrick saying, 'the more I think of it the more I think it madness not to move the catholic question',[44] while in February 1802 he complained to Holland that 'the not bringing on the catholic question is I think disgraceful, but you saw last spring how much it would have been against the grain'.[45] Later in 1802 there were rumours of Pitt's impending return to office on the condition that he would not raise the Catholic issue. Fox, however, believed that Pitt would do this despite his comments in his speech of 7 May 1801, and he told Robert Adair, another Whig MP, that 'My opinion of Pitt is not high, but I own I do not think him capable of this.'[46] He was again perhaps too generous to Pitt as this was what Pitt did two years later in 1804 when he replaced Addington as prime minister. It is clear from Fox's correspondence at this time that the Catholic issue was exercising his mind. It would also seem that it was more than just an issue of political expediency considering the lack of support from his allies on both sides of the Irish Sea.

The circumstances of the collapse of Pitt's ministry offered new hope to Fox and his followers. Pitt had been forced to resign over an issue that they supported, namely Catholic emancipation. Pitt had failed to introduce emancipation because of King George III's intransigence and the Foxites had always supported the superiority of parliament over royal prerogative (apart from their brief costly lapse during the regency crisis in 1789), so the issue was bound to excite them. The replacement of Pitt's ministry with that of Henry Addington, who owed his rise to power to his sycophantic attitude to the king, meant that Fox had a new target to aim his opposition. The issue that was most likely to embarrass both Pitt and Addington's administration, which had been formed explicitly to resist Catholic emancipation, was the Catholic question. If Pitt refused to support a motion for emancipation, then he could be accused of bad faith and his motives for resigning in 1801 would be in dispute, while it was an issue that could unite disparate members of the opposition from the Grenvillites to the Foxites against Addington. Fox, thus, in 1801 and in the early months of 1802, attempted to drum up support for Catholic emancipation. Yet he failed, much to his own disappointment, to bring forward a motion on emancipation because of the lack of support within his own party. Fox seems to have sincerely believed that Catholic emancipation would make a major contribution to solving the Irish question, as demonstrated by his passionate speech on the state of the nation in March 1801, but it was also the most important part of a political strategy aimed at bringing the Whig party out of the political wilderness in the new political environment created by Pitt's resignation.

In July 1803 the Irish question once again came to prominence with the outbreak of rebellion in Dublin. For Fox the insurrection in Dublin offered an opportunity to restate his Irish policy and to criticise the government's handling of the affair. His criticism was exacerbated by the involvement of his brother, General Henry Fox, in the events in Dublin. General Fox was the commander of the forces in Ireland in 1803 and was charged with quashing the rebellion. However, he mishandled the affair and his panic-ridden reaction was criticised by members of the Irish administration. Following the rebellion, he was dismissed from his post in Ireland and transferred to a new position in England. Charles James Fox, in a demonstration of family loyalty, leapt to his brother's defence both in private and in public. In a debate in the House of Commons in 1804 on the removal of General Fox, he defended his brother against the accusations of Charles Yorke, the home secretary, who himself was defending his brother Lord Hardwicke, the lord lieutenant in Ireland.

Fox's reaction to the insurrection in Dublin and his defence of his brother's actions has hitherto been neglected by historians. None of Fox's many biographers, from Lord John Russell in the nineteenth century right up to more recent authors such as John Derry and L. G. Mitchell, mention this episode in Fox's career. This neglect has been mirrored in most accounts of Emmet's rebellion.[47] In his recent exhaustive history of the rebellion, Ruan O'Donnell has mentioned the debates on General Fox's removal but has misjudged the motivation behind them, suggesting they 'served the interest of those who resented Fox's opposition to the renewal of the war with France',[48] but this interpretation fails to take into account the fact that Fox supported the motion that was proposed in parliament calling for an inquiry. Charles James Fox's reaction to the rebellion and the influence it had on the development of his Irish policy, in particular his attempts to find a new system of government for Ireland possibly involving the Prince of Wales, have also been neglected by historians and are addressed below.

Fox's initial reaction to the outbreak of rebellion in Dublin was to assume that it was linked to a possible French invasion. He dismissed the suggestion that the rebels were nothing more than a 'partial or accidental mob', but he wondered, if it was a serious attempt, why the rebels had not waited until the French had actually landed in Ireland or Britain. In a letter to Charles Grey he concluded that he could not understand it, but that it proved what he always suspected, 'that the accounts of a better state of Ireland were delusory in the extreme'.[49] His pessimistic view of the situation in Ireland was further expressed in a letter to his younger brother, General Henry Fox, the commander of the forces in Ireland, when he wrote 'All hope of this miserable business being accidental is now over, and the state of Ireland appears as bad as can be.'[50] He went on to criticise government policy and suggested that the rebellion would mean the continuation of military rule in Ireland and he remarked that this would be dreadful.[51] In a letter to Grey he suggested that the whole system of governing Ireland was wrong and that there must be a 'fundamental change . . . to give even a chance of further quiet there'.[52] Fox, despite his reservations about the system of government being operated in Ireland, did, however, support the actions of the Dublin administration towards the rebels. He told Grey that he believed that neither Lord Hardwicke nor his brother would 'consent to any cruelties'.[53] Fox's high opinion of the lord lieutenant, which was shared by Henry Grattan,[54] was, however, altered following Hardwicke's conflict with General Fox.

The dismissal of his brother, General Fox, as commander of the forces in Ireland led Fox to take a critical view of both the British and Irish administrations. General Fox had been accused of incompetence because of his conduct on the night of the rebellion. Lord Redesdale, the Irish lord chancellor, wrote that 'His conduct has destroyed all confidence in him, and I am persuaded nothing good can be done under his command.'[55] Modern historians have tended to agree with this analysis, with Patrick Geoghegan highlighting 'Fox's inept management of the city's defences'.[56] Allan Blackstock, while criticising Fox's actions arguing that 'he had all the credentials to be a disaster in Ireland',[57] has suggested that the conflict between Hardwicke and Fox predated the rebellion and was as much structural as personal. The Union had caused a division of powers between the lord lieutenant and the commander of the forces and the communications breakdown and power struggle it caused was 'brought to a head when Robert Emmet's followers staged their insurrection'.[58] The dispute had as much to do with the control of yeomanry patronage as it did with the events of the rebellion. Despite the endorsement of Redesdale's view by later historians, contemporary opinion was more divided. Lord Cornwallis believed that Fox was not to blame and wrote following an examination of the General's papers that 'it does not appear from them that in the business of that night any blame can be imputed to him'.[59] This view seems to have been shared by some in the British military establishment, and when Fox was removed from his post in Ireland he was given command of a district in England, and later served as governor of Gibraltar.

Charles James Fox defended his brother throughout this period. He seems to have been surprised initially by General Fox's recall and he sought further information before writing to him in September 1803. He was, however, at this juncture still ignorant about the reasons for his brother's recall.[60] By November of the same year Fox was better informed and he told Grey that 'the folly of the castle appears . . . to have been beyond belief, and the impudence of the government there if they really have (as my brother thinks) endeavoured to lay part of the blame upon him must be beyond the devil's'.[61] He also made reference to his brother's new post, saying that his appointment to the command of a home district by the Duke of York was 'a pretty strong mark of confidence'.[62] In March 1804 Fox was presented with a chance to defend his brother in public, when a motion was brought before parliament by a Sir John Wrottesley calling for an inquiry into the Irish insurrection. Wrottesley was not a follower of Fox but a Pittite and the inquiry into the rebellion was seen as an opportunity to unite the Fox, Grenville and Pitt wings of the opposition against Addington's government.

Wrottesley's motion was debated on 7 March 1804. It brought Fox into direct contact with Charles Yorke, the home secretary and brother of Lord Hardwicke. Both Fox and Yorke were upholding their respective family responsibilities in this debate, something that Fox acknowledged. He was prepared to vote for the inquiry unlike Yorke, and he commented that Yorke 'may be, and no doubt is a much better member of parliament, and a much better statesman; but in promoting this inquiry I consider myself the better brother'.[63] Fox attacked the government's persistence in attempting to disassociate themselves with the events in Ireland, while they continued to attribute blame to his brother. He argued 'that the infamy is theirs and he stands acquitted'.[64] The fault of the government was such that the only way they could defend themselves was, according to Fox, to 'blacken the character of the commander-in-chief', and here he made references to the pro-government Dublin newspaper, *Faulkners Journal*, which had made attacks on General Fox.[65] Apart from attacking the government's attribution of blame to his brother, Fox also pointed out that the government were at fault. He reminded the house that a letter about a possible rebellion sent by Hardwicke to the commander of the forces on 16 July had reached Fox only on 21 July because he had been conducting a tour of the island's military defences. He also attacked Hardwicke's decision to retire to the Phoenix Park on the day of the rebellion suggesting that 'The state of Dublin on that day presents a lamentable picture of a city deserted by all the efficient members of its government; and if danger was apprehended never was conduct so unaccountable.'[66] This vacating of the city by the government, Fox argued, may have been related to the Irish administration's desire to suspend *habeas corpus* and to introduce a martial law bill. He suggested that 'It might afford some suspicion that the insurrection of the 23rd would not have been so very disagreeable, had it not being [*sic*] accompanied by the murder of Lord Kilwarden and Colonel Brown.'[67] This was an early expression of a now discounted theory that Emmet's rebellion may have been a government conspiracy.[68] Fox had succeeded not only in disputing the allegations against his brother, but also in voicing his disapproval of the conduct of the Irish administration and especially the lord lieutenant.

Apart from his defence of his brother in the House of Commons, Fox also made more general attacks on the government's handling of the rebellion and on their Irish policy. He believed that the rebellion had demonstrated the inadequacies of the policy being pursued by Addington's government. In a debate on the king's speech at the opening of the parliamentary session four months earlier in November 1803, Fox took the opportunity to question the system being employed in Ireland. He told the House of Commons that he could see no reason 'to think that permanent tranquillity will be established . . . while the present system is continued'.[69] The hope expressed in the king's speech that those involved in the insurrection were convinced of their error was also challenged with Fox claiming that 'without a totally new system of managing the affairs of Ireland being adopted, a hope of the Irish being convinced of their error can hardly be expected'.[70] He believed that he would not have been doing his parliamentary duty if he did not highlight the misrepresentation, as he saw it, of the situation in Ireland, contained in the king's speech. But he was not content to be the only dissenter and he told the members of the House of Commons that they could consider themselves otherwise than guilty 'if they suffered themselves to believe in the continuance of Irish tranquillity, because the country is represented as now contented and because hopes are held out that this contentment is permanent'.[71] The themes that Fox had raised in his speech of 22 November were developed in his speech on Wrottesley's motion the following March. He suggested that the actions of the Irish administration were a compelling argument against the Union, 'For this parliament is unfit to legislate for a country, the executive administration of which it can not control.'[72] This statement was tempered, however, by his assertion that parliament must regain control of the Irish administration and that each MP must demonstrate that they are members for 'the whole empire, for Dublin as well as for Hertfordshire or Yorkshire'.[73] Fox's conception of the role of the Union parliament was clear: the Irish administration had to be accountable to parliament and members must serve the whole empire.

Fox was prepared to make constructive suggestions regarding the administration of Ireland as well as the negative criticisms made in the House of Commons. Like Pitt's resignation two and a half years earlier, the rebellion created an opportunity to raise the Irish question and Fox was determined not to let this one pass. His most audacious scheme involved the Prince of Wales. The prince had become increasingly interested in politics since the reappearance of his father's madness in 1801 and had continued to maintain close links with the Whigs. On 18 August 1803 Fox wrote to the prince suggesting that he take up the Catholic question. He believed that if the prince took up this issue that support would be forthcoming in Ireland, and 'not only from the Ponsonbys, the Duke of Leinster and their friends but even Mr Foster'.[74] Fox believed that the prince's support would unite the various opponents of the Union in Ireland. His belief that Foster would support Catholic emancipation at this juncture was optimistic considering Foster's vehement opposition to the measure in the past. Support for emancipation would remain 'antithetical to Foster' and he did not gain office in the Fox-Grenville coalition of 1806 partly, according to his biographer, because of Fox's hostility to anyone associated with 'the old castle', making his advocacy of Foster's support in 1803 stranger still.[75] As well as raising the question of supporting Catholic emancipation with the prince, Fox also raised the possibility of repealing the Union, but he confessed that he had no opinion on the matter other than a tendency to lean towards the negative. He urged the prince, however, to consult with Lord Moira, Lord Hutchinson, John Foster and George Ponsonby with regard to the dissolution of the Union. He also raised the possibility of the prince becoming the governor of Ireland, although he recognised that this would be objectionable to parliament. Instead, Fox argued, if the prince supported a conciliatory policy then he might 'open hopes to the dissatisfied people of that country . . . which might in some degree divert them from their connections with France'.[76] This generation of hope for the future was dependent upon the early succession of the Prince of Wales to the throne, not an unrealistic hope considering the state of the king's health. Fox's concentration on Ireland as the focus of the prince's political activity is interesting and shows the importance he attached to the subject. He told the prince that Ireland was 'the most endangered part of the empire, that on which you must employ your thoughts'.[77] The renewed fear of a French invasion following Emmet's rebellion had highlighted the need to find a solution to the Irish question.

On the same day, Fox wrote to Charles Grey outlining his plans. He told Grey about his suggestion to the prince regarding the formation of a government with explicit support for Catholic emancipation, and his belief that this would have a positive effect on Irish opinion. He confided to Grey, however, that he thought nothing would come of this plan because he considered the 'prince and his friends incapable'.[78] In particular, Fox did not think highly of Lord Moira, the prince's closest ally, although he confessed that if 'he can be right about anything it will be about Ireland', a reference to Moira's Irish connections.[79] In his letter to Grey he also declared his intention to write to Grattan and Ponsonby to ascertain their opinions on the present state of Ireland. His commitment to Ireland is obvious from these communications, but he warned Grey that this 'wonderful and unnatural activity' was confined to Irish affairs and founded on the grounds that 'if there is any chance, however small of doing good in Ireland, I know not how being in parliament, I can refuse attending to it'.[80] An arrangement with the prince, as Fox feared, failed to materialise, but despite the failure of this bold initiative, he told Grey that 'Ireland was still a serious business' which he ought to consider.[81] Fox's discussions with the prince and with Grey on Irish affairs at this time show his determination to utilise the rebellion in Dublin to criticise Addington's government.

Emmet's rebellion, like Pitt's resignation, had brought Irish affairs back into focus and Fox was determined not to miss this opportunity to attack Addington's Irish policy. Just as Ireland was the most endangered part of the empire, Irish policy was one area where Fox could attack the government. The formation of Addington's government on an anti-Catholic platform meant that they were vulnerable to attack on Irish issues, a vulnerability that was exposed with the outbreak of rebellion in July 1803. The accusations levelled at Fox's brother by the Dublin Castle administration following his alleged mishandling of the insurrection only served to increase Fox's antipathy towards the government. His hitherto ignored parliamentary defence of his brother combined with a simultaneous attack on Hardwicke's conduct in March 1804 demonstrated Fox's commitment both to his brother and to his cause: a new more conciliatory policy for Ireland. He was also able to utilise the rebellion to advocate a new policy for Ireland. The approach made to the Prince of Wales in August 1803 was influenced by events in Dublin and this novel plan showed Fox's commitment to Ireland. Fox throughout his career was interested in finding a solution to the Irish question, and through his Irish contacts he possibly had a better understanding of the Irish situation than many of his contemporaries. This interest was further emphasised when, in

1805, he introduced a petition on behalf of the Catholics to the House of Commons. But, as this chapter has shown, this was not an opportunistic action based solely on a desire to return to government, but part of a long commitment to Ireland and the Catholic question in particular, which had become one of the dominant components of his political life in the years 1801–3.[82]

Notes

1 Grattan to Fox, 12 Dec. 1803, *Memoirs of the Life and Times of the Rt Hon. Henry Grattan by his Son Henry Grattan*, 5 vols (London, 1839–46), V, p. 243.

2 L. G. Mitchell, *Charles James Fox* (Oxford, 1992), p. 252.

3 Martyn Powell, 'Charles James Fox and Ireland', *Irish Historical Studies* 33: 130 (2002), pp. 169–91.

4 Loren Reid, *Charles James Fox* (London, 1969), pp. 349–60; John Derry, *Charles James Fox* (Gateshead, 1972), pp. 382–95; Mitchell, *Charles James Fox*, pp. 178–93.

5 Holland wrote, 'The events in Ireland had so exasperated Mr Fox that he told me and others that his opinions on the subject were neither fit to be spoken in public nor even to be written in private'. H. R. Vassall, Lord Holland, *Memoirs of the Whig Party During my Time*, 2 vols (London, 1852–4), I, p. 128.

6 Oliver McDonagh, *States of Mind* (London, 1983).

7 Derry, *Charles James Fox*; Mitchell, *Charles James Fox*; Reid, *Charles James Fox*; David Powell, *Charles James Fox: Man of the People* (London, 1989); P. M. Geoghegan, *The Irish Act of Union: A Study in High Politics* (Dublin, 1999); G. C. Bolton, *The Passing of the Irish Act of Union* (Oxford, 1966).

8 A reference to the two poems that Fox composed upon the deaths of two dogs belonging to his friend and colleague General Richard Fitzpatrick's. According to David Powell, Fox should have been writing elegies to the Irish parliament instead. Powell, *Charles James Fox*, p. 250.

9 Fox to Gen. Richard Fitzpatrick MP, [undated, 1798?], Lord John Russell (ed.), *Memorials and Correspondence of Charles James Fox*, 4 vols (London, 1853–7), III, p. 281.

10 Fox to Lord Holland, 19 Jan. 1799, Russell (ed.), *Memorials and Correspondence of Charles James Fox*, III, pp. 150–1; and Fox to Henry Grattan, 4 Feb. 1799, *Life and Times of the Rt Hon. Henry Grattan*, V, p. 436.

11 Holland, *Memoirs of the Whig Party*, I, p. 143.

12 See for example Fox to Holland, 26 Feb. 1799, Russell (ed.), *Memorials and Correspondence of Charles James Fox*, III, p. 161.

13 See Debate in Irish House of Commons, 5 Feb. 1800, *Journals of the House of Commons, Ireland*, XX. Grattan's speeches relied less on skilfully deployed argument than on fusillades of pointed phrases and his quotations from Locke, Grotius etc. suggest that Fox may have influenced his arguments. For a description of his oratory see R. B. McDowell, *Grattan, A Life* (Dublin, 2001), p. 33

14 Debate in the House of Commons, 3 Feb. 1800, *The Parliamentary History of England from the Earliest Period to the Year 1803*, 36 vols (London, 1806–20), XXXIV, col. 1386.

15 Ibid.

16 Ibid.

17 Ibid.

18 Speech to Whig Club, 6 May 1800, *Life and Times of the Rt Hon. Henry Grattan*, v, pp. 196–7.

19 Ibid.

20 John Ehrman, *The Younger Pitt*, 3 vols (London, 1969–96), III, p. 509. This was a reiteration of the conclusion made by Richard Pares in his *King George III and the Politicians* (Oxford, 1953), p. 1.

21 Richard Willis, 'William Pitt's resignation in 1801, re-examination and document', *Bulletin of the Institute of Historical Research* 44: 110 (1971), pp. 239–57 at p. 257.

22 See Geoghegan, *The Irish Act of Union*, pp. 208–26, passim.

23 See, for example, Derry, *Charles James Fox*, pp. 385–7; Reid *Charles James Fox*, pp. 373–5, David Schweitzer, 'The Whig political connection between Great Britain and Ireland' (PhD thesis, University of London, 1982).

24 Fox to Richard Fitzpatrick, 3 Feb. 1801, Russell (ed.), *Memorials and Correspondence of Charles James Fox*, III, pp. 319–20.

25 Ibid.

26 Ibid.

27 See Fox to Dennis O'Bryen, Feb. 1801 (BL Add. MSS 12099, fo. 6).

28 Fox to Richard Fitzpatrick, 3 Feb. 1801, Russell (ed.), *Memorials and Correspondence of Charles James Fox*, III, pp. 319–20.

29 Fox to Lord Holland, 8 Feb. 1801, ibid., pp. 186–7.

30 Fox to the Earl of Lauderdale, 19 Feb. 1801, ibid., pp. 325–8.

31 Ibid.

32 Fox to Grey, Feb. 1801 [undated], Russell (ed.), *Memorials and Correspondence of Charles James Fox*, III, pp. 328–30.

33 Fox to Lauderdale, 19 Feb. 1801, ibid., pp. 325–8.

34 Debate in the Commons, 25 Mar. 1801, *Parliamentary History* XXXV, col. 1153.

35 Ibid.

36 Ibid., col. 1156.

37 Ibid.

38 Ibid., col. 1158.

39 Ibid.

40 Fox to Lauderdale, 19 Feb. 1801, Russell (ed.), *Memorials and Correspondence of Charles James Fox*, III, pp. 325–8.

41 Debate in the Commons, 7 May 1801, *Parliamentary History*, XXXVI, col. 642.

42 Schweitzer, 'The Whig connection', p. 334. See also Thomas Bartlett, *The Fall and Rise of the Irish Nation: The Catholic Question 1690–1830* (Dublin, 1992), p. 278.

43 Charles James Fox, *History of the Early Part of the Reign of James II* (London, 1808), pp. 38–9. See also J. Dinwiddy, 'Charles James Fox as historian', *Historical Journal* 12 (1969), pp. 23–34 for a full discussion of Fox's historical endeavours.

44 Fox to Fitzpatrick, 1801 [undated], Russell (ed.), *Memorials and Correspondence of Charles James Fox*, III, p. 334.

45 Fox to Holland, Feb. 1802 [undated], ibid., pp. 190–1.

46 Fox to Robert Adair, 1802 [undated], ibid., p. 387.

47 See Helen Landreth, *The Pursuit of Robert Emmet* (Dublin, 1949); León Ó Broin, *The Unfortunate Mr Robert Emmet* (Dublin, 1958); Patrick M. Geoghegan, *Robert Emmet: A Life* (Dublin, 2002).

48 Ruan O'Donnell, *Robert Emmet and the Rising of 1803* (Dublin, 2003), p. 174.

49 Fox to Grey, July 1803, Russell (ed.), *Memorials and Correspondence of Charles James Fox*, III, pp. 417–18.

50 Fox to Gen. H. E. Fox, 31 July 1803 (BL Add. MSS 37,053).

51 Ibid.

52 Fox to Grey, 8 Aug. 1803, Russell (ed.), *Memorials and Correspondence of Charles James Fox*, III, pp. 420–1.

53 Ibid.

54 See Grattan to Fox, 12 Dec. 1803, *Life and Times of the Rt Hon. Henry Grattan*, V, p. 243.

55 Lord Redesdale to Spencer Perceval, 16 Aug. 1803 in A. P. W. Malcomson (ed.), *Eighteenth Century Irish Official Papers in Great Britain*, 2 vols (Belfast, 1990), II, Private Collections, p. 342.

56 Geoghegan, *Robert Emmet*, p. 168.

57 Allan Blackstock, 'The Union and the military 1801–*c.*1830', *Transactions of the Royal Historical Society*, 6th Series, 10 (2000), pp. 329–51, at p. 337.

58 Ibid., p. 338.

59 Lord Cornwallis to Charles Ross, 8 Dec. 1803, *Correspondence of Charles 1st Marquis Cornwallis*, Charles Ross (ed.), 3 vols (London, 1849), III, p. 507. See also NLI MS 57 for a strong defence of General Fox's actions on 23 July.

60 See Fox to General Fox, 20 Sept. 1803 (BL Add. MSS 37,053).

61 Fox to Grey, 27 Nov. 1803, Russell (ed.), *Memorials and Correspondence of Charles James Fox*, III, pp. 434–6.

62 Ibid. See also his letter to Holland of the same day, Ibid., pp. 229–30.

63 Debate in the Commons, 7 Mar. 1804, *Parliamentary Debates*, I, col. 779.

64 Ibid., col. 780.

65 Ibid., col. 782.

66 Ibid., col. 785.

67 Ibid., col. 786.

68 For a discussion of this conspiracy theory see Geoghegan, *Robert Emmet*, pp. 39–43.

69 Debate in the Commons, 22 Nov. 1803, *Parliamentary Debates*, I, col. 1542.

70 Ibid., col. 1543.

71 Ibid.

72 Ibid., col. 788.

73 Ibid.

74 Fox to the Prince of Wales, 18 Aug. 1803, in A. Aspinall (ed.), *The Correspondence of George, Prince of Wales, 1770–1812* (London, 1967), IV, pp. 402–5.

75 See A. P. W Malcomson, *John Foster: The Politics of the Anglo-Irish Ascendancy* (Oxford 1978), p. 100.

76 Fox to the Prince of Wales, 18 Aug. 1803, in Aspinall (ed.), *The Correspondence of George, Prince of Wales*, IV, pp. 402–5.

77 Ibid.

78 Fox to Grey, 18 Aug. 1803, Russell (ed.), *Memorials and Correspondence of Charles James Fox*, III, pp. 424–6.

79 Ibid.

80 Ibid.

81 Ibid., p. 427.

82 I would like to thank Dr Patrick Geoghegan, who supervised the dissertation on which this chapter is based, for all his assistance and encouragement.

CHAPTER 4

'Unhappy is the man and nation whose destiny depends on the will of another!'

Social and linguistic perspectives on Robert Emmet's mission to France

Sylvie Kleinman

The great French chronicler of the 'human comedy', Honoré de Balzac, once stated that Daniel O'Connell had been one of the only three men truly worth meeting in the first half of the nineteenth century.[1] That two other major figures in Irish history, Theobald Wolfe Tone and Robert Emmet, had in their short lives met and parleyed with the most infamous of Balzac's great men, Napoleon Bonaparte, is a testimony to the internationalism of the United Irishmen. Both Tone's heroic overtures to the French Directory and private audiences with General Bonaparte (as he was then), and Emmet's noble but unsuccessful dealings with the increasingly despotic First Consul of France, are cherished if emotive episodes in the romanticised myth of Irish republicanism. But the shaping of Irish nationalist identity fed on the cult of disappointment, and the apportionment of blame on foreign others, who had either oppressed Ireland or fuelled her hopes, only to betray them. This was particularly true in the confused context of post-Union Ireland, when national self-identities were defined by the Franco-British conflict. Narratives of this decisive period regularly throw up the recurrent motif of Ireland distancing itself from France, in sharp contrast to the enlightened optimism of the 1790s. Understandably, a cult of bitter disappointment at yet another invasion that never was grew quickly after Emmet's demise, and rendered the French irrelevant to the development of his legend.[2] As Marianne Elliott has pointed out,

The quotation in the title of this chapter is by Theobald Wolfe Tone, 9 April 1796 (*The Writings of Theobald Wolfe Tone, 1763–98*, ed. T. W. Moody, R. B. McDowell and C. J. Woods (Oxford, 2001), II, p. 149).

'The future of Irish republicanism lay with Emmet's romantic legend of the noble victim and the imperialist [French] tyrant.'[3]

We are not surprised, therefore, to learn that the statement quoted in the chapter title was formulated in Paris, by an Irishman forced by political circumstances into exile from the cherished land of his birth, but having found an honourable asylum in revolutionary France. Though recorded by Tone, its despondent mood aptly introduces this discussion of Robert Emmet's mission to France, which proposes, however, to adopt a fresh approach to this much romanticised episode. While much of the 1798 historiography has, somewhat understandably, tended to focus on the political outcome of the Franco-Irish partnership – a failure – I shall reflect the cultural turn in Irish studies by discussing the communicative *process* underlying this significant chapter in Ireland's international relations.

In his celebrated polychrome rendering of Robert Emmet's interview with Napoleon, J. D. Reigh confidently transposed into print what oral memory had never doubted, namely the young Irishman's skills as a tactician and communicator.[4] Leaving nothing to the imagination, Reigh depicts Emmet boldly upright, dominating one half of the print, poised and ready for the exchange. We know all too well the outcome of that encounter, but as Patricia Palmer has incisively stated 'Historians are inclined to take the transparency of language for granted. They can cheerfully record the burden of a parley without wondering about the mechanics of precisely how it was conducted.'[5] Inspired by Palmer's query, this chapter will fill a much-needed gap in the historical narrative of 1798 by discussing the manner in which Emmet overcame the inevitable linguistic barriers raised during his mission. Without these insights into his intellectual abilities, and indeed those of other key United Irishmen, can one say that their history has truly been written?

A EUROPEAN GEORGE WASHINGTON?

Emmet's story was indeed one that easily lent itself to myth making, but in his comprehensive and insightful study of Emmet's short life, Patrick Geoghegan has established a clear connection between many facets of his life and that of the archetypal hero-quest.[6] Appropriately, a recurrent motif sees the hero drawn to a 'remote land of exile from which he returns to perform his . . . deeds among men . . . bringing back from his adventure the means for the regeneration of his society'.[7] Called to some 'high historical undertaking', the hero must survive a succession of trials and miraculous tests, and render 'back into the language of the light world the pronouncements of the dark'. The metaphor of decrypting hidden meanings is borrowed here to justify this discussion of how Robert Emmet made sense of a foreign tongue.[8] But a hero's existence is often punctuated by human-like failings, and thus Emmet's story symbolically begins with a paradoxical episode in the life of his own boyhood hero, which indirectly relates to Palmer's argument. About a quarter-century before his birth, in the densely forested wilds of western Pennsylvania, a skirmish between French soldiers and British colonial troops was to trigger one of the most colossal cultural propaganda wars in Western Europe, one in which Ireland would soon occupy a precarious position. The inexperienced 22-year-old militia commander on the English side, overly reliant on his Indian guide, had misinterpreted the moves of the French, and the ensuing confusion led to an exchange of gunshots. This resulted in the accidental death of Jumonville, the French-Canadian officer in charge and, much to the jubilation of his cocky British counterpart, the taking of several scalps. The French then captured the British fort and presented its commander with a statement. Once signed, it would confirm he had breached the rules of engagement, and accepted responsibility for the 'assassination'. But the British commander, son of a Virginian plantation owner and a surveyor by profession, refused to comply. Despite being fully familiar with the circumstances of the incident related in the statement, Lieutenant Colonel George Washington of the Virginia regiment insisted he could not sign. The text was in French, a language he did not understand.[9] This episode is said to have marked a turning point in an extraordinary career which (despite his apparent monoglossia) was to see Washington become an international hero, transforming his birthplace into an independent and democratic nation. His life fuelled the determination of many United Irishmen, most notably Theobald Wolfe Tone and the young and impressionable Robert Emmet. Vowing as a boy to become the George Washington of Ireland, Emmet would fulfil this pledge, seconding Malachy Delaney on a secret mission to France to lobby for an invasion and deliver his country from the yoke of British tyranny. However, unlike his hero, Emmet has left behind traces of his fluency and ease of expression in the language of Voltaire and Rousseau, and from today's multicultural self-perception, we may wish to think his mission to the continent, and noble overcoming of language barriers, made him a *European* George Washington.

Emmet enjoyed all the cultural benefits of his genteel upbringing, and in keeping with our assumptions on the educational attainments of the late eighteenth-century political élite, he grew up in a multilingual environment. A lifelong friendship was maintained with a Marquise Gabrielle de Fontenay, a French émigré who had settled in Ireland and tutored the Emmets in French, and her correspondence with both Robert and Thomas Addis has contributed to scholarship on the family.[10] It is said Latin and French were preferred as the languages of habitual use in the Emmet household, Irish spoken to the servants, and 'English seldom used, except in social life'.[11] Certainly as one of the more gifted pupils of the celebrated Whyte's Academy of Grafton Street,

Emmet would have been exposed to a curriculum of classical and modern languages. Theoretical models of language acquisition in the 1960s were somewhat disdainful of the methods employed by past generations, and rejected 'grammar translation' as it apparently discouraged spontaneous conversation and the development of meaningful communicative competence. If indeed translation laid much emphasis on written forms of language, and the syntactic exactitude which that implied, it also helped to develop a broad lexis and the familiarity of writing in a foreign tongue. Both Robert and Thomas Addis Emmet would put this skill to good use in France, though for purposes their language masters might well have shuddered at.

Furthermore, pupils may have spent solitary hours pouring over translations, but the whole education system revolved around that pivotal activity of the age, public oratory and the mastery of rhetoric. Emmet famously had been introduced to it by Whyte, who excelled in that discipline.[12] Public declamation evidently enhanced general communicative skills which, despite today's emphasis on orality and ephemeral language, are difficult to stimulate in a classroom environment. The experience of acquiring multiple languages is also known to be beneficial, and mastering the rules of rhetoric and sound argumentation would have rounded off Emmet's linguistic preparation for his mission to France, as we shall soon discover. Unfortunately one can say very little as to his short time in Trinity, as it was not until the nineteenth century that modern languages were taught in a formal and structured way, exams scheduled and degrees conferred. In 1775 the provost John Hely-Hutchinson had, it is true, introduced a regulation establishing professorships in Spanish, French, Italian and German, but the teaching was informal and complementary to the establishment of a Riding-House. Young 'gentlemen of Fortune' could thus, according to the Provost, be sent 'abroad more capable of receiving Improvements from their Travels', though Hely-Hutchinson would eventually discover that Emmet's time abroad had been a kind of 'parody of the Grand Tour which a young gentleman of his education might have made in happier times'.[13]

Any linguistic examination of Emmet's secret diplomacy is bound to be much graver and less colourful than the experiences of an earlier Trinity graduate, Theobald Wolfe Tone. The sorrowful testimony of his arrival in France, claiming to speak but an 'execrable . . . detestable jargon' reads like a true eighteenth-century narrative of misfortune, in which he cast himself as the suffering hero. However, his diary is a fascinating, if subjective, case study of goal-oriented language-learning in an adult.[14] Despite occasionally casting himself as a bungling Anglophone straight out of a period stage farce, Tone was quickly to gain fluency and leave a positive and lasting impression on the political and military decision makers he was to encounter. He could never have guessed, in his personal dealings with such notable figures as Napoleon and Talleyrand, that he was preparing the ground for the tireless efforts on behalf of Ireland that his friend Thomas Addis Emmet, and the younger Robert before him, would make in the early years of the next century. One will simply recall Tone's meeting with Napoleon in December 1797, then (only) the rising General Bonaparte, who had expressed curiosity at where the Irishman had learned to speak French. It is worth remembering that the Corsican had himself only learned the language as a schoolboy (through the grammar-translation method!) and is said to have felt inhibited at not shaking off a perceptible accent in French well into adulthood. This vignette contextualises Emmet's own contacts with Napoleon within the complex mosaic of languages and national identities which was then Europe. A final point worth stressing is that while the political events which unfolded in Ireland in the 1790s had been largely influenced by the Francophilia of the age, this did not necessarily mean that leading radicals were Francophones, that is fluent speakers of French. It is true that knowledge of foreign languages was widespread, but many (if not most) polemical works had been translated into English; participation in the cosmopolitan culture did not, therefore, necessarily require a command of the language.[15]

EMMET AND DELANEY'S 1800 MEMORIAL TO NAPOLEON BONAPARTE

> Nous venons de la part de nos concitoyens d'Irlande pour demander la cinquième fois le secours de la Nation françoise[16]

Historiographical narratives of Emmet's mission on the continent focus on the political dimension of his actions and, as his movements are thoroughly documented in the recent publications by Elliott, Geoghegan and O'Donnell, there is no need to revisit them.[17] The following discussion is therefore intended to complement theirs, and in particular contextualise the composition of the 1800 Memorial.

In sharp contrast to Tone, Robert Emmet left behind so few papers that his legend as heroic icon was easily constructed around the mystery of the unknown, or rare writings composed in dramatic circumstances, as underlined by Marianne Elliott.[18] But one text, written on the continent in the later summer of 1800 and one of the earliest examples of Emmet's determined rhetoric, had remained unknown until very recently. Given its ultimate purpose, it is also one of the most significant of his compositions, and like the corpus of documents archived in France which testify to their intensive lobbying there, is a significant (if heretofore neglected) part of the legacy of the United Irishmen.[19] Somewhat eerily, the clear penmanship of the Memorial is unmistakably the same 'strong firm hand, without blot, correction or erasure' as that of Emmet's celebrated last letter to William Wickham, written from his prison cell almost exactly three years later.[20] The 1800 Memorial, boldly intended for none other than Napoleon, is an informative but eloquent plea for assistance from France, formulated in virtually flawless French. Though it is signed with the names of both Robert Emmet and Malachy Delaney (the senior United Irishman on the mission), some of its phrases unmistakably echo other writings of Emmet's in English. But as they are in French, they add a unique dimension to his legacy. Thus vital clues to Emmet's legend have been found in translation, demonstrating how the political failure of his mission to France has tended to overshadow more positive facets of this episode, which merit closer scrutiny.

Though Emmet famously assumed various pseudonyms and practised several handwritings to confound the authorities, that text is unmistakably written in the same hand as others attributed to him, and despite the clandestinity of their mission its authorship is clearly marked as that of both Robert Emmet and Malachy Delaney, both names signed in the former's hand. Sent to the continent by a restructured United Irish organisation to renew negotiations for a French expedition, the two men travelled to Hamburg in late August 1800, and from there addressed the Memorial to General Augereau, commander of the French-controlled territory in Holland and with whom Delaney had served in the Austrian Army.[21]

Appended to the formal plea for military assistance, which the authors clearly wrote in the hope it would be forwarded to the First Consul, was a request for passports into France. Twenty years older than Emmet, Delaney was officially the senior member of the delegation, and one feared by Wickham as a man of considerable talents. While not wishing to diminish his contribution, scholars can be grateful that as the nominated secretary of the mission it was Emmet's task to draft the missive. The style of its rhetorical flourishes, and the manner of its eloquent plea to the French authorities for an expeditionary force, make attribution of at least some of the creative dimension to Emmet straightforward, as many phrases echo the *Manifesto to the Provisional Government* and the final speech from the dock. We have no indication of the extent of Delaney's own multilingualism save that he probably spoke German and had, at minimum, conversational French, a prerequisite for most officers at the time regardless of birth or allegiance. Given the incriminating potential of the Memorial, it is unlikely Emmet and Delaney called on third parties to assist with its composition, but as a confident and near-perfect composition in French, the Memorial is a dignified testimonial of the lobbying conducted in a foreign language by the United Irish. Finally, a handful of basic syntactic and orthographic errors indicate no assistance was sought from a literate Francophone. Essentially a functional text filed away in administrative archives, it remained unknown until recognised by Elliott as influential in Emmet's bid to gain an audience with the French, and translated extracts were published in an article commissioned for the special bicentenary issue of *History Ireland.*[22]

In late summer of 1800, the French archives of various ministries were already brimming with numerous documents relating to the political situation in Ireland, and various plans for incursions and invasions into the British Isles.[23] Of particular relevance were the tireless submissions of Général Humbert, increasingly sidelined by the current regime as a former ally of Hoche who embodied military valour in the name of the Republic. Relentlessly seeking command in a renewed strike at England, he had maintained a close connection with John Sullivan, his former aide in the Mayo expedition of 1798 and previously a staff translator at the ministry of foreign affairs, and had also befriended Thomas Russell and other exiled United Irishmen in Paris. Far from being the uneducated brute portrayed by historians overly reliant on biased secondary sources, Humbert was after all 'the first, the only French general to have skirmished with the English on their own territory'. Three memorials, two in the distinct hand of John Sullivan and thus the fruit of their collaboration, were sent to the authorities between July and October 1800, as the Emmet and Delaney Memorial was itself making its way to Paris. Arguing that an expedition would serve France on economic as well as military grounds, Humbert also called for the gathering of the United Irishmen in France into an Irish Legion, and laconically justified upholding 'l'espoir de la Nation Irlandoise, ce qui ne peut qu'inquiéter nos ennemis'.[24]

The Emmet and Delaney Memorial would thus not have arrived unexpectedly on anyone's desk. Succinctly presenting its arguments in just over one thousand words, it is dated using the revolutionary calendar, soon to be abolished but still a reminder of the upheavals France had known, as 28 fructidor 8 (15 September 1800). The text is addressed to the 'Citoyen Consul', and in the upper right-hand corner of the first folio we see two annotations in different handwritings confirming it was passed on from Talleyrand, once again minister for foreign affairs, to the 'premier consul' – Bonaparte. The latter's signature clearly overscribes the first line of the text. The opening lines immediately announce its purpose, an exhortative plea for assistance from the French nation: 'Nous venons de la part de nos concitoyens de l'Irlande pour demander la cinquième fois le secours de la Nation Françoise.' The authors go on to provide factual proof underpinning their request, namely that the controversial Union Bill passed earlier that year, 'n'a point adouci les mécontentements'. Vowing the armed Irish would take only twenty days' drilling to be worthy of fighting alongside the French, this section ends with a forthright appeal to emotion: 'est-ce que vous voulez nous abandonner?'

Next, vital facts were provided to sway decision makers, namely the extent of Crown Forces the French were likely to encounter, though admittedly accurate figures were hard to come by. One is reminded how light-heartedly

Tone had recorded Lazare Hoche's own *insouciance* on this very same issue: '"Oh", said he, as to opposition, "*Je m'en fous!*"', which Tone prudently refused to translate for his readers.[25] Emmet and Delaney though had remained rigidly formal, and went on to explain they were to keep the strictest secrecy, and avoid communicating with their compatriots 'here', meaning Hamburg. Unfortunately, Emmet and Delaney had been spotted by the double agent Samuel Turner. His information to Dublin Castle pointed to Emmet's preponderant role in the communicative aspect of their mission, as he stated: 'Several memorials were prepared by E.'[26] But Emmet, Delaney and other associates may well in turn have spotted Turner, as they requested passports to France under false names, 'afin que les malveillants de notre nation qui sont à Paris et payés par le gouvernement d'Angleterre ne reconnoisse point nos noms'.[27] Despite these apprehensions, and much to the delight of future generations of researchers, the Memorial is signed with their real names. The text closes with a religious allusion characteristic of both Emmet's other writings, and phraseology employed in the United Irish oath: 'nous jurons a la face du Ciel de repondre jusqu'a la derniere goutte de notre sang pour notre patrie'.

This manuscript, and its Gallicised expression of the pledge to sacrifice the very last drop of blood for the nation, would not have been accessible to those who later elevated Emmet's story to hagiography, and as such forms an important chapter of his legacy and that of the United Irishmen. Readers of the Memorial cannot doubt the self-assurance and autonomy Emmet would have possessed when, following up the written acts of communication, he would have had to engage in face-to-face interaction with senior French figures. Given Emmet's refined linguistic skills, the occasional grammatical errors embedded in the otherwise elegant (if at times dense) prose of the French Memorial take us by surprise. These discrepancies are attributable to an English speaker making interlingual transfers, and only one phrase could possibly have misled the reader. Nowhere is there conveyed an impression of incompetence in the overall abilities of the authors, shedding doubts on their abilities to mastermind an insurrection. Typical errors, which many speakers of French and English experience owing to the relative similarities of both languages, are explained by what are known as false friends of the translator, or *faux-amis*. Many words are spelled the same in both languages, and though they may share a common origin their meanings have diverged over time. In cases where words *did* share the same meaning, Emmet chose to use the English spelling (consideration being given that French spelling in 1800 was not the same as today). Random examples are '*déliverance*', spelled correctly in the second sentence of the text (without the /e/ in the second syllable), though the /e/ is clearly struck out further on in the manuscript, signalling the author's hesitation; '*passport*', spelled as in English three times, omitting the final /e/; '*compatriots*' (altering the word's pronunciation in French to 'compatrio(s)' [*sic*].

Semantic *faux-amis* are far more common, and can confuse the reader. We see this in the (incorrect) selection of the noun *épreuve*, no doubt resulting from its proximity with the English lexical item *proof*: 'Cinq cent mille hommes ont été compris dans l'organisation de l'Union irlandaise, l'entrée actuelle de ce nombre . . . est une *épreuve* d'une telle universalité de la [*sic*] sentiment qui environne ce corps' [my italics] The sentence intends to convey the idea that the high numbers having joined the ranks of the United Irishman (exaggerated, as stated above), despite cruel and constant persecution, is a *demonstration* of the feelings motivating that body. However, the author has predictably confused *preuve* (the equivalent for 'proof'), with *épreuve*, owing to a phenomenon known as initial syllable recognition. By the late eighteenth century *épreuve* was primarily employed in French to described an *ordeal*, and the verb from which that substantive evolved, *éprouver*, is also incorrectly employed further on: 'Nous vous offrons (ces hommes) . . . sans avoir le moindre doute de leur succès – car ils ont *éprouvé* leur force'. [my italics] This leads to a contradiction, or *contresens*, as literally translated the sentence means the force of the men has been *spent*, whereas the intention is to convey that they have *demonstrated*, or *given proof*, of their strength.

Certain errors made by non-natives demonstrate they have internalised rules and patterns in the language they are learning. To compensate for a conscious lexical deficiency, learners frequently coin new words which appear to conform to the rules of spelling and morphology in the language in question, referred to nowadays by applied linguistics as a creative strategy. The Memorial features such neologisms demonstrating Emmet's 'morphological creativity', such as *certainté*, a direct productive transfer of the English substantive *certainty*. Here it is used as a noun, and daringly formed by appending the nominal suffix /-té/ to the existing French adjective 'certain', that is certain + té. The authors, presumably Emmet, familiar with such nouns as '*sûreté*' derived from a similar construction, would produce a new word, also triggered in their mental vocabulary by the cognate English equivalent *certainty*. Though the correct French word would have been *certitude*, the sentence in the Memorial is perfectly coherent. A final innovative coinage further demonstrates (Emmet's?) strategic competence in terms of bridging lexical gaps, here in the transfer of a basic transitive verb of spatial displacement, often posing problems of transfer between the two languages: 'nous attendons ses [Bonaparte's] ordres pour *voiler* auprès de lui'. Where in English such transitive verbs are frequently formed using the name of the appropriate 'contrivance', as in 'to sail' where the noun 'sail' becomes the verb, French phrasal verbs of displacement often employ compound forms, such as 'mettre à la voile'. This was the correct form employed on one occasion by Edwin Lewins (a fellow United

Irishman educated in France), whereas Emmet's older brother Thomas Addis (equally fluent, but experiencing like Robert occasional and minor difficulties) had opted for the pragmatic but slightly unusual 'faire voile'.[28] More surprising, given the overall sophistication of the prose throughout the 1800 Memorial, is a basic gender error where instead of the article 'du', *sentiment* is preceded by the feminine articles 'de la'. Typical of English speakers is the omission of the definite article *le* before a title, as in 'nous espérons que général Augereau voudra bien . . . etc.', instead of '*le* général Augereau'.

Equally problematic is the formation of the perfect tense, as verbs using the auxiliary *to have* in English do not always use *avoir* in French. Through a process of backtranslation, the phrase 'des troupes . . . qui *n'ont* jamais *sorti* du royaume' is revealed as a direct transfer of the English '*have* never *left* the kingdom', whereas in French the verb *sortir* (when not followed by a direct object) is governed by the auxiliary *être*. The presence of these noble linguistic failures in a text intended for Napoleon Bonaparte – not a Francophone by birth – is almost paradoxical, and conveys a charming sense of 'otherness' in the author's voice which is confirmed in the process as that of a non-native. But internal correspondence between the French authorities makes clear that Robert Emmet was perceived as 'a single-minded negotiator with talents as a military tactician, at least on paper'.[29] This demonstration of how leading United Irishmen overcame linguistic barriers illustrates the central part of rhetorical persuasion in public discourse (practised not only in the mother tongue, but in Greek and especially Latin), and compositional skills acquired through study of the classics were easily transferred in any language. At the core of Emmet's legend is the transcendent oratorical skills he had displayed as one of the most memorable debaters of Trinity's College Historical Society.[30] Mandatory reading for the otherwise introverted and unassuming Emmet would have included the celebrated *Lectures Concerning Oratory*, delivered in the college by John Lawson and published in Dublin 1759. Possibly Emmet remembered one of Lawson's rules when planning his composition to Napoleon: 'You should, as much as possible, adapt yourself to the capacities of your audience . . . be perfectly clear, yet never tedious, unadorned, yet never insipid, close in reasoning, yet never obscure'.[31]

However, the art of oratory was also founded on the 'scaffolding' of the basic parts of the speech, and the Memorial replicates this essential structure. The language employed to persuade is intended to stimulate to laudable action, and appeals to emotion were not uncommon in this type of discourse. Rhetorical questions established a direct connection between sender and recipient of the message, as in 'voulez-vous nous abandonner?' Such requests were underpinned by the honesty of the sender's motivations, and innate truthfulness: 'nous nous fions à la franchise de notre representation et de nos demandes . . . par cette verité, nous demandons votre secours'.

Other stylistic effects – central to the appeal of polemical texts often read out in public – were triadic structures and emphatic repetition of key verbs:

> Nous vous offrons encore ces hommes. Nous les offrons, sans avoir le moindre doute de leur succès . . . Nous vous offrons davantage, de cette partie de la nation . . . Nous vous offrons la force réunie . . . Nous vous offrons la compensation ample . . . Nous vous offrons deux cent mille braves irlandois

We find this again in the second paragraph of the *Manifesto to the Provisional Government*, addressed to the 'People of Ireland', where the verb 'show' is repeated four times: 'You will show to the world . . . you will show to the people of England . . . you will show them'.[32]

Finally, the strategic alliance was cemented by a shared Anglophobia, and it is no doubt allegorical flourishes such as the following one which had prompted the informer Turner to allude, not to Emmet's French, but to the inflammatory nature of the memorials 'drawn up in the *usual language* of the party here': 'deux cent mille braves irlandois . . . dignes de combattre de coté de l'armée Françoise et *d'extorquer* la paix du Monde dans le *coeur* de l'Angleterre'. [my italics] The belligerent metaphor of ripping peace from England's very life-force is an early echo of the dramatic appeal in the opening phrase of the *Manifesto*: 'the only satisfactory proof of your independence . . . your *wresting* it from England with *your hands*'. [my italics] That same image is reiterated in his speech from the dock. This discursive style merely reflected the propaganda of the time, and the bilingual and skilful William Duckett had deemed such political communicative techniques 'l'arme la plus terrible dont on puisse se servir pour nuire à ce gouvernement [i.e. England]'.[33]

'. . . CETTE CONVERSATION'

Robert Emmet, Malachy Delaney and possibly John Grey travelled to Paris sometime between November 1800 and early January 1801, and they may very well have been the three Irishmen possibly giving pseudonyms, and referred to by Fouché, the Minister of Police, in a letter to Talleyrand signalling their arrival.[34] Upon entering France, these men had requested permission to go to the capital specifically to see the First Consul, this being a much more plausible version than that provided by Turner.[35] Stating that General Augereau had deemed the mission of so much importance, he was induced to 'quit his command and escort them [i.e. Delaney and Emmet] to Paris where he introduced them to the First Consul', certainly confers a disproportionate status on the informer's prey. Therefore one must look to French archives which none the less leave gaps, as Talleyrand glowingly describes to the First Consul an impressive memorial presented to him in person by 'deux irlandais' whom he received in early January 1801, and though they remain unidentified we will presume they were Robert Emmet and Malachy Delaney.[36] This second missive would appear to be a revised text from the September one, judging by the way Talleyrand describes its structure and content. Firstly, Emmet and Delaney seem to request an invasion of 30,000 troops in three landing points, in variance with the earlier version. Talleyrand then employs a most evocative turn of phrase to describe how the Irishmen portray the existing English forces in Ireland, certainly not in the first text: '[des] Irlandais recrutés de force, ou volontairement enrolés pour apprendre la guerre et la faire ensuite à leurs maîtres'. Finally, the 'authors of the *mémoire*' detail the broader consequences of the separation of Ireland, namely that it would lead to 'la ruine du commerce et du gouvernement anglois'.

The debate as to Talleyrand's corruption will not be reopened here, but despite cynicism among the United Irishmen as to the overall sincerity of the French, his favourable impressions seem genuine and suit the purpose of this discussion: 'Le mémoire des deux Irlandais est très bien fait, net, précis, et *noblement écris.*' [my italics] Qualifying the prose as 'noble' is a tragic irony, as we know that attribute would forever be collocated with Emmet's heroic failures. Talleyrand was then ordered by Bonaparte to have the two Irishmen liaise with the commander of the Armée de l'Ouest who would lead the expedition, and for that reason the Memorial was forwarded to Général Bernadotte. However, Bernadotte's letter acknowledging receipt is puzzling, as he thanks the minister for the attached mémoire which he infers is in English, adding 'je l'examinerai avec soin, dès qu'il sera traduit'.[37] Despite exhaustive research, this second memorial has not been located, therefore one must regretfully assume Emmet and/or Delaney chose for whatever reason not to make a second attempt in French. It is not impossible that Bernadotte's reply was hastily dictated and based on the assumption the memorial was in English. Possibly the Irish felt they deserved an invasion under the command of someone who mastered sufficient English to grasp the gist of a 'well planned, neat, precise and nobly written' military plan, though Lazare Hoche's reputation was never diminished by his monoglossia. Talleyrand himself had spent many years in Philadelphia, and could competently judge the stylistic quality of text in English. He was also intimately acquainted with various facets of the Irish question, and possibly when listening to Emmet he had been reminded of the eloquent overtures of his predecessors, Lewins and Tone, whom he had met in 1797–8. The Irish question would continue to pursue him, as ten years later he would receive an emotive petition from Tone's widow Matilda, requesting an extension of the pension attributed to William, her only surviving child and now a 20 year old enrolled at the Cavalry school of St Germain en Laye. Matilda's courage and firm resolve shines through in this letter she must deliberately have chosen to write on 20 June, Tone's birthday.[38]

In the process of inventing a nation, Elliott underlines that there is much selective memory and tendency to error-ridden historiography.[39] Despite having demonstrated so far that Emmet would have been a credible and efficient spokesman for the United Irishmen, in any language, regrettably one must be cautious and conclude that it is highly unlikely the meeting with Napoleon ever took place. In fact Emmet and Delaney had anticipated that a chance to 'merely communicate' with the First Consul may be turned down, as their request to do so concludes with the phrase 'si ce n'est impropre', that is, *improper*. That Napoleon ordered his minister for foreign affairs to liaise with these praiseworthy, but after all unaccredited secret Irish 'diplomats', and put them in contact with a leading military figure, was in itself impressive. After the events of July 1803, he would clearly state that senior members of his government were to be put 'at the disposal' of Thomas Addis Emmet and other United Irish leaders in France, but it would be untimely to personally grant them an audience.[40] One of Emmet's earliest biographies was in fact researched and written in Paris by Louise Comtesse d'Haussonville, a grand-daughter of the celebrated and controversial *salonnière* Madame de Stael. Possibly her mother would have recalled meeting Emmet as a young girl, and how his energy was expressed in his 'melancholy features'.[41] Deeply inspired by her subject, she states she had trawled in vain through French archives in a desperate search for what would have been 'cette conversation . . . entre le grand Bonaparte et [le] jeune enthousiaste irlandais'.[42] To the nationalist imagination, Robert Emmet is depicted in Reigh's 1895 print as a formidable interlocutor, who despite the ultimate failure of his efforts, had been received with dignity by the French leader, seemingly on his own as Malachy Delaney is 'airbrushed' out of history. In keeping with Palmer's pursuit of the true materiality of crucial political exchanges conducted across language barriers, one can certainly say that Emmet *would* have conducted his face-to-face negotiations in a skilful and credible manner, and without the need of an interpreter. He would have impressed the First Consul and his entourage with some of his characteristic turns of phrase preserved for future generations in the 1800 Memorial, and in their own language.

LE SPLEEN DE PARIS

Possibly too much has been made of Emmet's reclusiveness in Paris as a symptom of his political distancing from a despicable and increasingly despotic régime. In the process it is implied that he rejected the entire French nation, its people and culture. A rare and important eyewitness account of Paris at that time is provided in the occasionally giddy, but perceptive journal of Catherine Wilmot, who travelled to the continent with the Mount Cashells.

Their endless heady and glamorous engagements had been facilitated by the Peace of Amiens and they took full advantage of the increasingly *arriviste* climate of the Consulate's 'new' aristocracy. Having met Emmet, Wilmot attributed his reserve as a symptom of his 'extreme prejudice against French society', a fact reiterated by an informer who said he lived 'very privately'.[43] That his wish not to mingle with the French was not a consequence of language barriers, given his known competence in the host language, is a fact astutely observed by Elliott.[44] On a more pragmatic note, it is evident that Emmet was no fool and knew, like the less assertive Tone before him, that Paris would be 'swarming with spies and informers', many of them English posing as Americans. Having to be constantly on his guard among the substantial and vibrant community of Anglophones in Paris was demanding enough, before one was to take on any *malveillants* among the French speakers. Emmet may have been reputed to have fluent French, but he had learned the language as a polite accomplishment and practised it among peers in the familiar environment of lessons or drawing room chatter, back in Ireland. That he could confidently exchange colloquialisms at the local *restaurateur*'s is less certain, and we have little indication he sought to mingle among the common people. The social stratification of French society was only just adapting to the imposition of the French language as the national medium of communication, and regional dialects and patois were still prevalent. While the challenge of detecting false accents intended to convince interlocutors of assumed identities and nationalities may seem to belong in cloak and dagger novels, it was a daily reality then and one of which Irish exiles in particular were wary.[45] In one (rare) indication of Emmet' s light-hearted side, he shows he was no stranger to the age's fondness for poking fun at erudite usage of French, through the technique of phonetical exaggerations of Anglophone pronunciation. He thus describes in a letter how, by accident, he was reunited with his brother Thomas Addis at the Amsterdam Post Office: 'I believe the Messieurs were a little surprised to see us run and hug each other *à l'Irlandez* [*sic*] without going through the previous ceremony of taking off our hats'.[46] If indeed Robert Emmet's political disappointment manifested itself in deep melancholy, he would not have been the first to experience what French romantic poets like Vigny and Baudelaire would later term *le spleen de Paris*. Embedded in the Irish psyche of exile was a resentment of the host country, even if it provided welcome asylum. For Emmet this would have been temporary, as unlike Tone he never contemplated settling in France, and would not have engaged in the mental process of long-term commitment and assimilation into his new environment. Contemporary literature on culture shock clearly points to feelings of depression and, most poignantly in the case of Robert Emmet, manifestations of fatalism.[47] In many cases social isolation is seriously compounded by language barriers, but Emmet did not have this problem, and appeared generally comfortable in the company of the 'respectable persons' he is said to have met.

Yet insufficient emphasis has been placed on positive cultural influences which may have impacted on this still young and impressionable man. Given his lifelong passion for chemistry, he was drawn to the substantial community of scientists in Paris, among who were some of the greatest chemists of the age, and contemporaries of the brilliant Lavoisier. Emmet met Vauquelin, who before discovering chrome had been a student of Fourcroy, the latter co-author with Lavoisier and Berthollet of the groundbreaking 1787 nomenclature of rational chemistry which established a modern, systematic naming of chemical compounds. As O'Donnell has suggested, it was possibly to his master that Vauquelin had offered to introduce Emmet (merely described as one of 'the first chemists of the age'), but one takes mischievous pleasure in thinking that it may have been Berthollet.[48] While Emmet may not have wished to hear of his time as a scientific expert on Napoleon's *other* expedition of 1798 (Egypt), he would have expressed (if privately) interest in the formula for chlorate-based explosives Berthollet was shortly to publish. Further satisfaction at the possibility of this encounter can be gained in the knowledge that Berthollet was to vote for Napoleon's deposition in 1814. One may hazard the guess that Emmet would have met Fourcroy, a collaborator of Lavoisier and a pioneer of plant chemistry, who would have encouraged the young Irishman to visit the Jardin des Plantes (which Tone did visit).

Living for some time on the rue d'Amboise then the nearby rue de la Loi (shortly to resume its former name, the rue de Richelieu), Emmet would literally have been following in Tone's footsteps when out and about, as both were near the rue Vivienne where the latter lodged after his arrival in February 1796. We know much less of his leisure pursuits than we do of Tone's, and though informers depict him as dedicated to his mission, we must not assume Emmet too did not indulge in the occasional *flâneries*, living only a quick stroll from the Palais-Royal and the Louvre which had housed the Museum Central des Arts since 1793.

That Emmet was a sincere Christian, his poetry inspired by visions of divine consolation, has been discussed in Geoghegan's recent biography. He may, like Thomas Russell, have attended church services which the restoration of Roman Catholic worship had made the talk of the town in the autumn of 1801. Emmet must, like Tone, have 'lounged among the booksellers' under the arcades of the Palais-Royal, and it may have been there he had purchased his cherished copy of Templehoff's work on the Seven Years War, as well as a *Nomenclature* of French military regulations he alludes to in his speech from the dock. Most importantly, despite an eye affliction which became troublesome (and may partially explain his reclusiveness), Emmet had easy access to the Bibliothèque Nationale on the rue de la Loi. Apart from pursuing scientific and military interests, he may have found solace in reading Chateaubriand's seminal *Génie du Christianisme*, published to much acclaim in April 1802. This eloquent apology for faith heralded literary Romanticism, and the inherent poeticism of his work may have struck a chord with Emmet, and inspired the 'brooding, messianic verse' he penned before his demise.[49]

Mystery surrounds his last few weeks in France, an episode one would wish to have more insights on as he spent some time in Normandy, posing as a labourer and assisting an English tanner who had taken him in.[50]

* * *

> 'Quand mon pays aura repris son rang parmi les nations de la terre, alors, mais alors seulement, que mon épitaphe soit écrite . . .'

Not long after Robert Emmet's demise, his legacy and historiography – if not his epitaph – were already being written in France. Though it was not until 1858 that Louise d'Haussonville's biography was first published, it is clear Emmet had made a lasting impression on her mother. As a child she had been privileged to meet him at the celebrated salon of Madame de Stael, herself ostracised from Paris by the First Consul and soon to be exiled from France. Insufficient emphasis has been placed on any outspoken anti-Bonapartist views Emmet may have encountered in such anti-establishment gatherings, and certainly anyone who had met him could not have been unmoved when later reading his speech from the dock. His brother Thomas Addis who, from May 1803 to March 1804, persistently lobbied Napoleon and his Minister for War Berthier for a French-backed invasion, ensured its publication in both French and English in *Le Moniteur* and *The Argus* on 9 and 11 January respectively.[51] As an illustration of the impact of some of its most potent passages, Emmet's vow to receive the French if they came as enemies with a sword in one hand, and a torch in another, easily transcends language barriers and finds resonance with anyone familiar with his story:

> Si les Français, sans y avoir été invités par le peuple de l'Irlande, se présentaient avec des desseins hostiles sur nos côtes, je leur résisterais de tous mes moyens . . . mes concitoyens, je vous crierais d'acourir le fer d'une main, et la torche de l'autre, pour les repousser de vos rivages, ou pour les immoler sur leurs bords, plutôt que de les voir souiller de leur despotisme le sol de notre pays.[52]

As preparations for an invasion of Britain were intensifying in 1804, the poet Jean-François Tissot had composed a lengthy elegy entitled *Les Trois Conjurés d'Irlande, ou L'ombre d'Emmet*. He confessed in his introduction how moved he had been by reading in *Le Moniteur* the last speech of 'ce vertueux patriote', who had left so fine a monument of courage and breadth of spirit in addressing his judges before being condemned.[53] A sympathetic editorial had prefaced the speech, and guaranteed that Emmet's demise would capture the French imagination:

> The English government spared no artifice to make the French believe they were detested in Ireland . . . no efforts were held back to truncate and twist the speech which the young and unfortunate Emmet delivered before his judges . . . Whoever will read the little we are quoting from the speech of this young man taken in the prime of his life . . . will no longer wonder that he was for his compatriots an object of admiration and enthusiasm, and for English despotism and those who uphold it, the subject of alarm and horror.[54]

However, once the reader's eye notes authorship of this editorial is attributed to none other than the *other* object of much of Europe's alarm and horror – Napoleon Bonaparte – a certain malaise settles in, triggered by the dashed hopes he had given the Irish people. In exile, Napoleon is said to have expressed deep regret that he had not turned his attentions sufficiently towards Ireland, and though he had met Tone, who claimed a certain legacy in France, he must also have felt the shadow of young Robert Emmet over his own fateful decisions. Possibly too he could not forget the sharply worded, but dignified, pleas for Ireland's liberation sent to him by William J. MacNeven and Thomas Addis, vital sources in the history of the United Irishmen which have probably received scant attention because they are in French.[55] But there may be more far-reaching explanations to the dismissal of the Irish experience in France at this time than simply stating the French connection became irrelevant once the long-awaited invasion never occurred. In his incisive discussion on confused identities and allegiances in the immediate aftermath of the Act of Union, Bartlett points to a certain denial among historians of the increasing socio-cultural manifestations of Britishness in Irish daily life at that time, citing Colley's argument that this invention of Britishness was inextricably bound up with the war with France. In the same vein, Whelan qualifies as 'aggressive . . . the British imperial mission [which] crystallised identity formation', and Madame de Stael observed that British society stubbornly refused to incorporate foreign cultural influences. Thus the Irish had little choice but to partake in the repudiation of Francophilia which went hand in hand with the new Union.[56] I will borrow these points to suggest that in the vacuum left by justifiably turning its back on France, Irish self-identification has, since that time, placed disproportionate emphasis on asserting its voice in the Anglophone world. Given the overlap of the frontiers of the former British Empire, and that of the English-speaking world, relevant studies in Irish exile are bound to be over-politicised. Yet in diluting the partnership in revolution which was the strategic alliance between France and Ireland to one of abject failure, scholars are over-concentrating on the outcome and not the process itself. In her authoritative work on the subject, Elliott stressed the increasing sophistication and strength of the United Irishmen in their foreign diplomacy, which did not wane during the Consulate.[57] Throughout the decade of that partnership, the experience for the United Irish diplomats of formulating cogent arguments in a foreign language may have occasionally seemed laborious, but the effort deployed meant their political rhetoric matured and refined in the process. The wealth of archival sources recording their dealings with the French form a significant, if little known, chapter of their history, which is most certainly not the stuff of woolly myths.

As early as 1790, Tone had pointed to one of the great paradoxes of Irish identity, in asking how far Ireland was bound and concerned in His Majesty's quarrels with Spain 'unless it be that we speak the English language?'[58] This is linked to another paradox of Ireland's troubled past, namely that here, unlike other corners of the globe, colonial discourse could not ground its legitimacy in a primal act of visual differentiation based on the colour of one's skin.[59] This argument of Gibbons can be extended to encompass a recurrent motif in the Irish experience abroad, namely that *phonological* recognition of Irishness was immediate in English-language exchanges, whereas the very act of speaking French could mask a brogue. This would socially divest the Irish of their British subjecthood, freeing them to assert their own identity and political otherness. A common thread runs through the extensive manuscripts detailing official attitudes in France towards Ireland and the United Irishmen, namely that they were consistently described as representing *une nation, un peuple*, which to French perceptions could already claim its place among the nations of the earth. Consistently discussed between French officials as a definite and distinct grouping, the Irish are never analysed in the correspondence of the period according to their social or confessional allegiance. That such a strong impression of the resolve of this island was made in France was solidified during the short time Robert Emmet spent there. A fitting tribute to the enduring legacy of his mission is the reminder that it was in Paris that the English translation of d'Haussonville's biography was promptly published in 1858. But more stirring is the common sense of purpose that emerges from the teamwork which saw the project through, namely the two Young Irelanders John P. Leonard and John Martin, the original author, and Miles Byrne, the longest living survivor of 1798.[60]

This discussion began by stating that Robert Emmet's legend centred on his meeting with one so admired by Honoré de Balzac, and it is apposite that the second was another scientist, the zoologist Cuvier. But according to Balzac, the third man's reputation eclipsed even that of Napoleon. Unlike the Corsican, he claimed, Daniel O'Connell incarnated the entire Irish nation, whose right to exist had never been doubted by anyone in France having read Emmet's last words in *Le Moniteur*. We will therefore conclude by returning to those immediately recognisable words which incarnate his legacy, though in the version later produced by d'Haussonville. John P. Leonard in his heartfelt introduction attributed the popularity of the original edition to 'the sympathy which still exists in [France] for events relating to Ireland'. He found d'Haussonville's rendering into French of the speech from the dock so faithful to the universal impact of the original, that he quoted it in his own English version of the biography, and below is the most quoted of passages. In so doing, he proved through the skilful and dedicated art of the translator that language barriers were not to be blamed for tyranny, despotism, and the discord between nations: 'Qu'aucun homme n'écrive mon épitaphe, car aucun homme connaissant aujourd'hui mes motifs n'oseraient aujourd'hui les défendre . . . Quand mon pays aura repris son rang parmi les nations de la terre, alors, mais seulement alors, que mon épitaphe soit écrite. J'ai fini.'[61]

Notes

1 Grace Neville, '"I hate France with a mortal hatred": Daniel O'Connell and France', in E. Maher and G. Neville (eds), *France–Ireland Anatomy of a Relationship: Studies in History, Literature and Politics* (Frankfurt am Main, 2004), pp. 241.

2 Marianne Elliott, *Robert Emmet: The Making of a Legend* (London, 2003), p. 103.

3 Ibid.

4 Reproduced in the Robert Emmet Bicentenary Issue, *History Ireland*, 11: 3 (Autumn 2003), p. 34.

5 P. Palmer, 'Interpreters and the politics of translation and traduction in sixteenth-century Ireland', *Irish Historical Studies* 33: 131 (May 2003), pp. 257–77.

6 Patrick M. Geoghegan, *Robert Emmet: A Life* (Dublin, 2002), p. ix.

7 J. Campbell, *The Hero with a Thousand Faces* (Princeton, 1949), p. 38.

8 Ibid., p. 97.

9 B. Chadwick, *George Washington's War: The Forging of a Revolutionary Leader and the American Presidency* (Naperville Illinois, 2004), pp. 44–5; R. Roland, *Interpreters as Diplomats* (Ottawa, 1999), p. 72. David Bell's thorough 'Jumonville's death: nation and race in eighteenth century France' for cultural expressions of the Franco-British propaganda war, in David A. Bell, L. Pimenova and S. Pujol (eds), *Eighteenth-Century Research. Universal Reason and National Culture during the Enlightenment* (Paris, 1999), pp. 227–51.

10 Thomas Addis Emmet, *Memoir of Thomas Addis and Robert Emmet*, 2 vols (New York, 1915), II, pp. 26–30; Diary of John Martin (PRONI D 560/5). I am grateful to Dr James Quinn for indicating the Martin reference.

11 Ruan O'Donnell, *Robert Emmet and the Rebellion of 1798* (Dublin, 2003), p. 4.

12 Geoghegan, *Robert Emmet*, p. 52.

13 *An Account of some regulations made in Trinity College, Dublin, since the appointment of the present Provost* (attributed to J. Hely-Hutchinson) ([Dublin], 1775); M. M. Raraty, 'The Chair of German at Trinity College, Dublin 1775–1866', *Hermathena* 102 (1966), pp. 53–72; S. McMahon, *Robert Emmet* (Dublin, 2001), p. 29.

14 Sylvie Kleinman, '*Pardon my French*: the linguistic trials and tribulations of Theobald Wolfe Tone', in Maher and Neville (eds), *France–Ireland*, pp. 295–310.

15 Maire Kennedy, *French Books in Eighteenth-Century Ireland* (Oxford, 2001), p. 164.

16 AAE, CPA 593, ff. 288–9. The original orthography has been maintained in extracts.

17 Elliott, *Robert Emmet*; Geoghegan, *Robert Emmet*; O'Donnell, *Robert Emmet.*

18 Elliott, *Robert Emmet*, p. 133; Ruan O'Donnell, *Robert Emmet and the Rebellion of 1803* (Dublin, 2003), p. x.

19 AAE, CPA 593, ff. 288–9.

20 Elliott, *Robert Emmet*, p. 98; repr. in R. O'Donnell, *Remember Emmet* (Dublin, 2003), p. 125.

21 AAE, CPA 593, ff. 288–9.

22 Marianne Elliott, *Partners in Revolution: The United Irishmen and France* (Yale, 1982), p. 275; Sylvie Kleinman, 'French connection II: Robert Emmet and Malachy Delany's Memorial to Bonaparte, Sept. 1800', *History Ireland* 11: 3 (Autumn 2003), pp. 29–33.

23 AAE, MD 53; AN AF IV 1598; 1671; SHD (Vincennes) MR 1420–2.

24 SHD 1420/33–43; dossier Humbert 482 GB 2e série (84d).

25 Tone, 23 July 1796, *The Writings of Theobald Wolfe Tone*, II, p. 251.

26 31 Aug. 1803, NAI 620/11/130/26.

27 AN AF IV/204/1182. The register for documents requested from the French authorities in August–September 1800 summarises the Irishmen's request 'to be delivered from the English yoke', to which is appended Napoleon's approval. The phrase dealing with the specific passport request only identifies them as 'Robert —'.

28 'Thompson' (i.e. Lewins) to the Directory, 26 Apr. 1799, AN AF III 58/228/2/f. 24; Thomas Addis Emmet to Berthier, Minister for War, 10 Dec. 1803, AN AF 1672/2/204.

29 Elliott, *Robert Emmet*, p. 3.

30 Geoghegan, *Robert Emmet*, p. 75.

31 Lecture 21, J. Lawson, *Lectures Concerning Oratory* (1795), p. 393.

32 Reprinted in Geoghean, *Robert Emmet*, p. 288.

33 AAE Dossiers personnels vol. 25, f. 306.

34 15 Nov.1800, CPA 594: 82.

35 Secret information, 31 Aug. 1803, NAI/620/11/130/20.

36 CPA 594: 150r.

37 CPA 594: 150v.

38 Matilda Wolfe Tone to 'Monseigneur', 20 June 1811, SHD Tone file (17y [d] 14).

39 Elliott, *Robert Emmet*, p. 34.

40 Napoléon to the Minister of Marine, 8 Aug. 1803, Corr. de Napoléon, 7–8: 450, 6994.

41 Baroness d'Haussonville (Louise Comtesse de Broglie), *Robert Emmet* (Paris, 1858, 2nd edn); O'Donnell, *Robert Emmet and the Rebellion of 1803*, p. 173.

42 D'Haussonville, *Robert Emmet*, p. 88.

43 C. Wilmot, *Irish Peer on the Continent* (n.d.), p. 54; NAI 620/130/43.

44 Elliott, *Robert Emmet*, p. 37.

45 *The Writings of Theobald Wolfe Tone*, II, p. 364.

46 Emmet to John Patten, 7 Aug. 1802, NAI 620/12/146/30, cited in Elliott, *Robert Emmet*, pp. 40–1.

47 A. Furnham and S. Bochner, *Culture Shock: Psychological Reactions to Unfamiliar Environments* (London, 1986), p. 167.

48 O'Donnell, *Robert Emmet and the Rebellion of 1803*, p. 180.

49 Elliott, *Robert Emmet*, p. 88.

50 Geoghegan, *Robert Emmet*, p. 114.

51 For further discussion see also Elliott, *Robert Emmet*, pp. 101–2.

52 *Le Moniteur*, 9 Jan. 1804, extract reprinted in *Recueil des décrets, ordonnances . . . de Napoléon Bonaparte: Extraits du Moniteur par Lewis Goldsmith*, vol. 1, 1799–1804 (London, 1813), pp. 856–9.

53 J-F. Tissot, *Les Trois Conjurés d'Irlande ou l'Ombre d'Emmet* (Paris, 1804). As suggested by James Quinn, as Thomas Russell features as one of the *conjurés*, he had evidently left a positive impression on his Parisians hosts, possibly having met Tissot in literary circles. See also C. J. Woods, 'The Place of Thomas Russell in the United Irish movement', in Hugh Gough and David Dickson (eds), *Ireland and the French Revolution* (Dublin, 1990), pp. 83–108.

54 O'Donnell, *Robert Emmet and the Rebellion of 1803*, p. 856, which Lewis Goldsmith (editor of *The Argus*) attributes to Bonaparte. My own translation.

55 McNeven to the First Consul, 11 Jan. 1803, AAE, CPA, vol. 601/54; T. A. Emmet to the First Consul, 7 Sept. 1803, AN AF 1672/2/209–16. Both are in very eloquent French, Emmet's featuring minor errors, and are discussed in my PhD thesis (DCU, 2005).

56 Thomas Bartlett, 'Britishness, Irishness and the Act of Union', in Dáire Keogh and Kevin Whelan (eds), *Acts of Union: The Causes, Contexts and Consequences of the Act of Union* (Dublin, 2001), p. 256 and p. 246; Kevin Whelan, 'The other within: Ireland, Britain, and the Act of Union', in Keogh and Whelan (eds), *Acts of Union*, p. 24. Germaine de Staël, *De la Littérature considérée dans ses rapports avec les institutions sociales*, ed. A. Blaeschke (1998), p. 199, discussed in Clíona Ó Gallchoir, 'Germaine de Staël and the response of Sydney Owenson and Maria Edgeworth to the Act of Union', in Maher and Neville (eds), *France–Ireland*, pp. 69–82.

57 Elliott, *Partners in Revolution*.

58 Theobald Wolfe Tone, *Spanish War*, reprinted in *Life of Theobald Wolfe Tone Compiled and Arranged by William Theobald Wolfe Tone*, ed. Thomas Bartlett (Dublin, 1998), p. 270 Quoting this pamphlet also reminds us that it concludes with the phrase 'fixing the rank of your country among the nations of the earth' echoed in the last speeches of both Robert Emmet and Bartholomew Teeling before him, Tone having been inspired by a speech given by the MP Sir Laurence Parsons.

59 Luke Gibbons, *Transformations in Irish Culture* (Cork, 1996).

60 Diary of John Martin (PRONI D 560/5). Louise de Cléron, Comtesse d'Haussonville, *Robert Emmet*, trans John P. Leonard (Belfast, 1858); D. Holland at the Ulsterman Office.

61 Reprinted in S. Ó Bradaigh, *Bold Robert Emmet* (Dublin, 2003), pp. 106–7.

CHAPTER 5

'The reptile that had stung me'

William Plunket and the Trial of Robert Emmet

Maeve Ryan

To most, the 28 years between the Irish Act of Union and the concession of Catholic emancipation are neither fashionable nor particularly attractive. It is difficult to know whether this is a cause of the extremely vague and highly misleading nature of the historiography to date or its result. The lasting impression of these times is of an Ireland languishing between the passion of the Union debates and O'Connell's final triumph in 1829 in the murky pond water of political, economic and social stagnation, where nothing dramatic was attempted and nothing at all was achieved in the direction of either Catholic emancipation or any other general improvement of Irish prospects. William Conyngham Plunket, though politically influential across the wide spectrum from 1798 to the Irish Act of Union, the trial of Robert Emmet to the parliamentary debates of the Napoleonic wars and through the entire progress of the Catholic emancipation movement, is scarcely remembered in Irish history. Where he has attracted attention, it is to be castigated as a hypocrite, or worse, a villain. His greatest contribution to Ireland, his twenty years' work as the foremost champion of emancipation in the House of Commons, has been easily overshadowed by the more attractive theatrics of Daniel O'Connell, and has utterly faded from both popular memory and the pages of history. Indeed, it is only in relation to some of the greatest figures of this time that Plunket's name surfaces: as an enemy of Lord Castlereagh, a friend of Lord Grenville, a supporter and successor to Henry Grattan, and a politically like-minded ideological opponent and, at times, uneasy ally of Daniel O'Connell. Representing the crown against Robert Emmet in 1803, Plunket's powerful courtroom denunciation of Emmet's motivations immediately tainted him with allegations of personal dishonour, perfidy and self-interest. The character of Emmet then grew to mythic status, and the story of his trial and execution gradually evolved into a Christ-like narrative cycle of betrayal and tragedy, in which Plunket remained the villain. Thus as early as 1803, and in spite of over four decades of continued parliamentary activity in the cause of Catholic rights, he secured his only truly enduring place in Irish history as the hypocritical Judas whose harsh, self-serving invective as prosecuting counsel so stung the tender conscience of Robert Emmet and inspired him to stand before court and country to defend his honour. The resulting speech from the dock is perhaps the most famous Irish republican oration of all time, words which have haunted readers and listeners around the world, words repeatedly invoked across the following two centuries to rouse the slumbering giant of Irish defiance, real or imagined, and fuse strands of disaffection into a formidable opposition.

As neither a clear-cut protagonist nor antagonist, Plunket's fleeting appearances and peripheral place in the judgements of Irish historiography make a comprehensive evaluation difficult, even now. He has attracted little attention, aside from two rather problematic collections of selected letters and speeches, and been remembered only in very superficial ways, mainly as one of several government 'villains' responsible for securing Emmet's conviction and execution. Contemporaries alleged that Plunket had been a family friend of the Emmets and that representing the crown on this occasion was a betrayal both of that friendship and of the radical principles it was believed they had shared. This accusation has coloured most evaluations of Plunket's character and, by extension, evaluations of his contribution to Anglo-Irish politics during the early years of the nineteenth century. Investigating Plunket's controversial speech against Robert Emmet in terms of the wider sweep of his entire career reveals a consistency for which he has not generally been credited. Furthermore, there is perhaps the possibility that the controversy was deliberately created or sustained by a lie originating with the Emmet brothers.

Playing a central role in the Union debates, Plunket led the anti-Union 'party' alongside Grattan and made his mark by swearing violent opposition to the measure, swearing to 'resist [the Union] to the last gasp of my existence and with the last drop of my blood', and bitterly condemning the corruption and intrigue of Dublin Castle under the chief secretaryship of Lord Castlereagh.[1] A mere three years later, with his courtroom denunciation of Robert Emmet, it appeared that Plunket had sold his principles for personal advancement, and was in turn bitterly criticised for his role in securing the conviction, particularly in light of his promotion to the post of solicitor general shortly afterwards. Nonetheless, he earned a strong reputation for personal honour through his sustained, principled dedication to the Catholic cause, and for a time he was one of the most celebrated Irish public figures. This standing suffered irreversible damage, however, with his decision in 1822 to enter a ministerial coalition with Lord Liverpool's government, and his acceptance of the post of attorney general under Wellesley's administration. As O'Connell's star rose across the 1820s, and popular politics grew from being a terrifying spectre for the conservative ruling classes to a successful, potent and formidable reality, Plunket's style of strictly parliamentary agitation for limited compromise concessions became unfashionable. In his repeated attempts to reconcile a conservative distaste for unconstitutional agitation with a strong belief in confessional equality and personal liberties, 'Plunket was a Grenville Whig before the Grenville Whigs existed, and remained one after they had become extinct'.[2] He thus failed to negotiate the inherent tensions of his position to any party's satisfaction: to reconcile the increasingly urgent calls for a solution to Irish grievances in general, and Catholic in particular, with his natural instinct towards reform through progressive constitutional action. Extra-parliamentary popular incitement was anathema to him, above all the appeal to the spectre of the disgruntled masses as a political weapon. His lifelong position on this was inflexible: 'I am not the advocate of their intemperance.'[3] Until the new Catholic Association took root, this was a viable, indeed acceptable, position to maintain. Thereafter, as heavy criticism mounted, Plunket drifted further and further from the centre of the Irish political world, merely observing where he had once directed. Finally, with an elevation to the peerage in 1827 and the acceptance of the lord chancellorship of Ireland in 1831, Plunket set in train the destruction of any remnant of virtue still associated with him, and demonstrated a remarkable fondness for nepotism, securing numerous places and positions of advantage for his large family.

Contemporaries and historians alike have found it difficult to judge William Conyngham Plunket, and, in the absence of any personal memoirs or accessible and comprehensive body of correspondence, his doubtful virtue has left him with a shadowy status inevitably leading to marginalisation and oblivion. His invisibility in Irish history can largely be attributed to the times in which he lived, yet the inaccessibility of reliable source material has played no small part in the process. Unsorted and thus far under-utilised, Plunket's manuscript correspondence collection in the National Library of Ireland contains a number of crucial documents which have the potential to revise a number of important judgements long held on this particular period of history. Drawing from this collection, and pulling together various disparate sources, this chapter will seek to cast Plunket in a clearer light than he has previously enjoyed. It has been said that 'the story of William Conyngham Plunket is effectively the story of the relationship between England and Ireland in the first half of the nineteenth century'.[4] Perhaps if this is the case it is fitting that Plunket has, like many other significant aspects of these years, faded into the shadow cast by the towering pedestals of some of Ireland's greatest heroes and most consecrated events and assumed a place in history only as a foil: on the one hand, to the first celebrity of popular constitutional nationalism, Daniel O'Connell, and on the other, with a good deal more notoriety, to one of Irish history's greatest romantic icons, Robert Emmet.

By all accounts, it came as quite a shock to contemporaries, sympathetic, hostile and neutral, to hear the words Plunket spoke against Robert Emmet in the courtroom at Green Street on Monday 19 September 1803. Emmet had declined to challenge seriously any of the crown evidence and, once the case on the part of the prosecution was declared closed, Leonard MacNally rose to state that 'Mr Emmet says he does not intend to call any witnesses, or to take up the time of the court by his counsel stating any case, or making observations upon the evidence; and, therefore, I presume the trial is now closed on both sides.'[5] Plunket stood up regardless, and told the court that it was 'with extreme reluctance' that 'in a case like this, I do not feel myself at liberty to follow the example which has been set me by the counsel for the prisoner'.[6] In 'a most masterly performance', Plunket then recapitulated the day's testimony, seeking to prove Emmet 'the centre, the life, blood and soul of this atrocious conspiracy'.[7] Contemporaries who remembered fondly Plunket's violent rhetorical defence of Irish constitutional independence expressed disgust at his supposed abandonment of idealistic radical opposition and denounced him as a hypocrite and Castle mouthpiece for seeming to condemn the very people his words had rallied a few short years previously. Gone were the passionate vows to die before accepting Union. 'When I feel the hour of my dissolution approaching', he had then declared he would, 'like the father of Hannibal, take my children to the altar and swear them to eternal hostility against the invaders of my country's freedom'.[8] Now, a mere four years later, he ridiculed the 'frantic desperation of the plan of any man who speculates upon the dissolution of that empire, whose glory and happiness depend upon its indissoluble connection'. To sever the connection, 'to untie the links which bind us to the British constitution' would be to 'turn us adrift upon the turbulent ocean of revolution'. This would be contrary to both 'God and nature', which 'have made the two countries essential to each other, let them cling to each other to the end of time, and their united affection and loyalty will be proof against the machinations of the world'.[9] The government reacted to his apparent about-turn with surprise and glee, Chief Secretary William Wickham remarking that Plunket's effective declaration in favour of the government would 'be the death blow to the anti-Union party at the bar',[10] and, apparently as a reward for this service, Plunket was promoted to solicitor general in November 1803, provoking a further storm of gossip and speculation. Plunket decided in 1804 to declare it slander and sue the English radical writer William Cobbett for libel in response to accusations printed in the *Weekly Register* that Plunket had, in speaking against Robert Emmet, betrayed a personal friendship and disrespected the memory of Emmet's father. The paper claimed this accusation as coming from Robert Emmet himself and stated that he had, on the morning of his execution, denounced Plunket as 'that viper whom my father nourished', a family friend 'from whose lips'

Emmet had 'first imbibed those principles and doctrines which now, by their effects, drag me to my grave'.[11] The publishers of *Sketches of History, Politics, and Manners in Dublin in 1810* repeated a similar charge:

> Mr Plunket conducted the prosecution against this unfortunate young man with a rancour and virulence which shocked and surprised every person acquainted with his obligations to his father and family. Mr Plunket's reason for this conduct has never been made known, though it injured him very much in public estimation. Crown lawyers have at all times been of the blood-hound tribe; they seldom lose scent of their prey, either from considerations of gratitude or humanity.[12]

Suing for libel on both occasions, Plunket was twice vindicated and awarded damages. The truth or otherwise of the charge has long been debated, and it was most recently dismissed by Patrick Geoghegan's *Robert Emmet* as unverifiable and unlikely, the 'bitter tone' seemingly 'at odds with everything else Emmet said and wrote in his final hours'.[13] Nonetheless the allegation is still mentioned in most accounts of the trial and the faint mark of dishonour has always endured.

Censured not only for speaking against the brother of a former friend but apparently also against his political principles, Plunket then had to endure the further criticisms that his speech was both unduly harsh and totally unnecessary. Emmet had essentially conceded defeat, had effectively admitted to the crimes of which he stood accused and had refused to defend himself. So why did Plunket choose to speak? It could be argued that he had no choice, either in accepting the government's brief or in rising to speak against Emmet. 'It is at my particular desire', Attorney General Standish O'Grady informed Lord Norbury in response to MacNally's objections, 'that Mr Plunket rises to address the court and the jury upon this occasion'.[14] Peter Burrowes certainly felt that Plunket had no alternative, and Charles Phillips, recounting the incident after the interval of many years, agreed that for Plunket to refuse would have been tantamount to expressing approval for the conduct of the accused, something which, in light of his anti-Union activities, would scarcely be in his interests to do.[15] The overwhelming tide of public opinion sided with the cynical interpretation, however, and, like Cobbett's 'Juverna', considered Plunket a 'renegade'. Later commentators have been similarly divided: Plunket's only biographer, his grandson, David Plunket, in a characteristically wholehearted defence of his grandfather's honour and virtue, considered 'the severest censures' 'visited' upon him to have been deliberate and spiteful 'distort[ion]' of the facts 'to suit the purposes alternatively of party, malice and romance'.[16] C. J. Hoey, on the other hand, though a staunch admirer of Plunket's, regarded the incident as 'an unaccountable hour' in which he 'cloud[ed] . . . his character as an Irish patriot and as an advocate, with that merciless speech'.[17]

> No palliation can mitigate the simple censure, that his speech to evidence upon that occasion was a cruel and uncalled for assault upon a young heroic martyr, who had already surrendered himself frankly to his doom.

Yet Hoey criticised how far this 'censure' was taken, and how the facts were distorted:

> The publicists of the day, who sympathised with Emmet, or who, like Cobbett, hated Plunket's party or person, did not rest there. They declared that Emmet had attacked Plunket from the dock – which was a lie; that Plunket had been under the deepest obligations to Emmet's father and brother – which was also a lie; and that Emmet declared he had imbibed the opinions upon which he had acted from Plunket's teaching – opinions, now abandoned by Plunket for corrupt motives. This also is an assertion equally without foundation; but which has never yet been properly met by the apologists of Plunket's conduct.

Plunket's anti-republican sentiments, he argued, were nothing new or surprising:

> Ten years before, towards Tone, Plunket had evinced precisely the same sentiments. Violent and unfeeling as he was in their utterance, it is impossible to deny that they were in perfect consistency with the settled opinions which he had for many years held and expressed. In every one of his Union speeches he speaks of the attempt of the United Irishmen and the attempt of the ministry with equal abhorrence.

This was true in point of fact, and was something Plunket himself had often protested, with little success. That he believed in his own consistency, particularly his hostility to radical republicanism, there can be little doubt, and he always maintained that this was something very separate from his anti-Union and opposition status. As early as the 1790s, as he recounted to Sir John Newport in 1821 in a rare personal defence of his political conduct, he had acted 'in opposition to the Irish government', but 'at the same time' served it 'both as a soldier and as a member of parliament, marking in the most decided manner [his] hostility to the revolutionary party'.[18] In a review of the past two decades, he felt he had repeatedly shown himself to be a man 'willing to act disinterestedly and strenuously upon [his] sober and just views, yet [who] look[s] with terror to wild reform and public tumult'. Above all things he defended his right to 'feel . . . strongly' and 'express' those feelings 'without reserve'. Emmet's rising, with all its lower-class character and avowed aims of using such 'wild reform and public tumult' to effect massive constitutional upheaval, unsettled Plunket and provoked just such a display of strong feelings, expressed without reserve. Central to his political self-image was the distinction he drew in his own mind between his opposition, indeed active resistance, to the proposed incorporating legislative Union in 1799 and 1800, and the revolutionary ideals of armed secret societies. A convinced imperialist, Plunket was, like Grattan, fiercely loyal to the British constitutional connection, and although both had vehemently opposed an incorporating union, both had become reconciled to its reality. Above all, both were distasteful of all forms of unconstitutional agitation.

Plunket's opening remarks suggest that he, like Emmet following him, pitched his speech not to the narrow confines of a courtroom and the inevitable result of the trial, but to a wider, and far more volatile national audience. 'If this were an ordinary case', he claimed in his opening remarks,

> and if the object of this prosecution did not include some more momentous questions than the mere guilt or innocence of the unfortunate gentleman who stands a prisoner at the bar, I should have followed the example of his counsel and should have declined making any observation upon the evidence. But, gentlemen, I do feel this to be a case of infinite importance indeed.[19]

In an affidavit sworn in 1810 for the purposes of his libel suit then in train against the publishers of *Sketches of History, Politics, and Manners in Dublin in 1810*, Plunket stated his belief in 1803 that a strong speech against Emmet 'would be of some service to the public', highlighting 'the folly and wildness, as well as the wickedness, of the treasonable conspiracy which at that time subsisted'.[20] In doing so he recalled that he had

> remark[ed] on the unworthy use which the said Robert Emmet had made of his rank in society . . . endeavouring to dissatisfy the lower orders of labourers and mechanics with their lot in life, and engaging them in schemes of revolution from which they could reap no fruit but disgrace and death.[21]

Years later, when challenged on his motives by Charles Phillips, Plunket still maintained that 'the times [had] rendered [the speech] necessary'.[22] Plunket's biographers both defend the genuine integrity of his motivations, yet entirely disagree on the precise character of those 'times'. David Plunket argues that it was merely the 'passions of the fractious, idle and discontented' which brought about the rising in 1803, not genuine social disaffection, and that the conspiracy had deserved 'no name of respectability', being merely an unprincipled exercise of arbitrary anarchy by a small and insignificant portion of the lower orders.[23] The 'milder system adopted by the government since the Union', he argued, 'was already producing its effects, and material prosperity so long banished from the country by the violence of party passion began to return'. 'In fact', he declared, 'never did a moment occur less propitious for an attempt to sever the connexion between England and Ireland.'[24] In contrast, Hoey's defence rests on the image of a genuine threat requiring harsh counter-measures. Though the rising had been little more than 'an hour's scuffle with the police and the piquet, stained by an atrocious murder', 'the revolutions of '48 have taught the world that one well-directed blow to a capital city, against a government to which the people are disaffected, is like a spark of fire touching choke damp'.[25] A close examination of Emmet's plan of attack, and the calculations upon which this rested, led Hoey to the conclusion that the government had had an almost 'miraculous escape'. The accidents which had undermined the secrecy of the conspiracy were such that 'no human sagacity could have foreseen or ingenuity repaired. Napoleon Bonaparte might have failed in the same circumstances.' On the question of whether Emmet had 'reason to suppose that if he could seize on the capital he would be supported by the country', Hoey was quite clear:

> I think he had. The disaffection in Ireland at this date was more intense and pervading than it ever had been in Tone's time. The Union was ruining Dublin. The national gentry remained disgusted with the government. The Catholics perceived they had been deceived. The whole country was again ripe and alert for revolt.[26]

Approximately half of Plunket's speech was taken with running through the 'mass of accumulated evidence', and the testimonies of co-conspirators and witnesses, presenting it such that 'no man capable of putting together two ideas can have a doubt' of the obvious conclusion of Emmet's guilt.[27] Plunket then expanded on the philosophy and founding beliefs behind the conspiracy, what it 'avow[ed] itself to be' in contrast with the reality of Ireland in 1803. While the declared thesis of Plunket's speech was to prove the prisoner as the centre and life-blood of the conspiracy, his strategy in speaking to a wider audience was to demonstrate the 'meanness and insufficiency' of its resources by reducing Emmet's revolutionary ideals to delusions of despotic grandeur and by mocking the working-class character of some of its principal actors, such as the 'bricklayer' Quigley. This strategy was twofold: Emmet had to be seen to be the clear driving force, and the extent to which the corrupting influence of conspiracy had taken hold had to be built up to the status of grave public threat, particularly the possibility of foreign invasion. At the same time, the rebels themselves had to be shown to be contemptible, and their endeavour of a character to which success would mean the end of all recognisable forms of social cohesion. In short, revolution was to be taken seriously, but to be seen as seriously unappealing.

Plunket's aim first and foremost was to show to the middle- and upper-class world that there was no potential success, no attraction and certainly no dashing romance in this kind of disaffection. He was also very careful to distance the conspiracy from any connection to the anti-Union party, presumably with himself specifically in mind. The rebels sought 'revenge on account of the removal of the Parliament' and presumed to 'call upon the loyal men who opposed its transfer' in 1800.[28] How Plunket's language changed in the intervening three years! He had then called Union the murder of the Irish parliament, and had prophesied the impending end of Irish liberty. Now he spoke of Union as a 'transfer', a removal of the institution to Britain. In light of this rhetorical turnaround, it is unsurprising that the speech earned Plunket disfavour with many former colleagues and sympathisers. In substance, however, Plunket was not entirely disingenuous, and was at least correct in drawing a distinction between 'the men, who in 1798 endeavoured to destroy the parliament' and the anti-Unionists who had, in Plunket's words 'opposed its transfer', since many anti-Unionists, Plunket included, had appeared in arms to defend the political establishment against the 1798 rebellion.

Contemptuous of the working-class character of the conspiracy, Plunket went on to deny it the respectability of a genuine political movement. Mocking the proclamation of provisional government 'in its majesty and dignity', Plunket expressed incredulity that 'the miserable victims who have been misled by those phantoms of revolutionary delusion', 'the bricklayer, . . . the baker, . . . the old clothes man, the hodman and the hostler' dare to 'call upon a great people to yield obedience'.[29] Turning to address these men directly, Plunket counselled that this was a 'cause which [could] not protect itself' and merely 'expose[d] them to destruction'. 'Providence', he then reflected, 'is not so unkind to them in casting them in that humble walk in which they are placed. Let them obey the law and cultivate religion and worship their God in their own way.'[30]

The rebels did not seek what Plunket would term legitimate reform. The plan was 'not to correct the excesses, or reform the abuses of the government', nor was it to 'remove any specks or imperfections which might have grown upon the surface of the constitution, or to restrain the overgrown power of the crown'. Nor was it to restore any privilege of parliament, or to throw any new security around the liberty of the subject'. The conspiracy was separatist in design, and republican in ambition. '"A *free and independent republic in Ireland*": A 'high sounding name!' but Plunket questioned whether 'the man who used [it] understood what he meant'.[31] There was 'no magic in the name'; rather Plunket drew attention to other, recently formed 'free and independent republics' from which 'the most abject slavery that ever groaned under iron despotism' had been seen to grow.[32] Furthermore, there had been no 'great call of the people, ripe for change'.

> Had any body of the people come forward, stating any grievance or announcing their demand for a change? No, but while the country is peaceful, enjoying the benefits of the constitution, growing rich and happy under it, a few, desperate, contemptible adventurers in the trade of revolution form a scheme against the constituted authorities of the land, and by force and violence [seek] to overthrow an ancient and venerable constitution and to plunge a whole people into the horrors of civil war.[33]

Even 'the wisest head that ever lived', Plunket claimed, would have to 'pause and stop' a moment 'upon the brink of his purpose' before presuming to replace the ancient and venerable constitution with one of his own design, however ingenious, perfect and 'fitted to the disposition of the people' it might be, and even if 'a great proportion of the people were anxious for its adoption'. Without any mandate from the people, Emmet presumed 'to claim the obedience' of the Irish nation, to throw 'a sacred *palladium* . . . over the rebel cause' and to claim for himself the supreme authority to determine the values of right and wrong, treason and loyalty, under a newly constituted system solely of his own invention. Plunket labelled the supporters of this scheme 'the illiterate victims of the ambition of this young man', who, with the arrogance of youthful idealism, sought to lure the masses with promises of a better alternative system that, in all probability, he could neither provide nor control. There are shades of the hatred Plunket later reserved for the character of Napoleon, 'that vicious despot who watches with the sleepless eye of disquieting ambition and sits, a wretched usurper, trembling upon the throne of the Bourbons', evident in his disapproval of Emmet and, years later, in his assessment of O'Connell and other populist leaders. In stooping 'from the honourable situation in which his birth, talents and his education placed him, to debauch the minds of the lower orders of ignorant men with the phantoms of liberty and equality',[34] Emmet acted with a degree of the self-willed narrow-mindedness Plunket subsequently deplored in Napoleon:

> His vice was not merely selfishness, but self-willedness, which, when it attains its perfection, as I think it did in him, is nothing more or less than the principle of evil. This does not imply a love of blood, or a gratuitous pleasure in the misery of others, but simply a determination not to be controlled in the exercise of self-will, either by respect for God or for compassion for man.[35]

According to Plunket, Emmet, his principles 'poisoned' and his judgement 'perverted' by misunderstanding the terms 'liberty and equality', 'should feel remorse' for the consequences 'grievous to humanity and virtue . . . which ensued', and 'should endeavour to make all the atonement he can, by employing the little time which remains for him in endeavouring to undeceive' his followers.[36]

By the conclusion of his speech, Plunket had moved through the evidence to demonstrate that the focus of responsibility lay with the prisoner alone, who had, in framing the project, gathering support and articulating in print a manifesto for rebellion, been prepared to 'let loose the rabble of the country from the salutary restraints of the law' and the 'humble walk[s] in which they are placed'. He may not have explicitly sanctioned individual murders, but yet 'what claim . . . can the prisoner have upon the compassion of a jury . . . ?' Plunket asked. 'In the general destruction, which his schemes [must] necessarily produce', murder would be unavoidable. The rabble let loose would be like 'the winds of heaven', 'what power less than omnipotent can control them?'[37] Emmet's subordinate followers, Plunket claimed, were 'a blood thirsty crew' who had taken advantage of the opportunity of anarchic social revolution his proposed rising had provided. They would, Plunket speculated, perhaps have 'immolated' their leader once he, with his avowed political ends, had outlived his usefulness or attempted to impose order upon the new system. With palpable disgust for the 'phantoms of revolutionary delusion' which gave honest men unschooled in statecraft 'chimerical' notions of escaping their station in life, and dishonest men the opportunity to 'embrue their hands in the most sacred blood of the country', Plunket declared all separatist conspirators, of all kinds, as 'incapable of listening to the voice of reason, and equally incapable of obtaining rational freedom, if it were wanting in this country, as they are of enjoying it'.[38]

Plunket's aim was to show the country the destructive wastefulness of 'travell[ing] back into the history of six centuries' and 'rak[ing] up the ashes of former cruelties and rebellions', which, he pronounced, had 'long since passed away'.[39] The rebel cry, inciting the people to follow the example of 'new-fangled French principles', was 'a fraud upon feeling', and merely 'the pretext of the factious and ambitious working upon credulity and ignorance'. The main achievement of this speech, however, was Emmet's furious resentment, inspiring an eloquent and impassioned defence of the integrity of his motivations, the respectability of the conspiracy and the justice of rebellion. Considering Plunket's lifelong conservatism, his role in provoking one of the most famous and influential orations of all time was perhaps his gravest miscalculation. It was a legacy which would endure across a century of bloodshed, and would contribute in no small part towards the achievement of that aim against which he had pledged his honour and his life: the severance of the British connection.

The career advancement he earned by this display demonstrated that Plunket had indeed reversed some of the damage wrought by his unequivocal stance at the Union. Opportunistic it may have been, but this does not mean the underlying sentiments were necessarily insincere. Years later, speaking as prosecuting attorney general at a treason trial of far lower profile than that of

Robert Emmet, that of a Ribbon Society member, Michael Keenan, Plunket again denounced the involvement in political matters of 'men in the humblest class of society'.[40] Just as he had attacked such men for the presumption of attempting to reframe the constitution with Robert Emmet, he considered them 'entitled to the protection of the laws, and . . . both useful and respectable members of the community' only 'whilst they confine themselves to their proper situation'. But they simply did not 'possess . . . the place or information necessary to qualify them for the conduct of political affairs'. An active member of the predominantly Catholic Ribbon Society, Keenan was indicted in November 1822 on the grounds of 'the existence in [Ireland], of a society formed for seditious purposes, and to disturb the public peace' and his personal involvement in the administration of unlawful oaths for this society.[41] 'It [was] with great pain' Plunket felt himself called upon in his opening speech at the Keenan trial,

> in the exercise of [his] official duty, to lay before the public the very odious, dangerous, and disgusting conspiracy, by the machinations of which this country has been for some time infested, and its tranquillity exposed to hazard.

'For some time past', considerably more, he believed, 'than two or three years, a plan has been formed in *Ireland* for associating the members of the community by unlawful oaths and engagements, to resist the laws, disturb the public peace, and overthrow the established government'. Disturbingly, the society had 'framed' a complicated 'machinery . . . well adapted to revolutionary movements' by reference 'to [the] unfortunate transactions . . . [of] 1797 and 1798 [and] . . . subsequently 1803', on the basis of rebel cells anonymous to one another, hierarchically represented up to a national assembly. Somehow, Plunket informed the court, 'the plans of former societies of United Irishmen were found, and suggested the scheme of operations'.[42] It was 'at all events clear', he went on to say

> that it has been founded for the purpose of violating the law, and interfering with the constituted authorities – and more than all, of infecting all orders of the people with a spirit of infuriate disaffection and insubordination, ready for any plan of mischief, should the exigencies of future times give that occasion.

He was as contemptuous then as he had been in 1803 of this working-class attack on the sanctity of the British constitution. Keenan had 'attained the rank of a provincial delegate'. 'What do you suppose is the occupation of this man who has thought proper to make himself a legislator and to entertain the scheme of unhinging the laws and the government of this country, as exercised for centuries?' Plunket asked.

> He is a coal porter in the employment of a coal factor in the city of *Dublin.* Of similar classes are all the persons leagued in this combination against the state . . . carmen, low artisans, and others who, though not the dregs of society, are far below the order of persons competent to take a share in regulating the concerns of the state.[43]

He had remarked in a personal letter to William Magee in 1803 that Emmet's 'rebellion [had] been, in my opinion, very contemptible, and very little either of talents or property engaged in it, a few middling shopkeepers, most (if not all) of them the debris of the rebellion of 1798, formed the head of it and the lowest rabble the tail. Body it had none – The Catholics certainly have not been generally involved in it.'[44] By 1822, the character of anti-establishment subversion had assumed a confessional character not present in Emmet's day, with the rival activities of the Ribbon Society and the Orange Order featuring most prominently. Plunket explained this to the court in 1822: 'One feature' of the Ribbon organisation distinguished it 'from that of 1797 and 1798'.

> It was exclusively confined to persons of one religious persuasion – I mean to persons professing the Roman Catholic faith. This circumstance alone, on the face of it, stamps the association with every mark of danger and illegality.

He went on to argue that the fabric of a society was created to be unified, whether Protestant or Catholic or both, 'for mutual assistance and protection; and those persons who would narrow this system into any exclusive association, are the enemies of the law of their country'. He stressed the fundamentally antisocial character of exclusive power structures, and claimed 'there is no crime, however shocking or revolting, which some of the[se men] would not be ready to commit, and even introduce as part of the general frame' of their revolutionary social organisation. With echoes of the rumoured Despard conspiracy of Emmet's day, the Ribbon conspirators apparently plotted to present a 'shew of rebellion' in Ireland 'if certain public transactions in England should continue and break out into insurrection', which would to compel the English government to send the army to Ireland and 'thus leave the English insurgents to complete their work'. This plan 'ceased with the end of disturbances in England', but was replaced by something darker and a great deal more sinister. Plunket claimed that with the recent radical development of particular branches, those increasingly clashing with rival Orange lodges, 'another object in view' was to abandon ideas of toleration and coexistence under equality, and to entirely 'overturn the protestant religion, and establish the Roman Catholic in its stead . . . They proposed the utter extirpation of all protestants out of the country. There is nothing connected with horror', he warned, 'nothing revolting to the feelings of human nature, at which persons once linked in illegal associations, are not capable of arriving'. It was, he claimed, 'a most painful duty' to him

> to be obliged to direct the public attention to the existence of a conspiracy of this kind. But I should have been guilty of abandoning the trust reposed in me, and wanting in what is due from me to the government and the country, if I had not taken all means in my power to prevent its further extension.

While 'no immediate danger . . . is to be apprehended from persons of this character and description', it was nonetheless

> a formidable thing, an alarming thing, to know that a conspiracy is on foot, and has been going forward for years in the land – that bands of wretches have been from night to night meeting in the heart of this our city, endeavouring to poison the minds of all orders of the people, and prepare them for the perpetration of any mischief to which any future emergency may afford opportunity and temptation.

It was to be considered 'truly melancholy' that

> these infatuated people will not take warning: time after time have similar associations been formed; during the last twenty-five years they have become more alarming and dangerous; but one undeviating fate has attended them all, – the ruin and destruction of their promoters and abettors. A set of journeymen carpenters, porters and mechanics, to associate to heave the British constitution from its basis, and overturn the laws established by the wisdom of centuries! Wild and chimerical speculation! The highest good fortune which such infatuated wretches can expect, is to escape hanging.[45]

Plunket's political opponents seized and manipulated his harsh words against Michael Keenan and the Ribbonist conspiracy as a propaganda weapon against the Emancipation Bill he was preparing for proposal at that time. Publishing these *Extracts from the Speech of the Attorney General for Ireland on Opening the Trial of Michael Keenan*, the pamphlet directly lifted text from Plunket's speech to demonstrate the apparent contradiction in his perception of Catholic rights: on the one hand he claimed there was no threat to the British constitution in granting Catholic emancipation, and yet on the other he freely conceded the existence of a seething hotbed of resentment among the Irish Catholic lower classes, and more ominously, a pre-existing conspiratorial network linked with the radicals in England and with the separatist intention of overthrowing the British crown and administration in Ireland. Most disturbingly, he asserted that the Ribbon Society was built on fanatical

Catholicism, and this Catholic underground network was plotting a massacre of all Protestants. For years Plunket had pledged the innate fidelity of the Catholic subject, and the justice of 'tak[ing] the brand from his forehead and the bitterness from his heart'.[46] 'You do your duty as legislators', he had promised, 'and doubt not that they will do their duty as subjects'.[47] In a letter to the extreme Tory solicitor general, Henry Joy, a mere two years later, Plunket roundly condemned Sir Harcourt Lees's 'wild suggestions' that there had ever in recent memory been 'a conspiracy in Ireland for the murder of the protestants', as though he had never himself asserted precisely the same thing. He declared in unambiguous terms, 'I believe a more audacious, wilful falsehood never was uttered.'[48] By publishing selections of his speech at the Keenan trial his enemies publicly exhibited the contradiction in Plunket's personal politics in an attempt to further undermine his public credibility, already at this stage in very poor currency with pro-Catholic Whig and anti-Catholic Tory colleagues alike. It is very likely that, in a passion of disgust for Ribbonist subversion, he took an amount of rhetorical licence, since he had never before expressed a fear that Irish Catholics considered or countenanced any proposal to revisit scenes of 1641 upon their Protestant countrymen. Once spoken, however, the words could not be retracted, and the enemies of emancipation could claim that

> as on 17 April next, a Bill for granting further concessions to the R[oman] C[atholic]s is to be moved in the House of Commons by Mr Plunkett [*sic*]; it is of *vital importance* that the *conspiracy fully proved* (in Dublin on the 2nd , and on the 5th of November last,) to have existed for above *three years*, among the R[oman] C[atholic]s exclusively, for subverting the *constitution* in *church* and *state* and *destroying* all the *protestants*, should be made generally known; and also, that this foul papist conspiracy extends all over Ireland, and has connection with the radicals in England.[49]

Plunket had revealed in his speech against Emmet his patent contempt for lower class politicisation, and his speech against Keenan confirms that he still subscribed to these views decades later. From the days of the French Revolution, through the Terror, the 1798 rebellion, Emmet's abortive attempt and the rise of confessionally aligned secret societies since the Union, he had come to loathe and detest exclusive societies, denouncing them in 1821 as the 'insane attempts' of the 'blind and deluded' to eat into and corrode the hearts of the country, 'infecting the mass of its population with an habitual relish for mischief and insubordination'.[50] Incompatible with their own avowed ends, such as civil equality, freedom of speech and toleration, he believed them destined from their inception to end in crushing defeat or the triumph of despotism. It was his belief that exclusivity, particularly along confessional lines, merely legitimised sectarian violence and facilitated its exploitation for selfish material gain. He held that nothing could accelerate the dissolution of the Anglo-Irish bond faster than groups of radical extremists, and made it a fundamental tenet of his pro-emancipation platform that granting equal rights to Catholics would fatally undermine those radical groups masquerading as political lobbyists. Moreover, Plunket was certainly not alone in maintaining this deep suspicion of underground activity. Daniel O'Connell, for example, had personally witnessed some excesses of the French Revolution and the experience marked him with a lifelong aversion to 'useless outrages' and violent 'exhibitions of . . . strength'.[51] He firmly believed that 'Resistance is not right until legal authority is done away with, and the iron and red hand of power is raised against the people.'[52] Another leading figure in the emancipation movement, Bishop James Doyle, responded to the Ribbon activities in Dublin which led to Keenan's trial in November 1822 with a sermon to the diocese of Kildare and Leighlin counselling that the subversive 'design' of 'overthrowing the government established in this country by the divine permission' as 'opposed to the maxims and example of our divine redeemer, and of his apostles, and to the uniform doctrine of that church whose faith you profess'. People's 'motives . . . in forming this vain and senseless project', he denounced as 'not only wicked, but disgraceful to you as men and Christians'. In a comment revealing of the social and class conservatism of many Irish Catholic proponents of emancipation, ecclesiastical and secular, Doyle was led to 'conclude, dearly beloved . . . that the body of a nation is like, in some degree, to our own. The different ranks and orders which compose it are ordained of GOD, that the whole may be preserved entire'. He warned the people to go about their lives and to 'leave the legislature to pursue those means of improving your country which their wisdom will devise'.[53]

In 1813 Plunket had pressed the Commons that fulfilling the 'duty' of conceding this measure would 'give satisfaction to the honest and to the reasonable', 'separate the sound from the unsound', and 'leave the bigot or the incendiary stripped of all his terrors by depriving him of all his grievances'. Plunket saw in the proposed measure of Catholic emancipation the potential to diffuse the power of radical extremists while simultaneously granting a just reward to the loyal and the faithful, those deserving of political power and civil equality. Inevitably, this was the wealthier Catholic body. Any kind of political activity in the lower classes deserved to be crushed. He had made this distinction clear at the Keenan trial: 'Men in the humblest class of society' were unfit to judge the justice or necessity of any political decision, and any intervention in this sphere into which they were not born was an imposition which should not be tolerated. While they were 'valuable members of the community' this was only 'while they, by the exertion of their honest industry, in their humble callings contribute in their proper sphere to the public prosperity'. 'When they madly rush beyond that boundary', only evil could result.[54] The Ribbon Society had been

> founded for the purpose of violating the law, and interfering with the constituted authorities – and more than all, of infecting all orders of the people with a spirit of infuriate disaffection and insubordination, ready for any plan of mischief, should the exigencies of future times give that occasion.

However 'the present tranquil state of the world', Plunket was careful to state, 'affords no immediate prospect' of the successful implementation of such conspiracies.

Class conservatism and distaste for separatist republicans, such as Plunket demonstrated at both Emmet's and Keenan's treason trials and on many occasions in the intervening years, would not have provoked widespread disapproval or condemnation in the aftermath of the Emmet trial. Though the tragic, youthful figure of Emmet evoked sympathy and pity, the rebellion itself evoked little public support. Though a wide variety of political views certainly existed, many would have been in agreement with Grattan's initial assessment of the effort: 'this is getting up merely to be cut down; their hanging is of little moment, but they ruin the country'.[55] Thus the hostile response of contemporaries to Plunket's speech was not so much a reaction against his specific sentiments as the apparent lack of integrity in his decision to abandon his long-held opposition status and to speak in favour of the government. When this decision brought promotion and advancement to Plunket, it merely confirmed what many suspected: that the action had been cynically motivated, and rumours of a bond of obligation between Plunket and the Emmet family thrived. Though Plunket maintained that the Emmet trial had been of more social consequence than ascertaining the guilt or innocence of the accused, that 'the times [had] rendered it necessary', many suspected him of lying, even to himself. The Emmet *Memoirs* offers a succinct appraisal of this point of view:

> It was an entirely gratuitous act on the part of Mr Plunket to have seized the opportunity for uttering a violent philippic against the prisoner. As he had lost caste with the government in consequence of his opposition to the Act of Union, he hoped by this exhibition of patriotism to be placed again in the line of preferment. Although it is said he made a masterly effort, the effect was the reverse of what he had anticipated. It created a feeling of contempt for his course, even with many of those who were in sympathy with the government.[56]

The harshness with which Plunket personally denounced Emmet, particularly since Emmet had offered no resistance whatsoever to his conviction, appeared unnecessary to observers, even those hostile to the avowed aims of the young revolutionary. Many, already unimpressed by Plunket's political *volte face*, leaped upon rumours circulating in the aftermath of the trial that Plunket had betrayed both his basic personal principles and a personal debt to the Emmet family. Of all criticisms across a long public career, this was perhaps the most personally upsetting to Plunket, and that against which, on two separate occasions, he successfully staked his reputation in the libel courts. It is also perhaps the most disingenuous of accusations, for though Plunket made many errors of judgement, most notably his flagrant nepotistic abuse of later office, he could not be accused of inconsistency of principle, nor of ever having genuinely endorsed any kind of revolutionary action. In desperation and the heat of debate, he had spoken strong words in the dying days of the Irish parliament, yet from the earliest divergence of opinion between Paine and Burke on the character of the French Revolution, where Wolfe Tone and Thomas Addis Emmet had chosen the teachings of Paine, Plunket had always been firmly in the Burkean camp, and it was from this time that Plunket noted with regret the waning of his former friendships with Emmet, Tone and other intimates of his college years. In fact, by 1803, all friendly feeling, if any, which may ever have existed between Plunket and any member of the Emmet family must surely have been at a decided end since August 1798, when Plunket had personally denounced Thomas Addis Emmet in the Irish House of Commons. Referring to a pamphlet in which Emmet, Arthur O'Connor and William MacNeven, as State Prisoners, had defended themselves against the 'garbled reports' of government spin, Plunket rose in parliament to 'reprobate . . . in the strongest terms the publication which had been read to the house', declaring it to be 'a species of proclamation or manifest couched in the most libellous and insolent language'. He described the three authors as men who were 'signal instances of the royal mercy to all the open and concealed traitors of the country'; and declared them guilty of 'urging' the masses 'to rebellion and to the aid of a French invasion'. While he was careful to recommend that the government honour any agreement reached in good faith with these men, he nonetheless pronounced that all 'precautions' should be taken to prevent such figures from 'corrupting the public mind'. McNaughton, following on from Plunket's words, was far more direct: 'as martial law had not ceased, the persons in question, Arthur O'Connor, Thomas Addis Emmet and Dr MacNeven, should be immediately brought to trial and executed. R. R. Madden describes Thomas Addis Emmet's 'disgusted' reaction to Plunket's speech, and quotes from *Pieces of Irish History*, published in New York in 1807 by MacNeven and Emmet, in which the incident is thus described:

> A tempest of folly and fury was immediately excited in the House of Commons. Blinded by their rage . . . Mr. McNaughton and two virulent barristers, Francis

> Hutchinson and Conyngham Plunket, were even clamorous for having the persons who signed the refutation disposed of by a summary execution.[57]

Yet in a personal letter to Rufus King in April 1807, Emmet did not implicate Plunket in the incident, merely stating that in August 1798 'a proposal was made in the Irish House of Commons by Mr McNaughton, an Orangeman, to take us out and hang us without trial'.[58] The disparity between these two accounts is strange: if Emmet was so disgusted by Plunket's denunciation of him, why attribute the attack solely to McNaughton? Madden rather unconvincingly accounts for it by claiming that 'Emmet's disgust and indignation at the treacherous conduct of W. C. Plunket in his regard – namely, in hounding on the government to measures of severity against him and the other two state prisoners – prevented his making mention of the name of W. C. Plunket.'[59] Perhaps rather, Emmet came to realise that depicting Plunket's severity against his brother as a shock betrayal and a display of outrageous dishonour by a close personal friend would merely serve further to edify the tragic hero, and to contribute to the process by which he was already becoming an enduring 'martyr in the cause of liberty' as Thomas Russell had claimed at his trial. In an 1806 letter to Peter Burrowes bitterly denouncing the 'list of promotions' which included Plunket's most recent advancement, Addis Emmet declared that there were 'certain men of whom I never wish to think, because I cannot think of them without the strongest emotions of aversion and disgust, strong and warm as was my former friendship'.[60] Emmet is vague, perhaps deliberately, about when exactly this friendship cooled, and this letter has most often been cited to reinforce the impression that the Emmet family were shocked and appalled by Plunket's alleged betrayal, yet the evidence would suggest that they could not have been.

If, as appears likely, Robert Emmet would not have been under the impression that Plunket was a family friend, this would seem to indicate that he must not have been the source of the accusation. However, a letter in the Plunket papers casts considerable doubt over this conclusion. It is from Leonard MacNally to an unknown recipient, in response to a 'request . . . made of me, at the desire of Mr Plunket' who was at that time preparing his libel case against William Cobbett.[61] Although this 'impose[d] a task exceedingly disagreeable', MacNally undertook to oblige this request and to 'candidly state, as far as recollection enables me, what passed from Mr Emmet to me on the subject of Mr P's speaking to evidence on the trial of that gentleman'. MacNally then recollected a conversation he had with Emmet 'on the morning of his execution'. He claimed Emmet had described Plunket's 'speech to evidence as an unnecessary act, he having previously instructed and insisted on his counsel to put such questions as amounted to a confession'. Emmet 'animadverted on Mr P[lunket]'s perseverance with great asperity' and 'charged him with ingratitude to "the son of a father" in whose house and at whose table, he said, Mr P[lunket] had been often entertained with hospitality and friendship'. 'When a boy', Emmet claimed to have 'repeatedly heard him argue on the politics of this country and the indepence [*sic*] it ought to establish', and apparently declared that 'those arguments were founded on and supported by the very same principles as those which had induced him to risque life and every other consideration' in what he himself called 'a "weak and ineffectual struggle to separate Ireland from England"'. Passionately bursting forth with an extended quotation of one of Plunket's anti-Union speeches to prove this point, Emmet apparently then went on to lament Lord Norbury's interruption of his speech from the dock, asserting that the judge had '"interrupted [him] at the very moment, when, though mortally wounded, [he] was going to crush the head of the reptile that had stung [him]"'. MacNally's word carries little weight in and of itself since having been revealed as a spy betraying Emmet's trust to the government for personal gain, yet this particular letter has a striking ring of truth to it. MacNally had nothing to gain by relating this version of events. Plunket and his legal team were attempting to locate the source of Cobbett's information. MacNally would have had no reason to fabricate this story and pass it on to them. At best he would have been involving himself in a public and messy legal affair; at worst, he was implicating himself. It is impossible to know MacNally's motives in writing this letter. His reluctance to oblige 'Mr Plunket' in any way is palpable, as is his disapproval of the 'unnecessary act' of Plunket's speech to evidence. Would MacNally have fabricated these details for that purpose? Perhaps the potential trouble this might cause for MacNally was outweighed by his desire to see Plunket fail in his public defence of his reputation. Again, it is impossible to be certain, and his remark that it was his understanding that 'several conversed with [Emmet] [after leaving Newgate]' would appear to deflect the focus from MacNally himself as sole source of the anecdote. He was also careful to state that 'a literal quotation never came from me'. None the less it appears unlikely that MacNally, so adept at keeping his head down that his duplicity went unrecognised for decades, would spontaneously invent this story and draw the attention of an opponent as sharp as Plunket without any basis in fact. Furthermore, MacNally's representation of Emmet's expressions and general behaviour is wholly in keeping with his character as we have come to understand it and the sentiments he expressed, while out of sync with the noble, Christ-like virtue of the Emmet myth, fit with the angry passion of the young revolutionary. If MacNally's account is true, Emmet did not therefore '"die in peace with sentiments of universal love and kindness towards all men"'.[62] Rather he was nursing a furious resentment of the 'reptile' whose harsh invective had so stung him, and of Lord Norbury for denying him his moment of revenge. If these were the thoughts occupying him in his final hours, and if, as MacNally thought it 'very probable', he repeated the accusation to the 'several' who 'conversed with him' at Newgate, the Christian character of Emmet as he faced execution is coloured with a little more human passion than the myth allows.

The Plunket papers contain many more similarly intriguing letters. Plunket's professional duties during this period situated him in a position accessible to parliament and public alike, and his papers reflect correspondence with members of both. Spanning the juncture of 'old' and 'new' style agitation, this collection provides many surprising perspectives of the Irish administration and English executive, both as they functioned and as they were perceived, with significant implications for the study of the intersecting spheres of political, legal and social history. The papers reflect the environment in which the government of Ireland was administered throughout this period, particularly in the 1820s with the rising pressure of extra-parliamentary agitation and its evolution towards the form eventually taken by 1829. It must be considered as a remarkable shame that such little use has been made of this collection since its acquisition by the National Library of Ireland in 1970.

This is undoubtedly due to the state of disorder in which it has remained. The collection, when exploited to its full potential, will contribute a great deal to our understanding of the legal and social worlds of Catholic and Protestant Ireland, and will unlock some of the complexities of interaction between Irish popular politics and the narrow political circles of the parliamentary elite. If Plunket had left a comprehensive body of political papers, even a diary or personal memoir, it would have greatly simplified the task of piecing together his motivations and concerns. It is rumoured that he, in a fit of pique, destroyed the greater part of his collection. The remaining collection, fragmentary as it is and with many letters only in draft form and without any sense of continuity, unfortunately still awaits a comprehensive catalogue.

An active pro-Catholic politician for over four decades, Plunket clearly contributed more to his world than one controversial speech, now one of the few things for which his name is still mentioned. He may or may not have been compelled to assist the crown against Emmet, and he may or may not have had specific career advancement in view on the day he rose to speak. Perhaps he felt Emmet's refusal to defend himself set a dangerous example, and conveyed a potentially explosive message to his supporters: that the forum of the court had no jurisdiction to try him, that he was above the established law and outside the bounds of legal treason. Perhaps he simply felt determined to deliver a masterful speech he had evidently prepared with some care. His exact motives are elusive. What is clear, however, is that the sentiments he expressed were in keeping with his genuine opinion of subversive revolutionary societies and his fear of the potential outcome of revolution, and that he does not deserve a reputation for insincerity any more than he deserved to be remembered for betraying a family with whom he had no relationship by that time.

The period between the Union and the Famine of 1847 persists in being remembered as one of unrivalled political, social and economic stagnation, and it remains one of the few areas relatively untouched by the sweep of revisionism in the past half century. 'By no other man', Plunket's grandson and only biographer to date has argued, 'could th[e courtroom denouncement of Emmet] have been done with so much weight and authority as Mr Plunket'.[63] With conclusions as wildly inaccurate as this, it may well be time for a new, more balanced and reliable biography which will accurately represent the contents of the Plunket manuscript collection and, taking into account the sources provided by other repositories, will have the scope and range to open up all aspects of his 60-year public life.[64] It is likely that such a work would carry significant implications for the study of Plunket's many contemporaries, and, it is to be hoped, potentially open up the so far untold story of his times. Often obscured by more attractive figures and peripheral to history, Plunket himself has no real myth to break down, only a reputation which deserves to be investigated, if not to defend, at least to explain.

Notes

1 Speech on the proposed Union, 22–23 Jan. 1799, quoted in James Cashel Hoey (ed.), *Speeches at the Bar and in the Senate, by . . . Wm. Conyngham, Lord Plunket, Lord High Chancellor of Ireland* (Dublin, 1856), p. 30.

2 C. L. Falkiner, *Studies in Irish History and Biography, Mainly in the Eighteenth Century* (London, 1902) p. 203. Indeed Grenville's character suffered a good deal less than Plunket's for his stance on the Peterloo question, despite expressing identical views in his correspondence and in parliamentary debate.

3 David Plunket (ed.), *The Life, Letters and Speeches of Lord Plunket, by his Grandson the Hon. David Plunket; with an introductory preface by Lord Brougham*, 2 vols (London, 1867), I, p. 333.

4 Colum Kenny, 'Irish ambition and English preference in chancery appointments, 1827–1841: the fate of William Conyngham Plunket', Discourse delivered at the Daughters of Charity, Henrietta Street, Dublin, 7 October 1994 in W. N. Osborough (ed.), *Explorations in Law and History: Irish Legal History Society Discourses, 1988–1994* (Dublin, 1995), p. 174.

5 Thomas Addis Emmet, *Memoir of Thomas Addis and Robert Emmet*, 2 vols (New York, 1915), II, p. 201.

6 Ibid., p. 204.

7 Wickham to Pole-Carew, 19 Sept. 1803 (TNA HO100/113,f.167).

8 Hoey (ed.), *Speeches at the Bar and in the Senate*, p. 30.

9 Emmet, *Memoir*, II, p. 205.

10 Letter of William Wickham cited in Adrian Hardiman, 'The trial of Robert Emmet', unpublished paper delivered at the Royal Irish Academy, 28 Oct. 2003, p. 5. See also chapter 13 of this volume.

11 R. R. Madden accepts this version of events. R. R. Madden, *The United Irishmen, their Lives and Times* quoted in Patrick M. Geoghegan, *Robert Emmet: A Life* (Dublin, 2003), p. 260.

12 *Sketches of History Politics and Manners, taken in Dublin and in the North of Ireland, in 1810* (Dublin, 1810).

13 Geoghegan, *Robert Emmet*, p. 260.

14 Emmet, *Memoir*, II, p. 202.

15 Geoghegan, *Robert Emmet*, p. 240; Charles Phillips, *Curran and his Contemporaries* (n.d.), p. 311.

16 Plunket (ed.) *The Life, Letters and Speeches*, I, p. 204.

17 Hoey (ed.), *Speeches at the Bar and in the Senate*, p. xiv.

18 Plunket to Newport, 9 Jan. 1821 (NLI MSS PC 922 'Newport 1816–1821').

19 Emmet, *Memoir*, II, p. 202.

20 Affidavit sworn for *Plunket* vs *Gilbert and Hodges*, 1811, quoted in R. R. Madden, *The Life and Times of Robert Emmet* (New York, 1856), p. x.

21 Ibid.

22 Phillips, *Curran and his Contemporaries*, p. 311.

23 Plunket (ed.) *The Life, Letters and Speeches*, I, p. 206.

24 Ibid.

25 Hoey (ed.), *Speeches at the Bar and in the Senate*, pp. 82–4.

26 Ibid.

27 Emmet, *Memoir*, II, p. 205.

28 Ibid., p. 207.

29 Ibid.

30 Ibid., p. 208.

31 Ibid., p. 205.

32 Ibid.

33 Ibid.

34 Ibid., p. 208.

35 Plunket to Walter Scott upon receipt of his *Life of Napoleon*, 3 Sept. 1827 (NLI MSS PC 919 'Misc. 1827, 26 Aug–3 Sept').

36 Emmet, *Memoir*, II, 208.

37 Ibid.

38 Ibid., p. 210.

39 Ibid., p. 206.

40 *A Report of the Trial of Michael Keenan, for Administering an Unlawful Oath* (Dublin, 1822).

41 D. J. Hickey's and J. E. Doherty's *A New Dictionary of Irish History from 1800*, 2nd edn (Dublin 2003) marks the beginnings of Ribbonism as late as 1826, though Tom Garvin (*The Evolution of Irish Nationalist Politics* (Dublin, 1981)), devoting a chapter to 'Secret societies before the famine', calls Ribbonism a Catholic 'counterblast to Orangeism' right through the early decades of the nineteenth century, and says that by its peak, 1825–1845, the movement shared Orangeism's 'addiction to oaths, banners, sashes, emblems and parades'. The chapter only devotes a few lines to the Keenan trial, and the entire Ribbon controversy in Dublin at this time, which had drawn major distinctions between the avowed nationalism of the leaders arrested in November

and Ribbonism as a protection organisation which had very easily 'turned into a protection racket, evolving into ingenious and sinister method of pumping a good deal of money out of poor and intimidated men' (Garvin, *Evolution*, p. 41). The Keenan trial took place on Monday 4 November 1822, a short time before the notorious 'Bottle Riot' in Dublin, and its practical invisibility in accounts of this period is likely to be in no small part due to the attention then focused on the rising antagonism between Wellesley and the Orange leaders, and the resultant entanglement between attorney general and the defiant ringleaders of the riot.

42 *Report of the Trial of Michael Keenan*, p. 9.

43 Ibid.

44 Plunket to Magee, 6 Oct. 1803 (NLI MSS PC 923 'Magee 1802–1825').

45 *Report of the Trial of Michael Keenan*, pp. 5–14.

46 Speech on Catholic claims in British House of Commons, 28 Feb. 1821, in Plunket (ed.), *The Life, Letters and Speeches*, II, p. 61.

47 Ibid., pp. 22–3.

48 Plunket to Henry Joy (NLI MSS PC 919 'Misc. Apr.–Nov. 1824').

49 Anon, *Most Important Facts: Extracts from the Speech of the Attorney General for Ireland on Opening the Trial of Michael Keenan* (extracted from the editions printed in Dublin, Exshaw, 1822, London reprint, J. Hatchard, 1823).

50 Speech on Catholic claims in British House of Commons, 28 Feb. 1821, in Plunket (ed.), *The Life, Letters and Speeches*, II, p. 61.

51 O'Connell to Plunket, 7 Mar. 1826, in Maurice R. O'Connell (ed.), *The Correspondence of Daniel O'Connell*, 8 vols (Dublin, 1972–80), III, pp. 237–8.

52 Quoted in Michael Tierney (ed.), *Daniel O'Connell: Nine Centenary Essays* (Dublin, 1949), p. 102. There can be no doubting O'Connell's sincere hostility to genuinely destructive secret societies, and his keenness to maintain the legitimacy of the Catholic association, despite his often flagrant flirtation with violent rhetoric. In response to a charge that his language was inflammatory and needlessly violent, he replied 'A French author says – I do not quote him as an authority, for no man hates French infidelity and French republican opinions more than I do; but a French author says that "you cannot make a revolution with rose water". He would make it with blood – I would make it with public opinion and I would put a little Irish spirit into it'. Quoted in Tierney, *Daniel O'Connell*, p. 103.

53 James Doyle, *Pastoral address of Dr Doyle (Roman Catholic Bishop of Kildare and Leighlin) to the Deluded and Illegal Associations of Ribbonmen, &c. &c. as Read in the Several Chapels in his Dioceses, on Sunday, November 24th, 1822* (Dublin, 1822).

54 Ibid.

55 Grattan to Rev. Mr Berwick, 25 July 1803, *Memoirs of the Life and Times of the Rt Hon. Henry Grattan by his Son Henry Grattan*, 5 vols (London, 1839–46), V, p. 223.

56 Emmet, *Memoir*, II, p. 149.

57 R. R. Madden, *The United Irishmen, their Lives and Times*, 3rd series (Dublin, 1846), p. 77.

58 Quoted in Emmet, *Memoir*, I, p. 263.

59 Ibid.

60 Thomas Addis Emmet to Peter Burrowes, 19 Nov. 1806 (RIA MS 23/K.53/51) quoted in Geoghegan, *Robert Emmet*, p. 240.

61 MacNally to Unknown, 16 Jan. 1804 (NLI MS PC 922).

62 Madden, *United Irishmen*, quoted in Geoghegan, *Robert Emmet*, p. 264.

63 Plunket (ed.) *The Life, Letters and Speeches*, 1, p. 215.

64 For example, British Library: Wellesley (and others) (BL Add. MSS 37298–312 passim), Grenville papers (BL Add MSS 58963); National Library of Wales, 1818–27: C. W. W. Wynn, 'Coedymaen'; PRONI: Formal Papers as Lord Chancellor (D 3406/A/14); NLI, Grattan papers (MSS 27,799), O'Connell (MSS 33565), Newport (MSS 796); University of Durham: Grey of Howick collection, '1831–34: correspondence with 2nd Earl Grey'; University College London, Special Collections: Brougham papers (GB 0103 BROUGHAM BL, HB).

REINVENTING EMMET

CHAPTER 6

Missing Robert Emmet

William Godwin's Irish Expedition

Timothy Webb

I

William Godwin (1756–1836) visited Dublin and environs (with a brief excursion to Carlow Assizes) between 2 July and 12 August 1800 when he left on the packet-boat for Holyhead at four o'clock in the morning. Although his travels took him to Dublin at a very significant time in its history, and although his journey (or journeys) carries a range of suggestive references, it has been relatively neglected by most of his biographers and interpreted as little more than a colourful excursion. Yet his visit to Dublin and Carlow relates in interesting ways to his previous writings and to a number of his central concerns and was to play a part, directly or indirectly, in a passage in his own *Essay on Sepulchres* (1809) and in the work of his daughter Mary and of her radical husband Percy Bysshe Shelley. The main sources for Godwin's expedition so far located are to be found in his diary (more correctly, a sequence of diaries, still not fully published), in two long letters to his business partner James Marshall, who was looking after his business affairs and his young family in London, and in two carefully considered letters to Samuel Taylor Coleridge, who had become a close friend and correspondent in the preceding months and who, with his own children, had dined at Godwin's on the preceding Christmas Day.[1] These three accounts often confirm each other but the diary and the letters to Marshall include details which are unique to their own version of events; in particular, the diary entries tend to be skeletal and laconic according to Godwin's normal diary practice; while the letters are often more confidential, more descriptive and expansive, and particularly in the case of the Coleridge letter, more judgmental and analytical. Through its very austerity and its appearance as an uncontaminated document of record, the diary gives the impression of objectivity and perhaps even of comprehensive coverage; yet comparison with the letters to Marshall, the accounts of various people who encountered Godwin, and contemporary newspaper records (themselves often biased in coverage), clearly indicate that Godwin's accounts in the diary are not always what they seem. As in the case of other expeditions, Godwin is capable of making mistakes and he sometimes becomes confused about names or dates (which can happen in letters, too); most crucially, perhaps, the diary records are not complete and on occasion omit altogether people or events which feature lengthily in letters. While the diary remains a particularly rich resource, it must be interpreted with caution.

Godwin had more than one good reason to visit Ireland. Like many English radicals of his time, his political conscience had long been exercised by the affairs of Ireland, so his panoramic vision of contemporary European politics was not likely to neglect the troubling presence of the 'sister' island. Yet the pressing affairs of France never succeeded in drawing him across the channel, even if Mary Wollstonecraft had been an eyewitness of some key events in the French Revolution; nor did he visit any other European country, although he frequently travelled, with an appropriately curious and questioning eye, throughout the British domains. He continued to travel extensively in imagination, and read widely throughout his life, interesting himself far beyond the norm in foreign and constitutional affairs, but his voyage across the Irish Sea seems to have carried a unique status; he retained many Irish friends and connections yet never made a return journey to Ireland, although he lived till 1836. This gap in his itinerary seems all the more curious in view of a conversation which took place during his visit on 2 August 1800, apparently at John Philpot Curran's. Godwin recorded in his diary that the discussion ranged over several subjects and included talk 'd'une 2me visite'.[2]

In the event, it was Curran rather than Godwin who enjoyed the privilege of return visits. For instance, before the month of August was out, he called on Godwin in London (on the 29th). On 2 and 3 September he dined and slept at Godwin's while he again slept at Godwin's on 25 and 28 September and on 17 October. He dined at Godwin's on 9 September and on 4, 17 and 19 October (on the last two occasions with Wolcot and Porson, respectively); he accompanied Godwin to supper at Taggart's on 9 and Reynolds's on 29 September and at Fenwick's on 4 October; together they travelled on the Wimbledon coach to Horne Tooke's on 28 September; and he accompanied Godwin to dinner at Perry's on 28 September and on 18 October, and at Wolcot's on 20 October. He called on Godwin, not only on 29 August but on 6 and (together with Tobin) 27 October, while Godwin reciprocated by calling on Curran on 2 and 22 October. On 18 October Godwin and Curran called on Reynolds, Fuseli and Lawrence. Curran invited Godwin to dinner on 26 October while, shortly before the conclusion of his visit, Curran was part of a large breakfast party at Godwin's on 29 October. Godwin wrote to Curran on 17 November, 8 and 28 January, and on 3 February.[3] These details attest an intimacy, even a friendship, between Curran and Godwin which seems to continue the pattern of Curran's earlier visit to London and of Godwin's own visit to Ireland. These intimacies were consolidated by many later visits from Curran and, to a lesser extent, by visits from his children (briefly, Richard but recurrently, and with increasing frequency, Amelia). Much later, after the death of his father (to whom Godwin had publicly dedicated *Mandeville*), his biographer and youngest son William maintained an amicable correspondence with Godwin and was a frequent visitor. The fragmentary evidence of various letters, and the records lodged in the diary, also indicate that, especially in the early days, he maintained some sort of correspondence with Margaret Mountcashel, Henry Grattan, and Mary Wollstonecraft's two sisters (Eliza Bishop (1763–1833) and Everina Wollstonecraft (1765–1841)) who set up a school in Dublin. Both sisters visited him in London but Everina Wollstonecraft (whom he liked a great deal less) spent much more time in his company. The evidence of these Irish connections is cumulative and incontrovertible. On the surface, then, it is hard to believe that Godwin was not invited, or that he preferred not to make a return visit to Ireland.

II

The main overt cause of Godwin's Irish expedition was a pressing invitation from John Philpot Curran, KC (1750–1817). Curran, who had joined the Irish Bar in 1775 and taken silk in 1783, was perhaps the outstanding Irish advocate of his time, or even 'the first advocate in Europe' (as Godwin told Coleridge). He had been MP for Kilbeggan (1783–6) and Rathcormack (1786–97) and in 1800 he represented Banagher. Curran had first met Godwin in London in October 1799 and their initial meeting quickly developed into a lasting, if improbable, friendship. On the surface they shared an interest in the state of Ireland shortly before the passing of the Act of Union, which Godwin had publicly opposed in his writing and Curran in his speeches and interventions in the Irish Parliament and (some thought) in his regular defence of United Irishmen in the Irish courts. Curran's forensic activities, his notable defence of Archibald Hamilton Rowan and his ferocious verbal assaults on the tactics of government, led to general assumptions about his political persuasions which were challenged by his later acceptance of high office when he became Master of the Irish Rolls and a Privy Councillor in 1806; however, in 1800 most observers would have concluded that he was at least sympathetic to those who opposed the Union. It was hard to forget that he had represented not only Rowan but William Jackson, William Drennan, the *Northern Star*, Henry Sheares, Theobald Wolfe Tone, and James Napper Tandy. Perhaps

Godwin (like his eventual son-in-law Percy Bysshe Shelley) also admired the eloquence of his performances in the courtroom. Godwin and Curran were bound together by other factors which are harder to identify and teasingly paradoxical: for all his reticence in public, Godwin seems to have warmed to Curran's exhibitions of Irish wit and eloquence while Curran admired Godwin for his unquestionable intellectual eminence as well as some more elusive personal qualities. In Godwin's phrase, Curran was a 'charming creature', while Curran addressed Godwin as a 'sacred presence'.

Curran's first epistolary approaches on 22 October 1799 were effusive and embarrassing. To begin with, he admits that 'he had been a rake yesterday and did not get your kind letter till my return home at night'. He continues:

> I cannot but confess that at the first moment it [the thought of friendship] excited a sensation too like that of vanity, which however, on being a little questioned, soon retired and gave place to a better, because an humbler a warmer and less selfish feeling. I remember I did not use the word friendship. I then created a term to express the act of the mind when it wishes very kindly and respects very much. I felt at the instant that the word meant a great deal more, that it implied a mutuality and reciprocation of those sentiments and that in this extended sense I could not use it without presumption. You have very kindly relieved me upon that score; but were you perfectly aware that that what you might have intended as simple pardon might be strained into something like contract and engagement? If you were, I thank you and accept it cordially and gratefully. And have only to regret that the distance of our habitations prevent me from profitting [*sic*] by it as much as I should wish and endeavour to deserve.[4]

Even here, one can detect the characteristic rhetorical devices of the Curran style: there seem to be at least five doublets and one triplet in this passage. The idiom of the court is not far away either: the sensation which soon retires 'on being a little questioned' and Godwin's 'simple pardon' which might be turned into 'contract and engagement'. With whatever delicacy, and whatever surface jocularity, Curran seems to be telling Godwin that, even if unwittingly, he has now committed himself to an official 'friendship', which implies ' a mutuality and reciprocation' based on the combined sentiments of wishing very kindly and respecting very much. That Godwin has entered into a new contractual relationship is indicated by the fact that, for all his uncertainties and hesitations, Curran addresses him as 'my dear friend'.

Only a few days later Curran wrote again, after a visit from Godwin and a note. Much of this letter is devoted to advice concerning Godwin's relations with Elizabeth Inchbald (1753–1821), novelist, playwright and actress, who had retired from the stage in 1789 and who had dined at Kemble's on 27 October in a company which included Sheridan, Lawrence, Morris (the code name of Arthur O'Connor) and Kemble's younger brother Charles. With a certain amount of flattery combined with shrewd appraisal, Curran advised Godwin: 'with a woman like her certain forms must be gone thro before reconciliation is accorded, that may carry a man like you'. When she was alive, Mary Wollstonecraft had been more tart about the attractions of 'Mrs Perfection'. More significantly, perhaps, Curran also pointedly remembered his own growing friendship with Godwin. On Sunday, 'we talked over the table and the talkers'. He conceded that his choice of term (presumably, 'talk') might be questionable, but his impression of his own irresistible rhetorical force is vivid when he characterises himself with folkloric intensity as 'one who flung an Irish mountain upon one of them and reduced him to a listener'. In the same letter Curran frankly admitted his own unwillingness to leave London and to return to Ireland and revealed an agenda for further meetings with Godwin both in Ireland and in London:

> The extreme reluctance with which I turn my face to that [?]devoted region of misery throws a sort of air of final parting over an adieu. But I trust we shall meet again shortly in Ireland, and more shortly in England.[5]

On 8 June 1800 Curran wrote to Godwin from Dublin with an extended and pressing invitation. He began with a complicated, but not unusual, explanation of failures in correspondence (in which Godwin may have played his own part, since Curran observed that he had only written one letter). Curran's letter then modulated into a compliment to Godwin's abilities, a self-humbling presentation of his own insufficiencies in face of Godwin's superior capacities, and a flattering invitation to a country which was already experiencing the first effects of an impending Union:

> If I had not thought highly of your head and your heart, I would not have solicited your friendship, nor be so anxious as I really am to cultivate and retain it. To a man who has lost his country, and his liberty the friendship of a few men of a certain class is perhaps the only consolation that remains. My last letter which has been brought back to me by the negligence of its bearer was written chiefly to remind you of our conversation about this country, and the kind inclination you shewed to gratify my wish of seeing you in it. Permit me now to recall what then passed to your memory. And to assure you that nothing would make me happier[.] I have yet two months to remain here. I am too much a slave to have as much of your company as I [?]would wish, but I will treat you with perfect candour, and promise you that I will act as your host as I would if I were your guest. I have an house in town, and a cottage in the country within three miles of it, a spare bed in each, books in each, and a bottle of wine in each, and in each you will find the most absolute power of doing what you please as to idling, working, walking, eating,

> sleeping, &c. There are many here that know you in print and are much pleased with the hope I have given them of knowing you in person.[6]

One of those admirers was Lady Mountcashel (?1772–1835) 'who is now settled near Dublin for the Summer, [and] speaks of you with peculiar regard, mixed with a tender and regretful retrospect to past times & to past events with which you have yourself been connected'. Curran is here referring to the fact that Mary Wollstonecraft had been the influential governess of the young Margaret King when she worked in the Kingsborough household at Mitchelstown and in Dublin in 1786–7. By the time of Godwin's visit, she had become Lady Mountcashel after her marriage to Stephen Moore (1770–1822), grandson of the 1st Earl of Moira and (in the judgement of William Drennan) 'a patriotic if not democratic nobleman'.[7] She was so devoted to the memory of her governess that the name 'Mrs Mason' under which she later lived in Pisa was probably derived from one of her stories. In the event, Godwin did spend a good deal of time in her company, visited her at Old Court in Bray, discussed education with her, and was taken out by her to visit local scenery.

Curran was persuasive (or attempted to be) in various other ways. One attraction might be the presence in Dublin of their mutual acquaintance John Philip Kemble (in the event Godwin arrived just too late to see or meet him). Curran's insistence on the amenities of his own hospitality and his desire for Godwin's presence is partly balanced, or persuasively extended, by the appeal to Godwin's political curiosity. If Godwin comes to Dublin, he will be offering 'consolation' to Curran while observing 'a man who has lost his country, and his liberty'. Curran returns to the ambivalent point later in the letter: 'I think too you would feel a curiosity to see a nation in its last moments'. There were other inducements. As he told Godwin, 'it was the pleasantest time of the year', and the journey was not very long, involving only a drive in a mail-coach to Holyhead, 'and a ferry brings a philosopher, six shirts, his genius and his hat upon it from London to Dublin [and vice versa], . . . in 54 hours'. He had set out

> the pros and cons with as much fairness as can be expected from a person so much interested in your decision. If therefore it does not interfere with some material object or engagement, in the name of God [?]even trust yourself to the hospitality of those Irish barbarians with whom your nation is about to communicate her freedom and her wealth.

With the authority of 'an old traveller', he told Godwin, with pressing force, that preparation and baggage were crucial and that 'travelling in idea is a thousand times more tiresome than travelling in fact'. The invitation reached a disarming climax: 'Say to me then by a line that I may put your sheets to the fire. If you should land here in the night you will find your bed ready at No. 12 Ely Place, at any hour.' He also allowed himself to recall other episodes from his London visit:

> Do you remember a conversation or two between you Mr Fenwick and myself, in which I gravely delivered a lecture upon novel-writing, and very sagaciously pointed out the shoals on which bad pilots had struck in that sort of navigation. When I read St Leon I was surprised to find you had so dextrously avoided them: and if I had not unfortunately recollected that the work must have been finished before the lecture was given, I should probably have felt no little pleasure in thinking how much good writing was indebted to good criticism.

Precisely which occasion (or occasions) Curran was recalling it is not possible to say, but it seems likely that he was thinking back to October of the previous year. On 3 October 1799 Godwin called on Curran with Fenwick; on 7 October he called on Fenwick, where the talk was of Curran; on 10 October Godwin had tea at Curran's with Fenwick, while on 12 October he dined at Curran's where the two other dinner guests included Fenwick. In fact, the novel was published on 2 December 1799 while Godwin noted the publication of the second edition on 3 February 1800.[8]

Whatever the date (or dates) and whatever Curran's influence on the revised version, his concluding reminiscence is an ingenious addition to the argument since it contrives to introduce a memory which links Curran with Godwin and is flattering to his achievements in fiction, while acknowledging Curran's own critical limitations (the choice of 'unfortunately' rather than 'fortunately' is both revealing and a further example of self-abasement). Obviously, Curran is skilful at deploying a kind of verbal modesty: 'those Irish barbarians' is calculated to appeal, if jocularly, to the metropolitan sensibility of Godwin (and can be compared to Curran's public utterances in which 'barbarism' or 'barbarity' was usually an attribute of unfeeling tyranny and used with unqualified force).

Curran had two houses (as he says in his letter) but he writes of them in terms that are also modest, even self-deprecating. His 'cottage in the country' was The Priory at Rathfarnham (off Grange Road) which he had bought in 1790 when it was still known as 'Holly Park'. This 'cottage' was a large house set in 35 acres. It quickly became the setting of a significant salon. In 1798 Major Sirr deputed a guard to protect it until he was countermanded by Curran's friend, Arthur Wolfe (later Lord Kilwarden). In the event Godwin was to spend a good deal of his time 'at Mr Curran's barn (as he calls it)'. For example, he confides to James Marshall: 'I am now writing on Saturday, the 2nd of August . . . , & am seated quietly in Mr. Curran's book room in his rural retreat, 4 miles from Dublin'.[9] Yet for all its apparent clarities, the record leaves some room for doubts and uncertainties of definition. According to Godwin's own listing he was at Rathfarnham on 2, 6 and 15, 17, 26 (when Gould breakfasted and Grattan called unsuccessfully) and 31 July (when Glover dined and slept), and on 1 (when Glover dined and slept) and 10 August (when Godwin dined); and he records that he slept there on 8, 10, 11, 18 and 19 July. This is a bare computation, based on specific mentions of Rathfarnham, but the record seems to suggest that it was the centre of further festivities. For example, he tells Marshall:

> I saw Mr Grattan for the first time in Ireland, at Mr Curran's country house, on [Sund]Saturday, the 12th of July, ten days after my arrival in Dublin. He then dined with us, but it was in a numerous company, that afforded me very little opportunity of diving into his characteristic qualities. The next day however we went over to Grattan's own house, where we arrived in the evening, & slept that & the succeeding night. Mr Curran was obliged on Monday morning to go to Dublin to attend the courts, in consequence of which I had Grattan almost, though not entirely, to myself till dinner time, when Curran & another person, his companion, returned from Dublin, about 13 English miles.

For 12 July, Godwin's diary records at dinner Grattan, Granard, Pim, Hamilton, Moore, Burke, Wallis, McGray and Conway (presumably the general who had called after dinner at Lady Moira's on 9 July), though in this version Rathfarnham is not mentioned (and the 'G.' who sleeps at Rathfarnham that night is not identified). Godwin did have supper the next evening at Grattan's (having earlier dined with Curran at Lady Mountcashel's, presumably at Old Court), where the other guests were Curran, Gould, Hartley and Trotter. The simple verb 'sleep' confirms that, as his letter asserts, he did sleep at Grattan's on two successive nights. These episodes demonstrate how the reticence of the diary occludes not only significant dimensions of Godwin's Irish experience, but specifically, the centrality of Rathfarnham. To take one further example, on 15 July Godwin writes, 'Rathfarnham; Gould, Batley & Glover dine; Gould sleeps', while on 17 July he notes 'Rathfarnham; Delane, Skeys, Trotter & Batley dine'. From these cryptic notes, and the ambiguity of their punctuation, it is not clear whether the dining and sleeping took place at Rathfarnham or in Ely Place. While it is not possible to reconstruct these social events with complete exactness or certainty, there can be no doubt that Curran made much use of his house at Rathfarnham and that Godwin was frequently there during the time of his visit.

III

In Dublin Godwin was much sought after socially, though there are some surprising absences from his list of contacts. For example, he seems not to have met the Emmet family although, as Ruán O'Donnell argues, 'Robert Emmet had been influenced by Godwin's writings when a student in Trinity and would probably have attempted to meet the author had he remained in Ireland.'[10] Nor did he meet Robert Emmet's sister Mary Ann Holmes who was an admirer of the writings of Mary Wollstonecraft and of her husband, whose *Political Justice* (like her brother Robert) she had studied with care. Mary Ann was in touch with Margaret Mountcashel and was regarded as 'a respected member of a discreet circle of disaffected liberal intellectuals' but, at the time of Godwin's visit, she was in poor health.

Godwin's reputation went before him. He proudly reported to James Marshall: 'No one has been ignorant who I was; to no one in that sense have I needed an introduction; & by none, so far as I know, have I been received with an unfavourable prepossession.' Yet, even this apparently innocent statement requires some translation. There were two Godwins, or even three, and it is not entirely clear which version, or versions, they received without an 'unfavorable prepossession'. Godwin was widely known as a radical political philosopher and the author of *Political Justice* and for many, including Robert Emmet and his elder brother Thomas Addis Emmet, this must have been his main attraction. O'Donnell explains:

> In the 1790s Godwin, Locke and Voltaire were exploited by republican propagandists who mass distributed excerpts from inaccessible and expensive books in pamphlet form. These compilations, along with Tom Paine's *The Rights of Man*, reached a huge non-traditional readership in 1795–98 and contributed greatly to Addis Emmet's objective of 'making every man a politician'.[11]

As Kevin Whelan specifically notes, two of these pamphlets were circulated among the peasantry of the north, the first mainly compiled from Godwin, Locke and Paine, and the second from Voltaire, Volney and 'other atheistical writers'.[12] As this shows, Godwin was often linked with Paine, since both English writers questioned traditional beliefs and the received bases of social organisation. In Dublin, James Moore (d. 1803) of College Green was involved in publishing *The Rights of Man* in 1791, followed by a number of Paine reprints, and also produced 'the sole Irish edition' of Godwin's *Enquirer* in 1797.[13] Such was his commitment that he even put forward Thomas Paine for membership of the United Irishmen. This radical Godwin would have been a hero to many Irish people but a threatening presence to many others. The experience of William Drennan shows that in Dublin as in England reactions to Godwin's memoir of his late wife, Mary Wollstonecraft, were mixed and often roused hostility or evasion.[14] The third Godwin was the writer of fiction, of *Caleb Williams* and especially *St Leon* which had recently gone into a second edition and was much admired.

As the diary shows, Godwin was much in demand. Among those he met, usually at dinner but sometimes through social calls and in some cases more than once, can be listed Henry Grattan (1745–1820); George Ponsonby (1755–1817), 'who, I find, is invariably held the 3rd orator in Ireland' (on Godwin's visit to Carlow); Hugh Skeys (the widower of Mary Wollstonecraft's Dublin friend Fanny Blood who had once been a member of the United Irishmen and (according to Leonard MacNally) their point of contact with Grattan, and who had written on the news of his wife's death to invite Godwin to stay in Dublin); Mary Wollstonecraft's sisters, Eliza Bishop and Everina Wollstonecraft, whom he saw quite frequently, especially in the earlier stages of his visit; relations of Sheridan, probably including at least one of his two sisters, who had married into the Lefanu family, and perhaps his young niece; Hugh Douglas Hamilton, the painter (1740–1808); Joseph Cooper Walker, the antiquary; many lawyers, unidentified Dublin citizens, and (on his trip to Carlow) 'Buck' Whaley, Jonah Barrington, Judge Thomas Kelly and several members of the military. One of the first people he called on was William Drennan (1754–1820), who had been a highly significant figure in the early days of the United Irishmen, had been tried for seditious libel in 1794, when he had been successfully defended by Curran, and was a close friend of the Emmet family. Although he had reservations about Godwin, Drennan invited him to dinner where he met, among others, Robert Emmet's brother-in-law the barrister Robert Holmes (1765–1859), husband of Mary Anne whom Drennan had been attending when Godwin first called; Holmes had already spent some time in prison and would be arrested in 1801 and again after the 1803 rising, even though he was out of the country at the crucial period. Godwin was also invited to Moira House (where Pamela Fitzgerald had taken sanctuary) and dined among aristocrats who shared strong anti-unionist sentiments and kept in touch with the Emmet family. At various times Godwin went walking, riding, sightseeing, and sea-bathing, and he travelled on the new Bray Diligence on visiting Margaret Mountcashel.

These contacts were significant and suggestive. Recurrently and unmissably, though, Curran and the Curran family were at the centre of Godwin's Irish experience. Godwin expressed something of the impression which Curran himself made on him in an uncompleted letter to Coleridge which was drafted when he was still Curran's guest:

> Curran I admire extremely. There is scarcely the man on earth, with whom I feel myself so entirely at my ease, or so little driven back from time to time to consider

> of my own miserable individual [*sic*]. He is perpetually a staff and a cordial, without ever affecting to be the one or the other. The being never lived, who was more perfectly free from every species of concealment. With great genius, at least a rich & inexhaustible imagination, he never makes me stand in awe of him, & bow as to my acknowledged superior; a thing by the way, which *de tems à d'autre* [*sic*] you compel me to do. He amuses me always, astonishes me often, yet naturally & irresistibly inspires me with confidence. I am apt, particularly, when from home, to feel forlorn & dispirited; the two last days I spent from him, &, though they were employed most enviably in tete à tete intercourse with Grattan, I began to feel dejected & home-sick. But Curran has joined me today, & poured into my bosom a full portion of his irresistible kindness & gaiety.[15]

The diary demonstrates that he dined out in Dublin on not less than twenty occasions, at least ten of which involved John Philpot Curran on his own (Curran also accompanied Godwin on at least two calls), while (with two exceptions, discussed in the next paragraph) the others involved 'Cs' or the Curran family (which may be thought to include the father). Of course, there is no way to tell what is signified by 'Cs' and whether it always includes the whole family, or only parts of it. There are also at least 13 other occasions when Godwin seems to have dined at home, presumably at Curran's, though the children are only mentioned specifically on three occasions. It seems likely that he came to know one or more of the children well, both through these social occasions and because they may have encountered each other when he stayed overnight, or at breakfast.

On his first full day in Dublin Godwin records that 'C's' dine. On the following day (that is, 4 July) he notes that 'R & A, E & S Currans' dine, and that on the day after that (5 July) '4 Currans dine'. This is intriguing for more than one reason. It seems to suggest that on 4 and 5 July the younger Currans dined without their father (elsewhere in the diary Godwin scrupulously records the numbers when he dines with more than two members of a family). Secondly, and much more intriguingly, the entry for 4 July is the only occasion when we are given any clues concerning the identity of the larger Curran family, who are usually signalled as 'Cs'. Some of the identifications are easy: 'R' is Richard, 'A' is probably Amelia (though it could be Anne), 'S' is Sarah. But who is 'E' (a letter very clearly written by Godwin)? This letter does not seem to fit any of the Curran names. Jane, the eldest, eventually came with Amelia to visit Godwin in London; young William became close to Godwin many years afterwards. Possibly Godwin is in error. Just possibly, though, 'E' might stand for Emmet (that is, Robert Emmet) who is signalled here by a code which is largely impenetrable, except for the proximity to Sarah Curran, which might point to a connection which was generally unrecognised at the time but which seems to have been developing since 1799. If so, this would be the only recorded time that Godwin and Emmet came together in Ireland. It would also explain the apparent intimacy with which Godwin could write about Emmet in his letter to Shelley.

Short of further evidence, this conjecture must remain only pleasingly speculative. Godwin's connections with other members of the Curran family are unquestionable. Frustratingly, this is the only time that he specifically mentions Sarah nor does she seem to have visited Godwin in London (perhaps because he seemed too close to the father who had rejected her). Richard (b. 1775) later turned out to be a friend and associate of Emmet who wrote a letter to him shortly before he was executed which included a paragraph specifically addressed to Sarah. In the fullness of time, he called on Godwin in London more than once (for example, on 10 October 1804 he accompanied Everina Wollstonecraft on a visit, while on 9 May 1810 he had tea at Godwin's with his sister Amelia), though they never became close. Richard Curran, who had been held in England on treason charges in 1798 was 'the friend and private secretary of Valentine Lawless, an Emmet family associate held in the Tower of London from 8 May 1799 to March 1801'.[16] It was Lawless (1753–1833), later Lord Cloncurry, and once an energetic United Irishman, who in the fullness of time would be responsible for raising a memorial to the memory of Amelia Curran in the Irish College in Rome. Lawless was close to Colonel Edward Marcus Despard, also a United Irishman (and known to Godwin), executed in London in February 1803 and supposed by some to be associated with Emmet and his rising; he also knew the Emmet brothers, was friendly with Thomas Addis and dined with Robert on his last night in Paris. Some of this was still in the future and Richard Curran may have been reticent. Yet Godwin's diary includes one Irish entry which might throw interesting light on his contemporary reputation. On 30 July it begins: 'Asks of RC; talks of Strafford & Leland.' The entry for the previous day suggests that the unidentified speaker is probably Henry Grattan. As we shall see later, the conversation at supper at Grattan's on the previous night had turned to 'talk of O'Connor, Emmet & secession'. Given such a context, and given that the speaker was well informed, it is not impossible that the 'RC' who is the subject of enquiry was indeed Richard Curran.

Perhaps the least well known of the three children is Amelia, although she played a significant part in the Emmet story. When the Priory was raided by Major Sirr and his police cohort, it was Amelia who let them in and who took decisive action when Sirr entered Sarah's bedroom. As Patrick Geoghegan puts it: 'Taking advantage of the chaos, Amelia raced to the secret alcove where her sister had stored her letters from Emmet and began burning the entire correspondence; the police attempted to stop her but only succeeded in saving a "few scraps" which were "all in Mr Emmet's handwriting".'[17] In spite of her continued lack of recognition, Amelia Curran was at the heart of the

Emmet narrative. After a lapse of time, she became friendly with Godwin and frequently called on him and dined at his house from 1810 onwards. Eventually, she settled in Rome where she became friendly with the Shelleys (Percy Bysshe had met her at Godwin's) who settled next door at 65 Via Sistina. While they were all living in Rome from 5 March to 10 June 1819, the Shelleys and Claire Clairmont saw her almost daily. During this period, she painted portraits of all the family: Mary Shelley (two pictures which once belonged to Trelawny but are now missing); William Shelley (the only extant picture of the Shelleys' child, which is now in the Pforzheimer Collection in New York); Claire Clairmont (now in Newstead Abbey); and Percy Bysshe Shelley (the portrait by which he is still best known, probably influenced by Guido Reni's picture of Beatrice Cenci, which is now in the National Portrait Gallery in London). She became particularly close to Mary Shelley, who entrusted her with delicate assignments concerning the tomb of William (who had died in Rome), and who later wrote to her with the news of Percy Shelley's drowning (Amelia was not in Rome at the time but, when the letter finally reached her, replied sympathetically).[18] This connection is one of the ways (like the presence of Lady Mountcashel in Pisa) that the younger generation of Romantics kept in touch with the activities of their predecessors.

IV

Since Godwin visited Dublin almost three years before Emmet's public activities, he can hardly be expected to have been close to the action yet, as these first encounters show, he met or observed many of the principals and he must have been conscious that Dublin was in a precarious and potentially revolutionary situation. It is often impossible to tell how much he knew but, since most of his movements were in legal or political circles and since his visit was animated and driven by Curran, his level of awareness should have been generally high. On his first full day in Dublin (that is, 3 July) he dined with a substantial company, including Ridgway and probably Burrowes (spelt 'Burro.' by Godwin). William Ridgeway of Harcourt Street (who had been called to the Irish Bar in 1790 was to play a significant part in Emmet's trial, in which he appeared for the Crown, while later providing an official account of the proceedings in which Robert Emmet's speech appears more improvised and more staccato (in Norman Vance's term) than the seamlessly sonorous version with which most people have become familiar.[19] Ridgeway had also published a transcript of the trial of the Sheares brothers in which Curran had appeared for Henry and, initially, for John, who was ultimately represented by Leonard MacNally. He was one of the dinner guests at Leonard MacNally's on 10 July. He also features in the long list of legal names which Godwin provides for 5 August at Carlow though it must remain unlikely that Godwin actually encountered him there or that the list signifies anything more than a recording of his legal presence.

Peter Burrowes, KC (1753–1841), who had been called to the Irish Bar in 1785, was a distinguished lawyer, who was to represent Emmet at his trial (basically, because Curran refused to do so and perhaps because he was friendly with Thomas Addis Emmet); along with Thomas Addis Emmet, he had been a founding member of the Monks of the Screw, and he too had once been a member of the United Irish Society but soon separated himself from its proceedings. Although he was a friend of Wolfe Tone, and sympathetic to Whig solutions, he would certainly have regarded Emmet's rising as too radical and too extreme. Like MacNally, he provided information to government, though neither lawyer appears to have been aware of the other's dangerously delicate position. Though it seems likely that it was this Burrowes whom Godwin encountered, final judgment must be reserved. Is this the 'Burro.' with whom Godwin dined on 3 July? (There were two lawyers in Dublin at that time (Frederick and William) who bore the name 'Burroughs', and two (Alexander and Peter) who bore the name 'Burrowes'.) And can this 'Burro.' be equated with the 'Burroughs' who appears in the list of people Godwin met in 1800? Or the 'Burroughs' who called on Curran on 22 October 1803 when he was in London and had dinner with Curran, Godwin and others at Hamilton Rowan's three days afterwards? Or the 'Burroughs' on whom Godwin called with Curran on 2 October 1809?

On the next day (that is, 4 July), the guests at dinner (presumably at Curran's) included Burton (Curran's clerk), Richard Newton Bennet (who had been called to the Irish Bar in 1796) and, notably, Leonard MacNally (1752–1820), of Harcourt Street (according to the *Dublin Directory*) or Dominick Street (according to Thomas Bartlett). MacNally, who had been called to the Irish and English Bars in 1776 and 1783, was then best known as 'an able criminal lawyer' specialising in defence briefs, a hard-working and convivial member of the Irish Bar who had once been a reasonably successful writer for the stage in England. Perhaps he is best known today as the author of 'Sweet Lass of Richmond Hill', but he also wrote *Sentimental Excursions to Windsor and Other Places* (1781), an adaptation of Sterne's *Tristram Shandy* for the stage in 1783, and a number of farces and comic operas including *Robin Hood: or Sherwood Forest* in the next year. MacNally (who had once written under the name of 'Plunder') had been a member of the Whig Club of Ireland and an active member of the Society of United Irishmen before he became an informer, and he continued to maintain a damaging public reputation for political extremism (as late as 1806 Drennan was to suggest his unsuitability for high legal office by noting that he was 'a sort of Newgate solicitor, much looked down upon by the bar' and that he had been 'a notorious United

I[rishman]').[20] Godwin would have deplored the politics but he might have appreciated the combination of interests; he seems to have experienced a more than usual fascination with the law, while MacNally's connections with the theatre were especially likely to appeal to his taste. Like all his contemporaries, including those who knew MacNally much better, he can hardly have suspected that MacNally was in the pay of the British government and that his reports were taken seriously at a high level. After all, MacNally had been chosen for the defence of William Jackson; had reduced Curran to tears by his defence of Patrick Finney (Curran's own address on this occasion was so fluent that, as the Stockdale edition admits, 'To keep pace with the rapid flow of his eloquence, is impossible'); had been specifically nominated by James Napper Tandy; and was part of the prisoner's defence team in the Wallace trial at Carlow (in all four cases he appeared alongside Curran, whose patriotic credentials seemed impeccable). Godwin could not reasonably have been expected to know that MacNally was in the habit of communicating defence strategies to the Crown (as in the case of John Sheares); or to predict that, in the fullness of time, MacNally would feed Emmet's defence plans to the authorities or that, having done so, he would visit him in jail on the morning of his execution and retail their discussion, with whatever inaccuracies and advantages to himself, to the ears of government.[21]

For his part, MacNally was not slow to play the expected social card: on 10 July Godwin dined at his house, together with 'Fletcher, Ridgway, Colles's, Ginnis's, Shaws, C[urran]s, Burton & Mrs Featherstone'. There followed a long gap until Godwin recorded on 6 August, when he was attending the Assizes at Carlow, 'Meet McNally'. So far the intelligence records have not revealed any report on Godwin by MacNally, though it is possible that such a report was filed, and MacNally must surely have observed the radical English visitor with special interest.

This encounter was one of the ways in which Godwin unknowingly anticipated the drama of three years later by meeting many of the principals in the Emmet case. There were other instances. On 17 July he walked with Henry Bennet to St Patrick's and Kilmainham. Bennet had been among the dinner guests on 4 July and some years later he was to call on Godwin in London in the company of Curran whose legal practice he eventually inherited. It seems that he took Godwin on a sightseeing trip; there's not much which is surprising about visiting the cathedral famously connected with Swift (on 11 August Godwin records, 'Talk of Swift & criminal jurisprudence') or the Royal Hospital at Kilmainham (1680) which was generally agreed to be one of the most spectacular pieces of architecture in the city. But Godwin's entry does not specify the Royal Hospital, and 'Kilmainham' might also, or alternatively, indicate the daunting gaol which had been built nearby as recently as 1788.

Such a switch of perspective also allows for the possibility that on his jaunt of pleasurable instruction Godwin set eyes on the complex where Robert Holmes and Thomas Addis Emmet were to be imprisoned, which gave its name to the Kilmainham Treaty of 1798, and where Robert Emmet was to spend his last night.

There was also the case of John Toler, who was the attorney general at this time, but who would become chief justice of common pleas and be created Lord Norbury later in the year, and who would eventually preside at the trial of Robert Emmet with what most historians regard as a peculiarly bad grace. Toler (?1741–1831) had been called to the Irish Bar in 1770, and appointed solicitor general in 1789 and attorney general in 1798 (which gave him the interesting task of prosecuting the rebels of 1798). Toler is one of the villains of Richard Madden's history of the United Irishmen, where he is described as 'the Jeffries of Ireland' and severely criticised for his performance at the trial of the Sheares brothers, not least for his opposition to Curran's application for a brief adjournment when the trial had been in process for 15 hours. Toler's name features in Godwin's list of those who appeared at the Carlow Assizes though there is no indication that he and Godwin actually met each other. As Attorney General he was also the leading counsel for the Post Office in the much-publicised Wallace trial (which Godwin notes both in his diary and in one of his letters), so it seems likely, though not certain, that Godwin saw and heard him in action.[22]

Of course, however visionary his capacities, Godwin cannot have known what would happen in the ensuing years; but his meetings with United Irishmen, or with those who had once belonged to the society, and his regular encounters and discussions with those who were best placed to assess the condition of Ireland and its prospects, must have kept him constantly aware that Dublin was precariously poised and that revolution or invasion were never far away. Reminders of 1798 were often vividly present, while Curran, Grattan and others focused his attention on the effects of Union. Grattan, for example, effected at least one telling introduction:

> Mr. Grattan introduced me [to] a poor man, who had been twice half-hanged [seal and tear] 's troops in the rebellion. I had therefore the [seal] ?st of the transaction from the fellow's own mouth. The first time seven cars were brought & set on end, that seven villagers might be suspended from the tops of their shafts, to extort a confession of arms from them. The second time the poor fellow's wife, who was on her death-bed, crawled to the threshold to intreat for mercy for him in vain. She survived the scene, of which she thus became a spectator exactly ten days. God save the King![23]

In his letter, Godwin records this anecdote with no comment beyond the use of intrusive adjectives, the insistence that he was writing down an eyewitness account, and the final ironical injunction.

It was at Grattan's, too, that Godwin was sharply reminded of the wider political implications of the situation. His diary records that on 29 July he breakfasted at Old Court (Lady Mountcashel's) and (together with Lady Mountcashel, as a letter specifies) called on J. C. Walker, the antiquarian, famous for his study of the Irish bardic tradition. The entry continues: 'dine at Grattan's, talk of O'Connor, Emmet & secession (Macleod expected): no sleep'. That Godwin did not sleep was the result of a recurring psycho-physical ailment ('deliquium', as he politely calls it in the diary). But the discussion was genuinely exciting, even disturbing. 'O'Connor' was Arthur O'Connor (1763–1852), a revolutionary aristocrat who later married Condorcet's daughter, and was mentioned several times in the 1799 *Report from the Committee of Secrecy of the House of Commons*. O'Connor was a friend of Godwin, who entered his name in his diary both without concealment and as 'Morris', the pseudonym which he adopted while on the run from the British authorities. In the *Report* he was linked with McNevin and Emmet (that is, Thomas Addis), described as one of the members of the Irish Directory, and identified as one of those who actively encouraged the French to invade Ireland. At the time of the dinner in Grattan's he was in prison at Fort George in Scotland as was Thomas Addis Emmet (who is almost certainly intended here rather than his brother, though the recurrent ambiguity is unsettling). Emmet had been arrested on 12 March 1798 at the house of Oliver Bond, who had himself been defended by Curran on 24 July in the same year against a charge of high treason (that is, as Curran reminded the jury, of 'compassing or imagining the death of the King, and of adhering to the King's enemies').

The third name seems to suggest a Scottish context since it must be that of Colonel Norman Macleod, a strongly independent figure in Scottish politics who had publicly backed the rights of the people and who had behaved in a courteous and helpful way to Archibald Hamilton Rowan (another of Godwin's acquaintances) when he had been arrested in Scotland on a political mission only a few years before. The presence of Macleod in this list underlines that connection between Irish revolutionary politics and developments in Scotland which animated the London Corresponding Society and troubled those who drew up the *Reports* for the Committees of Secrecy of the House of Commons and the Lords. The Commons Committee, for example, reported that at a Convention of Delegates from the Societies of the Friends of the People throughout Scotland on 11 December 1792 the Irish emissaries had claimed 'that the cause of the United Irish, was also the cause of the Scotch delegates'. For all his moderation, Macleod was much impressed by the United Irishmen whom he described as 'this body of men in Ireland, distinguished by the love of liberty, and closely united in the same glorious cause of reform with the Friends of the People in Britain'. An address which was published in the *Glasgow Advertiser* in January 1793 paid tribute to their political thinking: there he had found 'as eloquent, as concise, and as perspicacious a definition of the word and the thing PEOPLE as ever was given of any of the objects of the science of government'.[24] It seems, too, that he was known to Godwin who records seeing 'Macleod, Tierney' on 14 March 1796 and who encountered him again at Debrett's on 19 April. Although the precise nature of his connection with Irish politics remains unclear, Macleod did visit Ireland in 1800, as predicted in the conversation at Grattan's – on a 'jaunt', says his entry in *DNB*, but one might at least wonder if something more substantial than diversion was involved for a man who had interested himself so heavily in political causes, even if he was near the end of his life (he was to die in the following year). What is most interesting, though, is the conjunction of the three names and the idea of 'secession'; it seems as if there was a current of discontent directed against the Act of Union, which was only to pass into law two days after the meal at Grattan's, on 1 August. Frustratingly, Godwin does not tell us who said what – 'talk' is deliberately unfocused – but the news about Macleod's visit must have come from another member of the company.

V

The first sign of Emmet's rising in Godwin's diary is an entry for 29 July 1803. This is in red ink and reads: 'Death of Kilwarden'. There is no mention of Robert Emmet or of a rising, nor is there any further comment. Godwin usually reserved red ink for special occasions: parliamentary votes, prosecutions, acquittals, executions and natural deaths. Like many of his contemporaries, he seems to have been affected by the piking to death of the lord chief justice of the king's bench. Both the individual diary entries and the summarising list (which includes many names for 1800) suggest that Godwin never met Kilwarden in person but, whatever his presumed politics, he seems to have recognised that this bloody political killing was an emblematic event. Lord Kilwarden was Arthur Wolfe (1739–1803) who had been called to the Irish Bar in 1766 and had been made solicitor general in 1787 and attorney general in 1789, before being created Baron Kilwarden of Newlands in 1798. He had presided at the trial of Wolfe Tone, and was widely regarded as a thoughtful judge and an agreeable personality, even though there were some who reprehended his judicial behaviour and were pleased that revenge should be exacted. Wolfe had been MP first for Jamestown and then, briefly, for Dublin City; whatever their political affiliations, he had been a good friend of John Philpot Curran, had been his convivial guest at The Priory (where, at a later stage, Godwin himself had been a frequent visitor), and had materially assisted his legal career. After the trial of Theobald Wolfe Tone, it was Kilwarden who had acted as presiding judge at the hearing on 12 November 1798 at which Curran made representations on behalf of the condemned Tone, and it was Kilwarden who attempted to suspend the carrying out of a sentence of death. Again, when James Napper Tandy (1740–1803) had appeared before three justices in the court of king's bench on 10 February 1800, one of those three judges was Kilwarden, who had intervened to remind the prisoners of their right to nominate counsel; the case had eventually come to trial on 19 May, when one of the chosen barristers was Curran and when Kilwarden had made a lengthy charge to the jury. We cannot be sure how much Godwin knew of this, but it seems likely that he had at least a sense of Curran's sentiments. In Ireland the judicial presence of Kilwarden was hard to avoid. Godwin recorded that there was a trial at the court of the King's Bench, which was in Kilwarden's jurisdiction, on 8 July; his diary entry might seem to suggest that he attended in person, but he left no impressions, so it is possible that he was simply recording a legal fact. Kilwarden was also one of the two presiding judges at the Carlow Assizes which Godwin attended in early August 1803 when he followed in Curran's legal footsteps.

Godwin was away from his normal London address on an extended trip to family and friends during the crucial period after Emmet's trial and execution. His diary suggests that he was out of town after 24 September and only returned on 11 October. Two days later (on 13 October when his *Life of Chaucer* was published) he enters 'Journals and Newspapers', a printed resource which, presumably, allowed him to catch up on recent events. On the same day, he called on Rowan and Joyce. The meeting with Rowan is particularly significant since it was Rowan, whom he had seen at tea on 8 September, who had written him a letter during his absence with reflections on the fate of Robert Emmet:

> Poor Young Emmet! He was endeared to me by my friendship & respect for his Brother, than whom I believe no purer character exists. He seems to have imbibed the sentiments his brother professed when I left Ireland. He always objected to a greater force from France than would merely serve as a nucleus for an Irish Army, & when I doubted the power of the Irish to keep their country alone, & quoted a very strong expression of Mr H. T. [Horne Tooke] to Ld Semple [probably Hugh Lord Sempill] & me one day we met there – I do not know whether you recollect it – That if Ireland attempted to separate herself from England he would intreat [sic] her he would hold her by the Skirts but if she persisted he would take his cudgel & bury her if he could – He made light of it & insisted there was nothing to fear – [25]

This letter is a testament to the growing closeness between Rowan and Godwin, but it is also significant in other ways. A shared interest in Irish political, and even revolutionary, matters partly explains why Rowan should write to Godwin in such terms, but the very existence of the letter and Rowan's apparent need to write it might also indicate that Rowan detected in Godwin a more than usual concern for the fate of the Emmets. Unfortunately, there is some ambiguity in the letter since it is not entirely clear whether Rowan's 'He' at the beginning of the fourth sentence and the concluding 'He' to which it is connected are intended to refer to Thomas Addis or to Robert Emmet. Horne Tooke's dogmatic and outspoken style, however, is immediately recognisable. The political conjunctions are also entirely credible. Hamilton Rowan visited Horne Tooke's house at Wimbledon, as did Sempill, who must have been known to Rowan since, together with Edward Fitzgerald, Rowan had also been a steward at an anniversary dinner of the Society for Constitutional Information at which Sempill presided.[26] Once again, Rowan's syntax is frustratingly vague but his mixed statement and question, 'I do not know whether you recollect it', seems to suggest strongly that Godwin was also present on the occasion Rowan remembers so vividly. The letter not only demonstrates Rowan's closeness to such matters but also implicates Godwin and anticipates his special and knowledgeable interest.

Certainly, Rowan and Godwin were linked in many and complicated ways. According to Godwin's own account, he had first met Rowan in 1793. In the following year Rowan had been tried for a libel in the Court of King's Bench in Dublin; he was defended by Curran who won the moral argument but lost the case. Stockdale's transcript of the trial is prefixed by an abstract of the information filed by the attorney general (that is, Arthur Wolfe), which begins with an address from the Society of United Irishmen at Dublin to the Volunteers of Ireland, specifically issued by William Drennan as chairman and Archibald Hamilton Rowan as secretary. The Stockdale transcript tells its readers that, after a passage on the 'irresistible genius of UNIVERSAL EMANCIPATION' 'Mr. Curran was interrupted by a sudden burst of applause from the court and hall, which was repeated for a considerable length of time'. This account of the trial carries a final note: 'Upon the conclusion of this speech Mr Curran was again for many minutes loudly applauded by the auditors; and upon leaving the court was drawn home by the populace, who took the horses from his carriage.' The occasion did not go unnoticed in London because on 14 April 1794 the London Corresponding Society unanimously resolved to 'convey the approbation of this society' to Archibald Hamilton Rowan 'for his unshaken attachment to the people, and for his spirited assertion of their rights'; to John Philpot Curran for his 'admirable and energetic defence' of Rowan 'and the principles of liberty, as well as for his patriotic conduct in parliament'; and to the Society of United Irishmen in Dublin, 'to exhort them to persevere in their exertions to obtain justice for the people of Ireland'. In turn, the activities of the London Corresponding

Society and of the United Englishmen were scrutinised in the detailed *Report from the Committee of Secrecy of the House of Commons Relative to . . . a Treasonable Conspiracy* (1799).[27] On 30 March Godwin acquired a copy (he recorded that it ran to 87 pages).

This trial left its impress on Irish imagination and political conscience. Rowan, who had been at its centre, remained a formidable figure fêted for example on his appearance in Philadelphia, although after the trial he seems to have lost much of his revolutionary edge and, following a period of imprisonment, redirected his energies. As his *Autobiography* remembers, he encountered and came to know Mary Wollstonecraft in Paris. He received several letters from her and was allowed by her to stay in her house in Le Havre after she had returned to England and before Rowan emigrated to America.[28] There he set up in calico printing on the banks of the Brandywine in Delaware where one of his employees was Mary Wollstonecraft's brother, Charles (1770–1818). When he discovered that she had married Godwin, he wrote to congratulate her but delayed in sending the letter (dated 15 September 1797 at the top) so that the original message of congratulation was accompanied by a postscript directed to Godwin in which he lamented the news of her death as reported in the newspaper.

Further correspondence might illuminate the dark period between the writing of this letter and Rowan's eventual return to England. Certainly, from the time of his return (Rowan reappears in Godwin's diary in July 1803) he became increasingly, if gradually, close to Godwin. On 24 July he and Wolcot (better known as 'Peter Pindar') dine at Godwin's, on 8 August he calls on Godwin but finds that he is out, on 14 August Godwin calls on him, while on 8 September the Rowans (plural) come to tea. The next period is punctuated by Godwin's summer excursion and by Rowan's letter with its reflections on the sad fate of 'Young Emmet' (who was executed on 20 September) and its memories of Irish politics. The friendship continues after Godwin's late-summer break. On the very day when he notes 'Journals & Newspapers' Godwin calls with M. J. (Mary Jane Clairmont, now the second Mrs Godwin) on Rowan and Joyce. On 19 October Rowan calls on Godwin with Boaden, on 22 October Godwin calls with Curran on Mrs Rowan and Mrs Reynolds, on 25 October Godwin dines at Rowan's with Curran, Burroughs, Miss Hamilton and Mrs Godwin, and on 4 November the Rowans come to dinner in a company which includes Miss Hamilton. On 3 December Godwin met Mrs Rowan. In the next year (1804) the contacts continued and even increased. On 23 January Mrs Rowan and Mary Lamb called on Godwin; on 31 January Rowan dined at Godwin's with Coleridge; on 3 February Godwin dined at Rowan's (where the company included 'Castle Brown' whom Godwin had met in Ireland); on 3 March Godwin dined at Rowan's; on 5 March Rowan called on Godwin; on 8 April Mrs Rowan and Mrs Beresford called on

Godwin; on the next day Godwin called on Rowan; on 30 April Godwin dined at Mrs Beresford's where the guests included Rowan; on 18 May Rowan called on Godwin; on 22 May Godwin dined at Rowan's where the guests included 'Plunkets, 3 Fitzgeralds, Defrezes & MJ & Mrs Beresford'; on 24 June the Rowans called on Godwin and gave a dinner in the evening. The diary records fairly numerous other encounters (including an expedition to the theatre) which show the gradual appearance of the whole Rowan family, including the father, and on at least one occasion the presence at dinner in Rowan's of Everina Wollstonecraft, who also calls on Godwin on 24 December in the company of '5 Rowans'. On 9 January 1806 Godwin and Rowan attended Nelson's funeral at St Paul's.[29] Such listing may be tedious but it does serve to establish that the relationship involved regular contact and was reciprocal, and that, among other things, it served to keep Godwin in touch with Irish visitors and Irish affairs.

The charting of Mrs Rowan's presence is also of special interest, though the record is hard to interpret and may be misleading. According to Ruán O'Donnell, Sarah Curran lived in Mrs Rowan's house at 1 Lower Dominick Street after she had been ejected from the Priory by her father: 'The Rowan family were on good terms with the Currans and seemingly looked after Sarah Curran in Dublin city until her future prospects were ascertained.'[30] In Dublin tradition, too, it was Mrs Hamilton Rowan, together with Elizabeth Fisher Hammond of 86 Rogerson's Quay and her 18–year-old son Joseph, who took Sarah Curran to visit the graveyard at St Michan's where they laid flowers which they had bought in Capel Street on the grave of Robert Emmet.

VI

At the very centre of events after Emmet's uprising, much against his own will, was John Philpot Curran who by now was a close friend of Godwin. On 8 August Curran sent a letter to Godwin in which he discussed the prospects for Godwin's protégé Thomas Cooper in Ireland where, in his view, Cooper might not find a proper scene for his talents. He talked of Godwin's sisters-in-law who, he said, 'always speak of you with great affection'. The letter also referred obliquely to other events which must have been much on Curran's mind: 'our public calamities, of which no man can see the probable end or consequence'.[31] This phrasing is so portentously generalised that one cannot deduce whether Curran was more concerned with the assassination of his patron and friend Arthur Wolfe or with the revolutionary activities of Robert Emmet, who was still on the run; or perhaps equally with both. This letter would have reached Godwin before he left London on his holiday excursion. It is possible that he also read accounts of Curran's defence of Owen Kirwan in the Session-House at Green Street which took place early in September, after Emmet had been captured but before the raid on the Priory. By all accounts, this was a curious performance which suggested that Curran was gravely distracted and had largely forgotten that his main duty was to defend his client.

Curran was anxious to bring the attention of the court to that 'never to be too much lamented fate of Lord Kilwarden'. He 'drew a character of him, as marked by the most scrupulous anxiety for justice, and by the tenderest feelings of humanity'. He hoped that the character of the nation would not be slandered by any false assumptions concerning 'the horror of the crime':

> The general indignation, the tears that were shed at the sad news of his fate, shew that we are not that nest of demons on whom any general stigma could attach from such an event; the wicked wretch himself, perhaps, has cut off the very man, through whose humanity he might have escaped the consequences of other crimes; and by an hideous aggravation of his guilt, has given another motive to Providence to trace the murderer's steps and secure the certainty of his punishment; but on this occasion the jury should put it out of their minds, and think nothing of that valuable man, save his last advice, 'that no person should perish but by the just sentence of the law', and that advice he hoped they would honour, not by idle praise, but by strict observance.

As usual, Curran has strong advice for the jury; but, however much he may suggest otherwise, the whole force of his argument makes it difficult for them to forget the character of 'that valuable man' in order to concentrate exclusively on their juristic functions. In the course of one weighty sentence, Curran includes not only a national exculpation from false rumours of guilt and a reproach to those who brought about such an unjust and untimely death, but a powerful tribute to the humane virtues of the late Lord Kilwarden.

His speech for the defence is concerned in the first place, and primarily, to establish the correct terms of reference for understanding Robert Emmet's revolutionary activities, although Emmet is never mentioned by name. This involves a rhetorical exercise which praises the amenities of the existing system at the expense of the revolution whose intention was to destroy it:

> By the judicious adoption of a mild and conciliatory system of conduct, what was six years ago a formidable rebellion, had now dwindled down to a drunken, riotous insurrection – disgraced, certainly, by some odious atrocities – its objects, whatever they were, no doubt, highly criminal; but as an attack upon the state, of the most contemptible insignificance. – He did not wonder that the patrons of burning and torture should be vexed that their favourite instruments were not employed in recruiting for the rebellion.

One might almost be forgiven for concluding that Curran was nostalgic for the outrages and excesses of 1798 which, after all, was 'a formidable rebellion'. His characterisation of Emmet's 'contemptible' rising as a 'drunken, riotous insurrection' would leave its impress on later interpreters, not least the generally sympathetic, if critical, Percy Bysshe Shelley and the cruel, but unforgettably vivid, caricaturist, George Cruikshank.

In a powerful passage Curran describes his own walk to the courthouse:

> I now . . . come here through a composed and quiet city – I read no expression in any face, save such as marks the ordinary feelings of social life, or the various characters of civil occupation – I see no frightful spectacle of infuriated power or suffering humanity – I see no tortures – I hear no shrieks – I no longer see the human heart char[r]'d in the flame of its own vile and paltry passions – black and bloodless – capable only of catching and communicating that destructive fire by which it devours, and is itself devoured. I no longer behold the ravages of that odious bigotry by which we were deformed, and degraded, and disgraced – a bigotry against which no honest man should ever miss an opportunity of putting his countrymen of all sects and of all descriptions upon their guard . . .

The rhetorical flow, and the sentence, continues with growing and seemingly tireless excitement. Curran is concerned to affirm the normality of a city which carries no obvious signs or traces of Emmet's activities, but the emphasis on what he cannot detect in the streets around him allows him to luxuriate in an exercise in the Gothic sublime. The 'odious bigotry' which has been happily avoided justifies a passage of stylistic excess which encompasses oratorical tropes ('deformed, and degraded, and disgraced'), frequent Biblical or religious references, and cumulative denunciation. As he says elsewhere in his address, the old conspiratorial politics were dead and the process of development had created something more thoughtful and widely shared:

> politics were not now, as heretofore, a dead science, in a dead language; they had now become the subject of the day, vernacular and universal, and the repose which the late system of Irish government had given the people for reflection, had enabled them to consider their own condition, and what they, or any other country could have to hope from France, or rather from its present master.

The force of Curran's argument is based not only on his imaging of a dead science or a quiet city but on his tribute to the British system of justice (or to that version of it which was available in Ireland after the Union) and specifically to the courthouse at Green Street:

> Even in this melancholy place I feel myself restored and recreated by breathing the mild atmosphere of justice, mercy, and humanity – I feel I am addressing the parental authority of the law – I feel I am addressing a jury of my countrymen, my fellow subjects, and my fellow Christians – against whom my heart is waging no concealed hostility – from whom my face is disguising no latent sentiment of repugnance or disgust.[32]

Coming from Curran in particular, such a tribute is unexpected and striking. The barrister who was so critical of the practices of government and so supportive of the United Irishmen now pays homage to the 'mild and conciliatory system of conduct', the restorative 'atmosphere of justice, mercy, and humanity'. The Act of Union is no longer a threat to be feared but a civilising reality to be celebrated. Though he can hardly have known that in less than three weeks Robert Emmet would stand trial and make his speech from the dock in this very courthouse, their sentiments on these matters must have been wildly discordant. Curran's speech may seem to be constrained by the framework of the case but it is directed at Emmet (and perhaps at his own children, though it is not clear how much he knew at this stage of events about his family's complicity with Emmet). His respect for 'the parental authority of the law' is both a recognition of the virtues of the judicial system and perhaps of the judges who presided over it (as Kilwarden had done) and an allusion to the ways in which his own authority had been ignored by Emmet and perhaps by his own children. Likewise, his emphasis on 'concealed hostility' and faces which disguise their real intentions can relate exactly to the ways in which Curran believes that he has been betrayed and deceived. His relief at addressing a jury of fellow countrymen and fellow Christians is animated, no doubt, by the widely promoted belief that Emmet's intention had been to draw in the French, who were both foreign and atheistical. Finally, although he names no names, the thrust of Curran's thought is unmistakable in such a context. The unfortunate Kilwarden has been mentioned by name but, although Emmet is centrally implicated in much that Curran says, he is never named specifically, either in this speech or in the earlier 'calamities' letter.

Given such attitudes, Curran's eventual behaviour in London should not be surprising. Godwin's absence from town at the crucial time of the Emmet trial means that the lack of a note in his diary (in red ink or otherwise) is a frustrating fact but carries no significance. Curran arrived in London somewhat later than usual but, because of Godwin's absence, it must be unclear what significance, if any, can be attributed to this late arrival. The first mention of Curran's presence is on 15 October when he dines and attends the theatre with Godwin – 'half Pizarro, and Turk's Head', says the diary. The next day Godwin called on Curran at the White Horse Cellar but found that he was not in. On 18 October Godwin records that Curran was expected, while on

21 October he was one of a large company at dinner (others included Fuseli and Tooke, while Kemble was invited to come after the meal). The next day Godwin called on Curran and, with Curran, on Mrs Hamilton Rowan and Mrs Reynolds, and was expected to dinner. The next day (23 October) Godwin called on Curran but found he was out. On 25 October Curran was one of the company who dined at Hamilton Rowan's. On 26 October Godwin called on Curran, who was later expected to dinner, as he was also expected on the following day.[33] Once again, the detail may be tedious but the record suggests a man who was actively part of social life, even if his visit was much shorter than it had been in the past or than it would turn out to be in the future.

The decision of Godwin and Curran to attend part of Sheridan's *Pizarro* is interesting, particularly in view of recent circumstances. Sheridan was, of course, a friend of Godwin, who had dined at the Lefanus' in Dublin and who would write to Alicia Lefanu more than once at a later stage. Curran had dined in his company in October 1799 and, at least once on the same occasion, he had also dined with Kemble who had created the role of the Inca hero Rolla to great popular acclaim. Godwin seems to have had a special interest in the play which had been first performed on 24 May, since he saw all or part of it on 17 September before the visit in Curran's company and again afterwards (on 20 and 31 October). But, beyond any personal connection, *Pizarro* seemed to address itself to the concerns of both men, especially Curran. On 6 December Coleridge dismissed it as 'a Pantomime' in a letter to Godwin but the evidence of these several viewings suggests that Godwin detected in it something of more substantial interest. Although Sheridan's play (freely based on Kotzebue) ostensibly dealt with the Peruvian resistance to Spanish invasion, audiences recognised that it could be applied to contemporary political realities, not least the threat of a French invasion. Sheridan's version, which drew on his own celebrated speech in the Warren Hastings trial, was also concerned with the British in India (as Fintan O'Toole has pointed out, Rolla's patriotic declamation to his troops, which is not in the original, and which introduces the contrast of vultures and lambs, is based directly on Sheridan's image of the British as vultures and the Indians as lambs). The play produced a complicated set of resonances which should not have been lost on Godwin, and especially on Curran:

> as well as containing an allegory of England and India, the play also presented a version of England and France and one of England and Ireland. The irreconcilables of Sheridan's politics – opposition to a French invasion, support for the United Irishmen – could be reconciled at least in the imagination.[34]

In view of the seemingly irreconcilable impulses felt by both men, their apparent sympathy and support for the United Irishmen, and their revulsion at Emmet's rising and its consequences, such an imaginative displacement could scarcely have failed to be of particular interest.

VII

In the fullness of time, there was a further aftermath. When Percy Bysshe Shelley decided to visit Dublin in February 1812 he was, in a sense, Godwin's disciple, though it would be some years before he became his son-in-law. Godwin provided him with introductions (he called on Curran but, when they eventually met, found him coarse and disappointing, and he wrote to Hamilton Rowan and Arthur O'Connor's brother, Roger). He seems also to have used the Stockdales as printers; Stockdale does not feature in Godwin's diary but either he or Shelley may have known that he printed Emmet's declaration of independence in 1803 and that he was imprisoned for taking part in the insurrection. Godwin was particularly concerned that Shelley might become concerned in revolutionary violence and was anxious to provide him with cautionary advice. When Shelley made it clear that he was no longer so optimistic about the immediacy of change, Godwin responded:

> I can now look upon you as a friend. Before, I knew not what might happen. It was like making an acquaintance with Robert Emmett [*sic*], who I believe, like yourself, was a man of a very pure mind; but respecting whom I could not have told, from day to day, what calamities he might bring upon his country; how effectually (like the Bear in the fable) he might smash the nose of his mother to pieces, when he intended only to remove the noxious insect that tormented her, and what premature and tragical fate he might bring down upon himself. Now I can look on you, not as a meteor and ephemeral, but as a lasting, friend, who, according to the course of nature, may contribute to the comforts of my closing days. Now I can look on you as a friend, like myself, but I hope more effectually and actively useful, who is prone to study the good of his fellow men, but with no propensities threatening to do them extensive mischief under the form and intention of benefit.[35]

This passage is part of a much longer letter which is intended to celebrate Shelley's change of mind but Godwin is also concerned, both here and in the larger contexts of his argument, to remind Shelley of the dangers of shedding blood ('Shelley, you are preparing a scene of blood!', as he had warned in a slightly earlier letter). He insists on the new status of their relationship; although he had begun a previous letter with 'My Good Friend', that previous version of friendship must have been provisional or driven by hope. Now, as the paragraph reminds Shelley by repeating the point on three occasions, Shelley has become a 'friend' in the true meaning of that word. The point of comparison is Robert Emmet but, although Godwin's argument seems to draw on autobiographical experience ('I could not have told from day to day', etc.), what he says here cannot be taken to prove that he knew Emmet in person or was anything more than a keen, and horrified, student of his tragic revolutionary trajectory. The force of 'I believe' might be read as a personal credo but it might also be taken as a second-hand affirmation which distances Godwin from the burden of direct knowledge or absolute truth. Godwin's assessment of Emmet might also be thought to owe something to the letter of Curran (compare the letter's 'what calamities he might bring upon his country' and Godwin's desire to save Shelley and the Irish people from 'the calamities with which I see your mode of proceeding to be fraught' with Curran's allusion to 'our public calamities'); and to the reminiscence of Hamilton Rowan (compare 'of a very pure mind' to Rowan's praise of Thomas Addis Emmet 'than whom I believe no purer character exists', in the letter to Godwin which tries to draw a link between the two brothers). Although such phrases are scarcely original in themselves, they may well carry a stronger trace of the earlier contexts in which they were employed by those who knew Emmet better than Godwin did.

In fact, Godwin was so pleased that Shelley had retreated from the revolutionary path that he 'immediately' wrote an explanatory letter to Curran on 24 March (the diary confirms this, and it also shows that on 20 January Godwin had written to Shelley and to Curran, and that Amelia Curran had called). As Godwin informed Shelley, he had told Curran

> that I supposed he had kept himself aloof from you on account of your pamphlet, &c, that at my importunity you had given up your project, and that, that being the case, I trusted he would oblige me by seeking the man, whom under different circumstances he had probably thought himself bound to shun.[36]

Quite apart from the biographical details, not the least interesting feature here is Godwin's assessment of the older Curran and his apparent coincidence with Curran's quietist views. On the spectrum of revolutionary politics, Curran and Godwin represent one polarity and Robert Emmet the other, while Shelley oscillates uncomfortably between the two. For some years Godwin had attempted to distance himself from the more violent implications of his own writings, especially *Political Justice* which he accused Shelley, among others, of misreading or taken as read. He insisted that he was a philosophical anarchist, not a supporter of bloody or revolutionary change. This tendency was confirmed by the violent history of the French Revolution (which Mary Wollstonecraft could report on in person and had considered in detail in her analytical study); [37] by the memories of Hamilton Rowan who recalled that 'though I was standing above a hundred paces from the place of execution, the blood of the victims streamed under my feet';[38] atrocities of 1798 in Ireland (Godwin's discussions with Henry Grattan brought him directly in touch with at least one example, and his journey to Carlow took him through Hacket's Town, 'late distinguished for its flourishing streets, but of which every house but two, including the church & the barracks, was reduced to a heap of ruins by the late rebellion');[39] and perhaps by the execution in Dublin of an informer whose fingers and toes were torn away by the crowd 'with the utmost greediness, to preserve as precious relics of their antipathy & revenge' (Godwin seems to equate this kind of mob violence with the excesses of the French Revolution by wrongly according to it the date of 14 July).[40] Godwin's interest in this case might have been further heightened if he knew that it was Curran, in his defence of Patrick Finney, who had publicly destroyed the credibility of this informer, Jemmy O'Brien, who took his orders from Major Sirr (other lawyers in the case included MacNally and Ridgeway). Finally, there was the execution of Robert Emmet whose blood, according to some accounts, was lapped up by the dogs in the street.

At least one other detail may claim our attention. Godwin compares Robert Emmet to the bear in the fable who does not recognise his own strength and who unintentionally damages his mother. In one sense, this may be seen as yet another patronising and deflating tactic (since it is aimed not only at the Emmet of past history but at the Shelley of history to be). To use his own terms, Godwin does often write to Shelley as an 'instructor' rather than a 'friend' and this paternal solicitude leaves its mark on the 'Emmet' letter. He was very conscious of the differences between generations and felt it his duty to protect 'young' Shelley by invoking the memory of 'Young Emmet'. Perhaps, too, the introduction of the fable is a sign of a parental discourse, or a cautionary tale, directed at children. One of Godwin's most successful publications had been the two-volume *Fables Ancient and Modern* which he had first published in 1805 under the name of Edward Baldwin. In it he told a version of Jean de la Fontaine's fable '*L'Ours et l'amateur des jardins*' (8.10) which he transformed into 'The Hermit and the Bear'. Godwin's version features a 'very old man' who was also 'a very good man, doing kindness to every body when he was able', with the consequence that 'every body loved him'. One of his kind services was to look after a bear which had damaged its foot. When the bear was cured, it returned the kindness of the old man by looking after him: 'The hermit was feeble and stiff of his limbs . . . ; so this bear climbed trees for him, and shook the boughs, and made the apples and chestnuts fall for the old man's supper'.[41] Unfortunately, the final outcome was far from happy. One hot day, the hermit had fallen asleep after a long walk and dinner:

> As the weather was sultry, the flies came about the hermit, and lighted on his face, and tickled him. The old man shook his head, but did not awake: the bear growled,

> but the hermit was in a sound sleep, and the flies did not care for his growlings. At last one saucy fly pitched upon the old man's nose. Now, thought the bear, I shall have you; and with that he took up his paw to give the fly a good knock. The fly was killed; but the poor hermit's nose was terribly bruised, and after a time turned quite black. Immediately the hermit awoke, and began to be very angry; but he put up his hand to his nose, and the dead fly fell upon it: he then knew what the bear had been doing. Go, go, said he to the bear, shaking his head with the pain: I will always do you all the good I can, but we will not live together any more.[42]

Godwin's version, which is already less threatening than its original in which the old man is unwittingly killed by the bear, concludes with a moral which expands but takes the rhyming edge off the French ('*Rien n'est si dangereux qu'un ignorant ami;/ Mieux vaudrait un sage ennemi*'): 'He that admits into his company an awkward and ill-matched favourite, will sometime or other have reason to grieve, even for things that were intended in kindness.'[43]

This is the fable that Godwin wished to draw to the attention of Shelley. He had previously referred to it in a letter to Alexander Jardine (?1740–99), a soldier and political radical, who had proposed to Charles James Fox that Godwin should be sent on an expedition to France, but without consulting Godwin himself in the first place. Godwin reacted in a personal and troubled letter in which he asked: 'Are you the friend of liberty or the enemy?', and again, 'Are you my friend or my enemy? I cannot tell'. He was affronted that Jardine had planned for him to 'put myself into the mouth of that "dangerous wild beast of prey, Robespierre", for the purpose of making myself the martyr, not of truth as you imagine, but of falsehood'. He further expressed his indignation by referring to La Fontaine's fable: 'Next you treat me personally like the bear in the fable, who struck off his master's nose in attempting to kill a fly that had settled upon it.'[44] The reference suggests not only that the fable had made a special impression on Godwin but that he associated it with unfortunate or doomed interventions in revolutionary situations. In the French original, the bear breaks its master's head and kills him but in Godwin's letter to Jardine and his fable for children, the well-intentioned bear only injures its master's nose (the detail about the nose turning 'quite black' seems to be Godwin's invention). In the letter to Shelley, the victim of the bear's misplaced benevolence still suffers from a damaged nose but, perhaps significantly, is transformed from his master to his 'mother'.

The pertinence of this allusion and the specific naming of Robert Emmet after this long silence serve to show that his example had registered with Godwin and that it had made a deeper impress than one might imagine. Godwin did not allow himself the ambivalent force of Coleridge's annotation: 'Emmet = mad Raphael painting Ideals of Beauty on the walls of a cell with human Excrement.' Nor did he write a passionate letter, like Coleridge, in which he identified himself with the young enthusiast but thanked God that he had been spared from such irrevocable actions;[45] he did not write a long poem, like Southey, which exhibited sympathy for Emmet's vulnerabilities while passing judgement in a higher court and defending the superior virtues of a truly 'English' justice; nor, like Shelley, did he show the influence of Emmet's oratory, behaviour and poetry in his own writings, not least in the poem 'On Robert Emmet's Tomb'.[46] From such tributes and identifications, partial or otherwise, he was spared by age, by temperament, by contacts and by ideology. Yet, as the letter to Shelley clearly demonstrates, he was well aware of the example and, whether he encountered Emmet in person or not, the figure of the young Irish radical was firmly lodged in his consciousness.[47]

Notes

1 I am grateful to the Bodleian Library, Oxford for permission to cite and quote manuscripts from its Abinger Deposit. In the interests of economy, I shall refer to this collection as Dep. Godwin's diary runs to 32 notebooks (Dep.e.196–227) but his trip to Ireland can be traced in the entries of Dep.e.205. His letters to Marshall are cited from Dep.b.214/5 and his letter to Coleridge (which was partly printed by C. Kegan Paul) from Dep. b.227/8(a). For Christmas Day, see E. L. Griggs (ed.), *Collected Letters of Samuel Taylor Coleridge*, 6 vols (Oxford, 1956–71), I, p. 553.

2 Dep.e.206, f. 7r.

3 Details from Dep.e.205.

4 Dep.b.215/6.

5 Ibid.

6 Ibid.

7 Jean Agnew (ed.), *The Drennan–McTier Letters: vol. 2 (1794–1801)* (Dublin, 1999), p. 586.

8 Dep.e.204, f. 42r.

9 Dep.b.214/5.

10 Ruán O'Donnell, *Robert Emmet and the Rebellion of 1798* (Dublin and Portland, Oregon, 2003), p. 164.

11 Ibid., p. 37.

12 Kevin Whelan, 'The United Irishmen, the Enlightenment and popular culture', in David Dickson, Dáire Keogh and Kevin Whelan (eds), *The United Irishmen: Republicanism, Radicalism and Rebellion* (Dublin, 1993), p. 276.

13 David Dickson, 'Paine and Ireland', in Dickson, Keogh and Whelan (eds), *The United Irishmen*, p. 135.

14 See Agnew (ed.), *The Drennan-McTier Letters*, p. 382.

15 Dep. b.227/8(a). A second and fuller version can be found in the J. Pierpont Morgan Library in New York. Cf. quotation on p. 112 above.

16 O'Donnell, *Robert Emmet and the Rebellion of 1798*, p. 43.

17 Patrick M. Geoghegan, *Robert Emmet: A Life* (Dublin, 2002), p. 218.

18 Dep.c.516/1 (see also Dep.c.524).

19 Timothy Webb, 'Coleridge and Robert Emmet: reading the text of Irish revolution', *Irish Studies Review* 8: 3 (2000), pp. 303–24.

20 Jean Agnew (ed.), *The Drennan–McTier Letters: vol. 3 (1802–1819)* (Dublin, 1999), p. 481.

21 For a detailed consideration of Leonard MacNally, see Thomas Bartlett (ed.), *Revolutionary Dublin, 1795–1801: The Letters of Francis Higgins to Dublin Castle* (Dublin, 2004), pp. 38–46.

22 Dep.e.205, f. 7v.

23 Dep.b.214/5.

24 Cited in E. W. MacFarland, *Ireland and Scotland in the Age of Revolution: Planting the Green Bough* (Edinburgh, 1994), pp. 96, 79.

25 Dep.b.215/6.

26 Christina and David Bewley, *Gentleman Radical: A Life of John Horne Tooke 1736–1812* (London and New York, 1998), p. 136.

27 Michael T. Davis (ed.), *London Corresponding Society, 1792–1799*, 6 vols (London, 2002), VI, p. 12.

28 See Lyndall Gordon, *Vindication: A Life of Mary Wollstonecraft* (London, 2005), p. 249.

29 For St Paul's, see Dep.e.208, f. 12r.

30 Ruán O'Donnell, *Robert Emmet and the Rising of 1803* (Dublin and Portland, Oregon, 2003), p. 184.

31 Dep.b.215/6.

32 Cited from *Speeches of John Philpot Curran, Esq.* (Dublin, 1805), pp. 285–6; also pp. 289–90, 287, 284–5, 291.

33 For details, see Dep.e.206.

34 Fintan O'Toole, *A Traitor's Kiss: The Life of Richard Brinsley Sheridan* (London, 1997), p. 347.

35 Mark Philp (ed.), *Collected Novels and Memoirs of William Godwin. Volume I, Autobiography, Autobiographical Fragments and Reflections, Godwin/Shelley Correspondence, Memoirs* (London, 1992), pp. 76–7 (corrected from the MS where 'most' is certainly 'nose').

36 Ibid., p. 76.

37 Mary Wollstonecraft, *An Historical and Moral View of the Origin and Progress of the French Revolution; and the Effect it has Produced in Europe* (London, 1794).

38 William H. Drummond (ed.), *The Autobiography of Archibald Hamilton Rowan* [1840] (Dublin, 1972), p. 238.

39 For a fuller description, see *Essay on Sepulchres*.

40 In fact, the execution took place on 21 July.

41 William Godwin, *Fables Ancient and Modern* (London, 1819), p. 17.

42 Ibid., p. 18.

43 Ibid., p. 19.

44 This early example has been brought to my attention by Pamela Clemit who includes the details and the text of Godwin's letter to Jardine in Pamela Clemit and A. A. Markley (eds), *Mary Shelley's Literary Lives and Other Writings*, 4 vols (London, 2002), IV, pp. 69–71.

45 For Coleridge's reactions, see Webb, 'Coleridge and Robert Emmet'.
46 For Shelley, see Timothy Webb, '"A noble field": Shelley's Irish expedition and the lessons of the French Revolution', in Nadia Minerva (ed.), *Robespierre & Co.: Atti Della Ricerca Sulla Letteratura Francese della Rivoluzione* (Bologna, 1990), pp. 553–76.
47 As Pamela Clemit has reminded me, the Abinger deposit also includes handwritten copies of Robert Emmet's speech and part of a letter which may be addressed to Sarah Curran. Unfortunately, there is no record of when these copies were made or how, if at all, they relate to William Godwin.

For help, encouragement and detailed advice I would like to thank Andrew Nicholson and Pamela Clemit.

CHAPTER 7

Robert Emmet and Nineteenth-Century Irish America

Charles Fanning

No other Irish historical figure had so powerful and lasting an effect on the consciousness of Irish America in the nineteenth century as Robert Emmet. In American culture there were a great variety of opportunities to engage ideas about Emmet – ranging from individual, solitary contemplation to experiences within the family to public, communal occasions. Alone, one could glean the essence of Emmet's sacrifice by reading his speech from the dock or a lyric poem about him. One could also find the larger story in one of the many available biographies. In the home, one could gaze upon the image of Emmet on the parlour wall. A solemn familial gesture was possible in the giving of Emmet's name to a child. In the wider world, one could belong to an organisation named after Robert Emmet where parish, social, or Irish nationalist business was conducted. One could gather to bear witness to the speech and the story in dramatic form at a range of venues – from school halls to amateur theatricals to professional productions. And one could participate in formal observances celebrating the dates of Emmet's birth or death.

The power of the idea of Robert Emmet springs, of course, from his place in history as a figure of wholly admirable personal courage and as a hero of the struggle for Irish freedom from British rule. However, with that clear authority, there followed, as the night the day, opportunistic exploitation for a variety of less admirable aims and agendas. This essay provides a survey with examples of some Irish-American uses and misuses of conceptions of Robert Emmet in oratory, poetry, narrative, the visual image, bestowal of the name on a person, place, or organisation, dramatic performance, and ceremonial event. I shall also look briefly at some of the healthy critical perspectives on Emmet as an exploited commodity that emerged late in the nineteenth century from inside Irish-American culture.

Edward McSorley's fine, neglected novel *Our Own Kind* provides an example of the power of the Emmet ideal in Irish America near the end of its time of greatest vitality. Published in 1946, it describes the coming of age of the orphaned Willie McDermott, born, as was McSorley, in 1902, and raised by his Irish immigrant grandparents in Providence, Rhode Island. A 'chromo of Robert Emmet on the wall'[1] over the kitchen table is the lodestone for the relationship between the boy at age ten and his grandfather, Old Ned McDermott:

> Bold Robert Emmet was their refuge, their well of courage. Dear Emmet standing there in the courtroom face to face with the British judges that condemned him to his death and ordered his noble head cut from his body and thrown to the dogs in the dirty Dublin streets to be devoured by them. They would stand beneath the picture and his grandfather would say, 'Here, Will, now I'll read what Emmet said'. Or perhaps the boy would seize the old man by the arm and beg him to read what Emmet said. Their arms would be around each other or the boy would stand in front of his grandfather while he read. Sometimes they would read it together, the old man going slower so that the boy could keep pace with him. The old man's brown eyes would never waver an instant from the picture, although he might now and then shake a fist at the judges or perhaps, 'when the grave opens to receive me', his voice would be lowered a trifle.
>
> 'When my country takes her place among the nations of the earth, then, and not until then, let my epitaph be written', they would always read together. Each passionate word eternally damning the bewigged judges and especially [Willie's aunt] Nora for daring say [that his grandfather] could not read.[2]

By the time Willie realises that his grandfather has the speech by heart and is, in fact, illiterate in English, Willie has absorbed his grandfather's version of Irish history, in which Emmet and O'Connell stand for the right and wrong ways of proceeding towards the nationalist goal. The McDermott family is paradigmatic of a three-generational immigrant/ethnic process. Old Ned is a foundry worker with strong ties to the old country; his children, Willie's aunts and uncles, look towards Catholic American middle-class respectability; the boy is drawn to what he sees as his grandfather's more authentic, unpretentious ground-sense. Backed by the parish priest, the aunts and uncles prefer O'Connell to Emmet, but Old Ned sets them straight in no uncertain terms: 'I heard tell [O'Connell] was after Emmet, hunting him down with a blunderbuss', and that 'if a union man raised his voice in Dublin, the great Dan would shove a fist down his throat, and a big fist he had, too'. Moreover, 'the great Dan didn't give a damn whether the farmer had enough land to grow a dish of potatoes in or not. And why the hell should he? Sure the O'Connells owned half of Kerry'. Old Ned concedes that

> A man must free himself of his own ignorance before he'll free anything. But more than learning is needed to free Ireland and always was. Emmet had the right way

> for that, see; Emmet was for the sword and the gun and the hell with them all. Now O'Connell there had his chance, they say, that Emmet never had. But he was always for palavering with them – and God knows some of it had its place, too – but the sword is what's needed in the last run. They can talk and talk, but it's the sword will have the loudest voice in the end.[3]

Willie is thus prepared to side with his grandfather and the rebels against the other members of his family and the local priests when news of the Easter Rising hits Providence: 'Street by street, building by building, the bitter losing fight was fought every night from every newspaper they could get, even the raucous Boston paper with the flaming red headlines, the paper his grandmother said shouldn't be let into the house.'[4]

THE SPEECH

From very early on, Robert Emmet's speech from the dock had a life of its own in the United States. It is reported that a Mrs Hamilton from Dublin declaimed the speech on American stages as early as 1806, and it had countless performances throughout the nineteenth century and into the twentieth century – in venues formal and informal, in theatres, schools, parish halls, and parlours. The first great historian of early Irish America, George Potter, tells us that the speech 'was learned by heart by the generations'.[5] The importance of oratory in the struggle for Irish freedom was a constant theme at nationalist gatherings in the United States. As Boston's John E. Fitzgerald maintained in1888: 'Without brave hearts with eloquent and golden tongues to preach the gospel of Irish liberty from platform, rostrum, and felon's dock in every decade, the national spirit would long ago have died in the Irish heart.' Fitzgerald further declared that 'the dying speech of Robert Emmet, if no other were left, is sufficient to keep alive lofty patriotism and evoke tender sentiments at all times'.[6]

Emmet and his speech were associated with parochial education in the United States from quite early on. When Irish labourers and their families came to Lowell, Massachusetts, to build canals and work in the mills in the early 1820s, they established their own 'Irish schools' on the 'Paddy Camp Lands'. By 1830 they were able to convince the Yankee town fathers to help subsidise what was *de facto* Catholic education. By 1835, 469 children were enrolled, and two years later, the Lowell *Courier* praised the excellent preparation of these students for the public secondary school by citing as their models 'a Sheridan, a Burke, a Grattan, and an Emmet'. Oratory was a subject, and certainly these children were learning the speech.[7] Nearly a hundred years later, in James T. Farrell's novel *Young Lonigan*, at the Chicago parochial school graduation of young Studs Lonigan in 1916, the better students receive their 'Irish history diplomas' in addition to the ordinary sheepskin.[8] Indeed, the speech as learned by heart is still having influence. The writer and musician Terence Winch, raised in the Bronx in the 1950s, had a poem selected for *Best American Poems of 2002*. In his note for the anthology, he explains that 'in the last stanza, there's a bit of an echo of the famous Speech from the Dock by Irish patriot Robert Emmet, executed in 1803. I had memorized the speech in high school.'[9] The list of Americans for whom the speech has had significance goes on and on, and stretches from Abraham Lincoln's Illinois self-education in the law, to Robert E. Lee's West Point, to the 'Irish flats' of San Antonio, Texas, where its recitation was a regular feature of Saturday night entertainments as early as 1842.[10]

Emmet's speech was first published in America separately as a pamphlet (which included a portrait of Emmet) before 1810. A second pamphlet was printed in New York in July 1811.[11] Several later editions followed, at least one, in 1879, with a facing-page translation of the speech into Irish. Also in 1879, Patrick Ford's New York *Irish World* ran a full-page Irish translation of the speech, and for the next five years, Ford offered for sale separate copies of this version 'printed in the Irish character' and suitable for framing.[12]

The Speeches of Charles Phillips, the Sligo-born Catholic barrister and noted (if not notorious) speaker, had five American editions from 1817 to 1820. With the fifth and subsequent editions, this popular book included 'an appendix, containing an account of the last moments and speech of Robert Emmet'.[13] Then came *Irish Eloquence, The Speeches of the Celebrated Irish Orators, Phillips, Curran, and Grattan, To which is Added, the Powerful Appeal of Robert Emmet, at the Close of his Trial for High Treason, Selected by a Member of the Bar.* This was first published in Philadelphia (Kay, Mielke & Biddle) in 1832. Fourteen editions followed, the latest in 1857. First published in 1868 in Ireland and in 1878 in the United States, the Sullivan brothers' phenomenally successful *Speeches from the Dock* also contributed to the wide availability of Emmet's speech. By 1897, eleven American editions had appeared in New York City, Boston, and Providence, Rhode Island. It is safe to say that no piece of oratory by someone other than an American has ever been more readily available or better known in the United States.[14]

THE LYRIC MUSE

Virtually all of the nineteenth-century American songs and poems about Robert Emmet embody the purely instrumental motive of advocacy for the cause of Irish nationalism. At the same time, all such creations are free of disguised self-promotion. No one wrote songs or poems to make money or win public office. Thomas Moore's songs 'She is far from the land' and

'Breathe not his name' were of course widely performed in the United States. Songs composed in America were also heard in music halls, parish halls, and middle-class parlours of a Sunday afternoon. The sheet music of one of the most popular songs, 'Emmet's Last Words: When Erin shall stand 'mid the Isles of the Sea', was published in 1853 in New York City, with retail distributors in Detroit, Cincinnati, St. Louis, San Francisco, Portland (Oregon), and Quebec. One stanza ends: 'Till my country shall stand like a gem 'midst the free,/ Till then let my epitaph unwritten be.'[15]

The poems certainly came from everywhere. They were written by the Irish-American literati, most of them journalists, both secular and clerical; by educated professionals not otherwise involved in literature; and by autodidactic town laureates from all over the country. Most can go without repeating here (or anywhere else, for that matter), but let me cite just one of each type. My vote for the best of the poems goes to John Boyle O'Reilly's 'The Patriot's Grave', written for Emmet's centennial birthday and read at the exercises at Boston's Tremont Temple on 4 March 1878. Only eight years before, O'Reilly had escaped from penal servitude in Western Australia, and was already editor of the *Pilot* and an esteemed spokesman for Irish America.[16]

An ambitious 84-line poem in three different stanza forms, 'The Patriot's Grave', illustrates O'Reilly's gift for conciliation. He credits both parliamentary and physical force:

> With one deep breath began the land's progression:
> On every field the seeds of freedom fell:
> Burke, Grattan, Flood, and Curran in the session –
> Fitzgerald, Sheares, and Emmet in the cell!

And his conclusion is an artful echo of Emmet's famous speech:

> Chord struck deep with the keynote, telling us what can save –
> 'A nation among the nations', or forever a nameless grave.
>
> Such is the will of the martyr – the burden we still must bear;
> But even from death he reaches the legacy to share:
>
> He teaches the secret of manhood – the watchword of those who aspire –
> That men must follow freedom though it lead through blood and fire;
>
> That sacrifice is the bitter draught which freemen still must quaff –
> That every patriotic life is the patriot's epitaph.[17]

In the second category is 'Robert Emmet', by George E. McNeill, identified as a 'well-known labor agitator', in the *Boston Globe*, which published his poem in 1903. Here is a stanza indicative of the type:

> Weeping, we kneel around thy unmarked grave,
> A countless throng, the old, the young, the brave;
> Our swords remain unsheathed, our harps unstrung.
> In other lands remote, where Freedom's fires
> Illume our homes and patriot love inspires,
> With loving hearts thy name and fame are sung.[18]

From the autodidacts, local loyalty demands a few lines from the self-published 'Daniel O'Connell Came from There' of P. J. Pendergast, a grocer at the turn of the century in my hometown of Norwood, Massachusetts:

> Robert Emmet martyr slain
> Thought Ireland's freedom to proclaim
> But he was trapped in an English snare
> He was taken unaware he was executed there
> Because Robert Emmet came from there.[19]

THE STORY

The earliest American published narrative of Emmet's insurrection and trial appeared within a year of the event in Baltimore in 1804: *Forensic Eloquence, Sketches of Trials in Ireland for High Treason, etc.* This was followed by *The History of the Late Grand Insurrection; or, Struggle for Liberty in Ireland, . . . To which Is Added, a Short Account of the Insurrection by Emmet, with His Famous Speech Made to the Court Before Judgment*, published in Carlisle, Pennsylvania in 1805. These were both reprinted from British sources.[20] The standard Irish nineteenth-century lives of Robert Emmet were also readily available in American editions. John Doherty's 1836 *Life, Trial, and Conversation and Times of Robert Emmet* appeared first in New York in 1845 and again in 1850. R. R. Madden's 1844 *Life and Times of Robert Emmet* was published in New York in 1856, and again in 1857 and 1880. The noted Boston Catholic publisher Patrick Donahoe also brought out an edition of Doherty in 1852, and Donahoe's New York rival P. J. Kenedy published an edition of Madden. In response to the influx of Famine immigrants, at least nine separate editions of three different Emmet biographies were published from 1845 to 1857 in New York, Boston, Philadelphia, and Charleston, South Carolina.[21]

In the later nineteenth century, at least four original American versions of the Emmet story were attempted. All of the titles suggest a similar slant on the subject: Dennis O'Sullivan, *Robert Emmet, or True Irish Hearts* (1880), Varina Anne Davis (the daughter of Jefferson Davis, President of the Confederacy), *An Irish Knight of the Nineteenth Century* (1888), Greg Morehead, *Robert Emmet the Irish Patriot: The Romance of His Life* (1902), and *Robert Emmet: A Survey of His Rebellion and of His Romance* (1904), by Louise Imogen Guiney.[22]

This 'romantic' slant on the Emmet story is related to a set of ideas that can be labelled 'American Celticism'. These are traceable to Matthew Arnold's 'Celtic touchstones', which were glossed by John V. Kelleher as 'Titanism and magic and piercing melancholy and doomed bravery and ineffectualness and verbal sensuality and splendid dream-haunted failure and the exquisite spiritual sensitivity of the Celt.' As reinforced by the methodical mistiness, *fin-de-siècle* escapism, and wholesale retreat from the mundane of the 'Celtic Twilight' in its simplest translatable terms, the result was a heady brew much quaffed in Irish-American artistic circles. In fact, Kelleher contends that the best single example of the formula came from the American side. This was Shaemas O'Sheel's 1911 poem, 'They Went Forth to Battle But They Always Fell', in which it is argued that the Irish have always lost because they have always been distracted from the dreary concerns of the world, including the waging of war, by 'a secret music'.

> Ah, they by some strange troubling doubt were stirred,
> And died for hearing what no foeman heard.

'Here then', says Kelleher, 'is the new view of Irish history which explains defeat and removes its sting . . . They were beaten because, in other words, they were *fey*, doomed by their own spiritual sensitivity. One notes that the music or the word that did the dirty work was inaudible to the crass but competent enemy.'[23]

It has been my view that American Celticism allowed some of Irish America's creative folks to be 'Irish' in ways aesthetically acceptable to the American cultural mainstream of genteel respectability, while ignoring unpleasant and embarrassing aspects of Irish-American life – Fenian circles, the raids on Canada and the Dynamite campaign, the well publicised urban 'Irish problems' of poverty, disease, crime, and violence, the first flexing of New World political muscles – all, of course, resulting from the continuing flood of new immigrants set in motion by the Great Hunger.

Louise Guiney provides a solid case in point. A talented member of the *Boston Pilot* circle of writers, she was the daughter of Tipperary immigrant and American Civil War General Patrick Guiney. Like John Boyle O'Reilly, she found herself a mediator between Irish and Yankee Boston cultural life. Her first poems appeared in the *Pilot* in 1880 when she was 19, and five years later she dedicated her first book of essays to her Brahmin mentor, Oliver Wendell Holmes. A trip to Ireland in 1890 provided first-hand exposure to the burgeoning literary renaissance there. She met all the principals and became good friends with Katharine Tynan and Dora Sigerson. Guiney was caught between two contrasting roles as the child of a revered Boston Irish and Catholic hero and a writer with literary aspirations towards which the gatekeepers were all Anglo-Saxon Protestants. She solved the tension by moving permanently to England in 1901, where she lived frugally in Oxford while continuing to write until her death at the age of 59 in 1920.[24]

A pure strain of American Celticism appeared in Boston, where the pressures of anti-Irish and anti-Catholic nativism and the weight of an Anglophile literary establishment were especially strong. Although much more accomplished than most, Guiney's literary work still fits the Celticist mould in many ways, and her Emmet book exemplifies a version of his image that was acceptable in high-toned Christian Irish America.[25] Her aim is nothing less than the separation of Emmet's sacrifice from its worldly political context.

Subtitled 'A Survey of His Rebellion and of His Romance', Guiney's book gives short shrift to the former. Though her father had been a famous general and a supporter of the cause and her grandfather had been involved in the 1798 rising, she is not an advocate for the physical force movement in Ireland. Guiney devotes only ten of her book's 104 pages to the rebellion itself, and she explains its failure by a determined effort to distinguish Emmet from his fellow conspirators. First, his followers let Emmet down because 'he leaned overmuch, not on human goodness, but on human intelligence in making opportunity: and it failed him'. Guiney draws out this point with a curious artistic simile that has a further distancing effect: 'He was like the purely literary playwright labouring with the average theatre audience; he was never in the least, for all his wit, cunning enough to deal scientifically with a corporation on whom hints, half-tones, adumbrations, are thrown away.'[26] Moreover, 'treachery was at work and running like fire in oil under the eyes of one who could believe no ill of human kind'.[27] In her concluding assessment, Guiney blames 'English gold and English terrorism' for Emmet's abandonment by his 'humble colleagues at home', and she stresses that 'there is a great unwritten chapter of perfidy behind his lonely ineffectual blow struck for national freedom'.[28]

Further distancing of Emmet from his rebellion comes in Guiney's description of the 'many unknown, unprepossessing insurgents' who turned out on the evening of 23 July as 'the drunken refuse of the city taverns', and even as 'diabolical changelings'. In the event, she continues, 'the spirit of rowdyism, private pillage, and indiscriminate slaughter took the lead', most notably in the mob's murder of Arthur Wolfe, Lord Kilwarden, 'the one unfailingly humane and deservedly beloved judge in all Ireland'. In a startling reference to the Phoenix Park murders of 1882, Guiney further declares that Kilwarden's was 'a fate paralleled only by the unpremeditated assassination in our own time of that other kindest heart, Lord Frederick Cavendish'.[29]

Having surgically removed Robert Emmet from his rebellion, Guiney tells the rest of her tale with like intent. She sees Emmet's lingering in the Wicklow Hills for Sarah Curran's sake as 'a mad deed', but admirable. She dismisses Anne Devlin as 'a servant, a peasant wench who was devoted to him'.[30] She refers to the separate sketches found in Emmet's cell labeled 'R. E., head' and 'R. E., body' as evidence of 'the detached humour possible to an easy conscience'.[31] She dwells upon the romance of Sarah Curran's story, citing as gospel Washington Irving's 'The Broken Heart' and Moore's 'She is far from the land'.[32] Although she quotes liberally from the famous letters, Guiney says very little about the speech from the dock and does not quote much of it. The speech is simply too nationalistic for her purposes.

Guiney's work of apolitical apotheosis comes together in her argument that Robert Emmet is a 'universal', rather than a narrowly Irish hero. And yet, she also tries to have her cake while eating it by sticking closely to Arnold's Celtic touchstones in her delineation of Emmet's character. First, he is a figure belonging in 'the antique world, with its heroic simpleness'.[33] Emmet's Trinity classmate Charles Phillips is quoted with full credence: 'Everyone loved, everyone respected him; . . . [he] might be said to have lived not so much in the scene around him as in the society of the illustrious and sainted dead.'[34] Guiney also declares that Emmet died 'a single-minded Christian, never quite out of touch with the Church in which his holy mother had brought him up'.[35] Finally, the author moves into the mystic by asserting that Emmet enjoys lasting renown because 'his large soul has, like a magician, pieced together his broken body, the symbol of his broken, mistimed, and because mistimed, unhallowed effort. But only his own soul has done it, and by a power within.'[36]

To an extent, Guiney's hagiography rests on a solid sense of Emmet's extraordinary iconic position. Early in the book, she remarks that 'His is one of several historic instances in which those who have wrought little else seem to have wrought an exquisite and quite enduring image of themselves in human tradition.' She calls Emmet 'a living legend', the subject of stories told by 'peasants gathered around a peat fire in the long evenings'. Further, 'a certain coloured print, very green as to raiment, very melodramatic as to gesture, hangs to-day in the best room of their every cabin, and stands to them for all that was of old, and is not, and still should be'.[37] At book's end, Guiney comes around again to this concept by analysing the portraits sketched on the trial day by Petrie, Comerford, and Brocas. Dismissing Petrie's sketch (based on the death mask) as 'somewhat heavy and glowering, and distinctly wry-necked', she praises the other two as 'hav[ing] given us a face to look at which one instinctively believes in. It is stamped with concentration and resolve, but has in it something serene and gentle and sweet.' And yet, her preference for the Brocas sketch – it is her book's frontispiece – stems from what can only be understood as its *fey* quality. By virtue of 'the slight upward curve of the perfect eyebrows at the inner edge', says Guiney, the portrait conveys 'a faun-like idiosyncrasy' which adds 'a final whimsical attraction to a sad young face which a child or a dog would readily love'.[38]

After character, comes the argument from 'Fate', in which Guiney also includes Sarah Curran: 'To mark the look of this Robert, hungry for the heroic, the look of this Sarah, mystical as twilight, is but to forecast casualties . . . To be an Emmet at all meant to get into trouble for advanced ideals. To be a Curran meant to have a keen intelligence always besieged hard, and eventually overcome, by melancholia.' To Guiney, their shared tragedy is only appropriate:

> A *révolution manquée* with an elopement; expatriation with a marriage certificate; a change of political front with the parental blessing – all look somehow equally incongruous and out of key with those sensitive faces [i.e. Robert's and Sarah's] elected, let us say, to better things. Their story, with all deductions which can be made, has already done something to deepen the sense of human love in the world, and to broaden the dream of human liberty. Perhaps either of those games may be considered as always worth the candle.[39]

Guiney wants to move the idea of Emmet from the grimy particulars of Ireland in 1803 to the empyrean of the abstract. To this end, she attempts to set him entirely outside history, by declaring that 'History, a tissue of externals, cannot afford to take account' of the pure sacrifice of an Emmet. The historian sees only the 'rashness and the immediate ruin consequent upon it . . . Hence it falls out that certain spirits are finally given over, with their illegitimate deeds in arm, to folk-lore and balladry. Of these are Charlotte Corday, and John Brown of Ossawatomie, and Robert Emmet.' Guiney's peroration is the Celticist's argument from otherworldliness with a vengeance:

> We understand too well what social havoc these pure-eyed hot-hearted angels bring in their wake, when they condescend to interfere with our fixed affairs. They call into being in their own despite our most self-protective measures: measures, in short, which amount to an international coalition against the undesirable immigrant. Relentless inhospitality to such innovators, in every generation and in every clime, is the habit of this planet . . . The executed meddlers, however, often take on an unaccountable posthumous grace, and may even be approached upon anniversaries in a mood none other than that of affectionate congratulation. The anomaly of our own situation has passed with their death.[40]

As a cultural document in its turn-of-the-century moment, this text is very rich. Guiney's reference to idealists and visionaries as 'undesirable immigrant[s]' to the mundane world gains unintended resonance when it is recalled that she had been hounded from her position as postmistress in Auburndale, Massachusetts, in 1894 by a campaign of the virulently nativist American Protective Association.[41]

BECOMING AN IMAGE

The famous quotation from Yeats, 'Emmet died and became an image', is literally on the mark.[42] John Kelleher has said that when he was a boy in Lawrence, Massachusetts (he was born there in 1916), one of two pictures could be found all over the city on Irish-American parlour or dining-room walls – either Robert Emmet in the dock or Daniel O'Connell refusing to take the oath. As the McSorley novel suggests, it was usually one or the other – not both.[43] Certainly, there were Emmet pictures, both lithographs and chromolithographs (after the colour process was introduced at mid-century), everywhere in nineteenth-century Irish America. The most successful producers of mass-market art in America, Currier and Ives, were well represented. Nathaniel Currier had painted a picture of Emmet in the dock that became the model for their widely distributed print versions, which were available for purchase by wholesale, retail, mail-order, and through house-to-house peddlers. Their small-folio 'foreign scenes', mostly of England and Ireland for the immigrant trade, sold for as little as 60 cents (coloured) or 20 cents (black-and-white).[44]

Currier and Ives offered three different images of Robert Emmet, all in the small-folio format. The most elaborate, *Robert Emmet: Dublin on the 19th of Sept., 1803*, features a full-length portrait of Emmet standing in a courtroom surrounded by judges in wigs and robes. A fair portion of the speech appears as well. This is most likely the picture on the wall in McSorley's novel. They also offered a print of *Emmet's Betrothed*, a portrait of Sarah Curran dressed in black with her left hand on the frame of a harp and the first stanza of Moore's 'She is far from the land' in one corner.[45] Other companies also offered prints. For example, Emmet's execution was pictured in prints sold by Gies & Company in Buffalo in 1878 and by J. Kirwen (place unlisted) in 1883.

A range of other media was represented as well. The Briggs Company of America, which published lantern slides of historical events and travel scenes, offered melodramatic images of Emmet's speech and his execution in their 'English History' series of lantern slides. In the mid-1860s, American bonds sold to benefit the Fenian Brotherhood featured Emmet's picture, along with that of Wolfe Tone and an Irish wolfhound, and a commemorative plate carrying a portrait of Emmet was sold in the United States in 1880 to raise money for the destitute in the west of Ireland. Most implausible, perhaps, but indicative of one glaring strain of mixed motivation, was the appearance of the execution scene on an American cigar box label.[46] Visual citation of Ireland's patriot hero appeared at the two most important American international fairs bracketing the end of the nineteenth century. A bust of Emmet was displayed at the World's Columbian Exposition in 1893, and the Irish Village at the Century of Progress World's Fair in 1933–4 featured, all in a row on one street, replicas of the facades of the homes of Edmund Burke, Daniel O'Connell, and Robert Emmet. Finally, the Kerry-born sculptor Jerome Connor, who lived in the United States from 1888 to 1925, created a number of bronze castings of a statue of Robert Emmet in 1916. The Actor Brandon Tynan posed and Connor also consulted the trial sketches and death mask. The completed statues span the continent, standing at Dupont Circle in Washington, DC, in the town square of Emmetsburg, Iowa, and in Golden Gate Park in San Francisco.[47]

NAMING RIGHTS

The historian George Potter tells us that '"Robert Emmet" as a given name was as standard as Michael or John' throughout the nineteenth century.[48] Certainly, Irish Americans were calling their children after Robert Emmet well on into the twentieth century. Just to name a few, we have Emmet Kelly the circus clown (born in 1898), Emmet Larkin the historian (born in 1927), and M. Emmet Walsh the actor (born in 1935). When I was growing up in Norwood, Massachusetts, in the 1940s and 1950s, this was still going on. I was reminded of this well before I started thinking about the present essay. In reading Alice McDermott's novel, *Child of My Heart* (2002), I came upon this passage in which the 15-year-old narrator is talking to her eight-year-old cousin:

> I told her I could remember the name Robert Emmet. I said I had once asked my mother, probably when I was about your age, who Robert Emmet was, and she, after a long pause, had said he was an Irish patriot her father had been particularly fond of. I said no, he was a little baby boy, the one I was talking about. A little baby boy still in a blanket. That's the Robert Emmet I was talking about.
>
> Later on I found out that before me, my mother had had another baby who'd died just as he was being born and who was baptized Robert Emmet by the delivery room nurse because that was the name my grandfather offered when my father was asked and had no response to give.[49]

Names are always crucial in McDermott's fiction. Because they are so often withheld, when we get one, it registers. In *Child of My Heart*, for example, we never learn the narrator's surname, and her given name (Theresa) isn't mentioned until half way through the book. The novel is set in about 1960, which puts Theresa's birth year at 1945, and her stillborn brother's at least a year earlier. (We are told that her grandfather died in March 1945.)

All of this matches with what the novel caused me to remember – that I had a second cousin named Robert Emmet Drummey, born in Norwood in 1941. Like McDermott's narrator, my cousin was the grandchild of Irish immigrants who had come to America at the turn of the century. The name of 'Robert Emmet' meant as little to us in the late 1950s as it did to the fictional Theresa. It was a curiosity at best, and one that no one pursued. But of course the name had meant something to Bobby Drummey's parents and grandparents. And theirs was probably the last American generation for which such a vestige of unforced emotional resonance could attach to Emmet's name. It is, however, worth noting that, by this time, the naming had been a convention for 140 years.

A number of American places have also been named for Robert Emmet. Most were founded in the middle years of the nineteenth century in implausibly far-flung locales. Typical here is Emmetsburg, Iowa, settled in 1856 by six-wagons-full of Irish immigrants by way of central Illinois, and staked out and named two years later by three speculators from Fort Dodge named Hoolihan, Cahill and Cavanaugh.[50] One of Jerome Connor's statues of Emmet stands in the court-house square. Emmetsburg is in Palo Alto County, but a few miles north is Emmet County, Iowa, the setting for Leo R. Ward's fine 1941 novel of rural Irish America, *Holding Up the Hills*.[51] The state of Michigan also has an Emmet County, way up north, almost to the upper peninsula. There are also towns called Emmet (or Emmett) in Kansas, Nebraska, and Arkansas, and Emmett, Idaho, is in the copper-rich Boise Basin, where an 'Emmet circle' of the Fenian Brotherhood flourished just after the Civil War. And Emmet Park in Savannah, Georgia, is one of the few (though far from sufficient) reasons why these days that city has a huge St Patrick's Day parade.

A short-lived but important Irish-American nationalist group was the Emmet Monument Association (EMA), founded in New York City in March 1855 by exiled Young Irelanders Michael Doheny and John O'Mahony. An innocuous title to those not in the know, the name followed Emmet's speech by implying that Irish freedom would have to come before any monument could be erected. The association was strongest in New York but had affiliates elsewhere, notably in Boston. After dissolution owing to internecine strife in 1856, a permanent committee of 13 remained on the job, and it was they who petitioned James Stephens to organise the Fenian Brotherhood in 1858. Many militia companies that had been associated with the EMA went over en masse to the Fenians, and from there to service in the American Civil War, some keeping the association with Emmet's name all along the way.[52] One of these was Chicago's Emmet Guards, a Fenian-supported militia company which became a founding part of the Union Army's Western Irish Brigade under Colonel James Mulligan.[53] Another was the Robert Emmet Club of Cincinnati, Ohio, founded in 1855. There were other Fenian circles named after Emmet in Boston, New York, Philadelphia, Richmond, Virginia, Virginia City, Nevada, Boise, and Sacramento.[54]

Later in the century, many affiliated Clan na Gael camps in the American West took the name of the Robert Emmet Literary Association. These included Clan camps in Michigan, Colorado, Utah, and Arizona. The celebration of Emmet's birthday was the big annual event, but we can assume that precious little literature was discussed at the meetings. The weightiest of these was the camp in Butte, Montana, which inducted 804 men from 1881 to 1911. Because these western camps were full of miners, they doubled as labour organisations.[55]

DRAMATIS PERSONAE

Moving on to dramatic representation, I have looked at six different plays about Robert Emmet that were performed in nineteenth-century America. Three of these – by James Pilgrim, Dion Boucicault, and Joseph I. C. Clarke – are quite well known. *Robert Emmet: The Martyr of Irish Liberty* by James Pilgrim, an Englishman who turned out a number of melodramatic vehicles for the famous Barney Williams, was first performed in 1853 to mark the fiftieth anniversary of Emmet's death. This play had several published editions. Quite a tangled web, it was cut down from twelve scenes to four by the American playwright Charles Townsend, better known for his staging of *Uncle Tom's Cabin*.[56] Dion Boucicault's *Robert Emmet* was 'taken over' (or plagiarised) from an 1881 script of Frank A. Marshall, commissioned by Henry Irving for the London stage, but shelved because of its provocative nature in the context of the Irish Land War and the Phoenix Park murders. Irving gave the play over to Boucicault, and his version opened in Chicago in November 1884.[57] First performed in 1887, *Robert Emmet, A Tragedy of Irish History* was written by Joseph I. C. Clarke, an Irish-born journalist and balladeer who emigrated to New York City in about 1862.[58]

My other three Emmet plays are less known, or perhaps unknown. These were available to me because I live in Carbondale, Illinois. B. M. O'Boylan, about whom I can find no information, published *The Rebels; or, The Irish Insurgent Chiefs of 1803, An Historical Drama in Five Acts*, in 1894 in Newark, Ohio.[59] According to WorldCat, the only copy anywhere happens to be in my home library at Southern Illinois University. I found two more Emmet plays in our Sherman Theatre Collection.[60] These Emmet plays, both entitled *Robert Emmet*, are unattributed – I'll call them *Sherman A* and *Sherman B* – and undated. *Sherman A* is extraordinary because it is handwritten on the quartered back sides of nine different, colourful posters advertising melodramas, one of which is dated 1904. This could be a sign of popularity or piracy or both. *Sherman B* is a typescript using the 'stenotype' process, and thus must also be vintage 1900 or so. These two new plays are entirely different from any of the four published versions that I looked at. Certainly, there are plenty more out there.

Because the material is varied, I am assuming that my sampling of six plays is representative. To begin with, all embody the tension between relatively altruistic and self-serving aims that characterise American uses of the Emmet legacy. Naturally, all six feature Emmet's trial and speech from the dock, and in four this is the final scene. Five of the six plays take place entirely within the crucial three months of July through September, 1803.

Five plays include the love story of Emmet and Sarah Curran, and in all five it is a post-rebellion attempt to meet with Sarah that leads to Emmet's capture, thus enforcing the message that the love of a woman leads to Emmet's downfall. This point is mitigated, however, by the fact that in all five plays the disastrous tryst is set up by the machinations of an informer. Four of the six plays end with Emmet gazing off into the distance or up to the sky, having just delivered his speech from the dock. The obvious staging of apotheosis is reinforced by Emmet's last words in two of the plays. In Pilgrim, Lord Norbury declares Emmet convicted of treason by the King of England, and Emmet points to the sky and says 'My King is there!' In Clarke, Sarah Curran collapses at Emmet's feet, and he gazes upwards and tells her, 'Remember, our next meeting shall be there.' In Boucicault, as we shall see, Emmet's climactic apotheosis is literal.

Only two of the six plays stress the nationalist theme over the love story. James Pilgrim avoids the distraction of the romantic relationship by the ingenious ploy of giving Emmet a wife – Maria. Pilgrim also plants the implication of latter-day American help for the cause by sending off Darby and Judy, two of his stalwart peasant co-conspirators, to the new world. Their feast of whiskey and mutton and the cry 'Hurrah for America' end scene one of the last act, which is followed immediately by Emmet's trial. When the verdict is read, Emmet gives his grieving wife a decorous kiss, then calmly delivers his speech. In O'Boylan's play, *The Rebels; or, The Irish Insurgent Chiefs of 1803*, Sarah Curran has a relatively minor role, though her botched meeting with Emmet does lead to his capture. True to his title, O'Boylan includes Thomas Russell and Michael Dwyer as major characters, and Emmet's trial occurs as Act Three of five acts, followed by Dwyer's assumption of revolutionary leadership and an ending tableau of a ship full of rebels about to be transported to Australia. From the prow, Dwyer delivers an exhorting, patriotic speech.

Joseph I. C. Clarke's *Robert Emmet: A Tragedy of Irish History* begins as a nationalist narrative. Act I, set in 1800 in Lord Charlemont's Dublin house, provides historical deep background: Thomas Addis Emmet is in a Scottish prison and about to leave for America; his brother Robert's plans to continue working for Irish freedom have already caused a warrant to be issued for his arrest; the Act of Union, about to go into effect, is sure to provoke increased revolutionary activity. By the end of Clarke's play, however, the tone has shifted decidedly to the narrative of star-crossed love. Emmet's sentence and speech constitute the second of the play's final three scenes. It is sandwiched between two emotional appearances by Sarah Curran. In the first scene, she attends the trial and dissolves into hysterical weeping. In the third, she visits Emmet in prison on his last night, and as they declare their undying love, a bell tolls and the masked hangman enters to take the condemned man away. The play ends with the stage direction: '*Bell tolls again*; MISS CURRAN *shrieks and falls senseless to the floor.*'

The Clarke play's elaborate publication in New York by G. Putnam's Sons in 1888 suggests the sustained interest in the story through the century and before the run-up to the 1903 centennial. It is a lovely artefact of book-making. The seal of the United Irishmen is stamped in gold on the green cover and appears again on the title page, and the seals of Thomas Addis Emmet and Robert Emmet punctuate the ends of two acts. In addition, there are tissue-protected reproductions of the Comerford and Petrie trial sketches and of Emmet's autograph.[61]

O'Boylan's play has a preface, in which he spells out what were certainly two key aims of all these Emmet plays. He wants first of all to put 'a true and clean picture of Irish life on the stage', thereby countering 'the thing known as the stage Irishman'. He goes on to explain that 'I chose the subject of the present play because it supplied some of the best types of Irish manhood and patriotism, and afforded an opportunity of pointing out the causes that keep Ireland in bondage.' He hopes to emphasise 'the one grand thought that *Ireland must be* free'.[62]

Several contemporary reviewers of the Emmet plays measure success in these very terms. However, the pragmatic theatre-business motivation of filling the seats often ran counter to both aims. My six Emmet plays share a number of crowd-pleasing conventions which both reinforce the stage-Irish stereotype and deviate from historical accuracy at the expense of clear articulation of the nationalist theme. First, several include a subplot of happily resolved romance among minor characters, in counterpoint against the tragic Emmet–Curran relationship. Pilgrim avoids the star-crossed lovers by having Emmet married, but he also relieves the dark dénouement by sending rebels Darby and his pregnant lover Judy off to America. In Clarke, servant Rose Malone and Wicklow rebel Martin Burke plan to marry on the night Emmet is arrested. In O'Boylan, two minor characters become engaged and Marie Burke marries rebel chief Michael Dwyer and seems ready to accompany him to Australia at the play's end. Both of the Sherman plays feature weddings of minor characters, and in *Sherman B*, the contrast is enforced by having the wedding and Sarah Curran's last meeting with Emmet, leading to his capture, take place in the same act in the same churchyard.

Second, there is a good deal of disguise and mistaken identity in these plays – some of it obviously for comic relief. In Pilgrim, Darby dresses up as an old woman to avoid capture and Emmet himself tests the loyalty of his followers by masquerading as an old man. In *Sherman A*, Major Morrison and a government spy dress as an old man and woman to infiltrate the rebel camp in Wicklow, and in *Sherman B*, Major Sirr, who has never met Emmet, mistakes him for a loyal subject and deputes him to go looking for himself.

Third, despite the gravity of the main plot, music and dancing figure in several of the American Emmet plays. In Pilgrim, cheers and music follow an implausible close call – Emmet saves Lord Norbury's life – at the end of Act I, and a celebration marks Darby and Judy's American wake in Act III. In Clarke, Sarah Curran shows her mettle by singing a rebel song at Lord Charlemont's house in Act I. She does the same thing at 'Mr and Mrs Plinket's home at Sea Point, near Dublin', in *Sherman B*, which also includes a nationalist song from the Wicklow rebels. O'Boylan's odd play is oddest in its extensive use of poetry, dancing, and singing. Major speeches by Thomas Russell, Michael Dwyer, and Emmet himself are rendered in a species of blank verse – blessedly abjured in the transcriptions of Emmet's manifesto and speech from the dock, which O'Boylan's preface declares 'are taken literally from Madden's life'. Through the course of the play, music abounds. Russell and Emmet sing a duet about the Irish Brigade, Dwyer's fiancée sings a song in her sleep – about Emmet, not Michael, two minor characters plight their troth in a duet, and the play ends with a 'Song and Chorus' of hope for a future successful rising.[63]

In the matter of over-the-top pandering to the audience, Boucicault's *Robert Emmet* deserves special attention. There is no way of knowing how much was 'taken over' from the Marshall/Irving conception, but Boucicault certainly put the stamp of his own showmanship on his version. In the romance plot, Sarah Curran at first pretends to be married to Emmet to keep a nationalist crowd from attacking her father and Lord Norbury. Later on, the lovers agree to be married at night by a Catholic priest, Father Donnelly, and it is in his cottage that Emmet is ambushed by Major Sirr's troops. There is also an alternative romance in the provision at play's end of two tickets for America to rebel Michael Dwyer and Emmet's faithful servant Ann [*sic*] Devlin. There is cross-dressing in that Dwyer enters the play disguised as an old woman, 'Mother Magan'. (This was Boucicault's role in the original production in Chicago in November 1884. His son and daughter were also in the play.) And there is music, as Ann [*sic*] Devlin's brother Andy, a faithful Emmet supporter, sings contemptuous songs about the Duke of York ('The Duke of York was a damned bad soldier,/ From Dunkerque he ran away') and Major Sirr ('Now Major Sirr/ He is a cur,/ And his kennel is the Castle').

In addition, Boucicault takes the prize for bloodshed. In none of the other five plays does a character die on stage, but sensational deaths end each of Boucicault's last three acts. This is also the only play of the six in which any part of Emmet's rebellion takes place in view of the audience. At the end of Act II, the unruly mob attacks shopkeepers and passers-by at College Green, and when Lord Kilwarden arrives to make peace, he is killed by a pike thrust. Boucicault mitigates the effect here by making the murderer Michael Quigley, who is this play's government spy pretending to be a rebel. Robert Emmet comes on the scene just after and cries out, 'Ireland was murdered by that blow!' In Act III, Andy Devlin is mortally wounded in the ambush in which Emmet is captured by Major Sirr.[64] The fourth and final act ends with two sensational death scenes. In the first, the traitor Quigley sits in a shed at Ringsend counting his money. He is surprised by Michael Dwyer, disguised in a false beard and 'huge carman's coat' on his own way out of the country with Ann Devlin, who shouts out, 'Kill him, Mike! Kill him!' 'Never fear!' replies Dwyer. He chokes Quigley into unconsciousness, throws him into a boat, and he and Ann row out into the Liffey, 'to poison the tide' with the traitor's body. The play concludes with Emmet's execution and literal apotheosis. Needless to say, none of the other plays attempts this, and to bring it off, Boucicault utilises a firing squad. Emmet gives a purse to his jailors, kisses a portrait of Sarah Curran, shouts out, 'God bless my country!', and falls to the stage in a volley of shots. Here are Boucicault's directions for the ending tableau:

> The black flag is raised. Bell tolls. Stage dark . . . The wall behind Emmet slowly opens. A vista of pale blue clouds appears. The figure of Ireland clothed in palest green and with a coronet of shamrocks in her hair descends slowly; and bending forward when she reaches the spot behind Emmet, she kneels. Two children at her feet, R. [ight] and L. [eft], draw slowly back the body of Emmet until his head lies looking up into her face.

The *Chicago Tribune* reviewer of the premiere declared that 'Boucicault is a master of popular melodrama, but in this instance he fell between the two stools of melodrama and tragedy'. Furthermore, the use of stereotypical 'stock characters' is noted: 'the villains and heroes might be transferred from one drama to another with only a change of names'.[65] The play made little money, and Boucicault never revived it before his death in 1890. The playwright had been vilified for years in the Irish-American press for his hefty contributions to the stage-Irish stereotype. A few months before the opening of his Emmet play, the *Chicago Citizen*, the weekly sounding board of radical nationalist John F. Finerty, had railed against 'so-called Irish dramas' with their 'verbose bravery, the mimic treason, the *amadhaun* plots, and vulgar manner and sentiments of the players'. Finerty named Boucicault and Harrigan and Hart as prime offenders.[66]

Other American Emmet plays illustrate the popularity of the material through the century. These include a lost play from the 1840s by Nathaniel Harrington Bannister, an American actor-playwright from the Southern states; a play by Julius Tietze Tietzelieve which had New York editions in 1882, 1897, and 1902; and the play *Robert Emmet and the Days of 1803* by Dubliner Brandon Tynan, which had a long New York run in 1902 with its author in the starring role, and was published in the city that same year. This play had a very successful three-week run in Chicago in June 1903, where it managed to please even John Finerty, whose review summarises well the balancing act that was Irish-American historical melodrama:

> While the play as a whole is of the best class of Irish drama of serious purpose, it has a well interwoven comedy element and enough of stirring melodramatic touches – never overdone by the players – to thrill the pulses of the auditors without failure and set them always to demonstrating a most undisguised delight in every triumph of the hero.[67]

Emmet plays were also put on often by smaller stock companies and amateur groups. Most of the ones I have found date to later in the century, and many were part of the run-up to the centennial of Emmet's execution. However, I believe that the positive connotations of the Emmet dramas also contributed to the big campaign against the stage Irishman which gathered steam from the 1880s, reinforced by the emergent Irish-American middle class and spearheaded by the Ancient Order of Hibernians. No one familiar with this campaign should ever have been surprised at the negative audience reactions to Synge's *Playboy* in Dublin in 1907 and on the Abbey's first American tour in 1911. From 1875 through 1905, sites of plays about Robert Emmet included Wilmington, North Carolina, Troy, New York, the University of Notre Dame in Indiana, Providence, Denver, and Milwaukee (in German), Newark, New Jersey, Burbank, California, Pittsburgh, Philadelphia, and Spokane, Washington.[68]

Valuable detail can be found about one such Emmet play that was put on in St Louis. The 'Irish love drama, *Robert Emmet*' by Dr P. T. Cunningham, a local dentist active in Irish and dramatic circles, played yearly from 1904 to 1910. The play starred Dr Cunningham as Emmet, supported by a cast of 100 local amateurs, and featured Irish songs, dances, and 'bagpipe music'. The prospective audience was assured that the play 'is written along historical lines, eliminating anything like caricature and presenting a truthful portrayal of the Irish character'. Listed highlights for all five acts were as follows. Act I takes place in Paris, where Robert Emmet pleads with Napoleon for aid to Ireland. In Act II 'the famous Wicklow hero Michael Dwyer' sings a song in Irish, '*Fainne geal an lae* – the Dawning of the Day'. In Act III, Anne Devlin refuses to betray Emmet, 'at cost of her life'. Act IV contains Emmet's betrayal, arrest, trial, and speech from the dock, and Act V 'includes many beautiful and touching stage pictures, among them being Sarah Curran's visit to Emmet's grave, and closes with an apotheosis of Emmet'. The following year, Dr Cunningham founded the Emerald Stock Company in St Louis, pledging to work against the stage-Irish caricature.[69]

EMMET EVENTS

In nineteenth-century Irish America, the great commemorative Emmet event was his birthday, 4 March. In the later part of the century, many of these observances were the result of combined efforts by local chapters of the United Irish League of America (which was closely allied to the Parliamentary Party in Ireland) and the Ancient Order of Hibernians (the nationally organised voice of middle-class Irish-America). Often there were competing meetings sponsored by Clan na Gael, physical force advocates and inheritors of the mantle of the Fenian Brotherhood in America. These meetings took place all over the United States, in towns and cities both large and small. In the medium-sized Irish community of St Louis, Missouri, for example, were three nationalist organisations – two moderate and one 'radical' – and all marked Emmet's birthday with separate yearly evenings of oratory, recitations, and music.[70]

In March 1884, the Chicago Irish sponsored three different Emmet events, each representing a separate community within the greater whole. Gathering at a downtown Loop venue were the 'Irish Nationalists of Chicago', the established middle-class movers and shakers with ties to the larger Irish-American nationalist movement. They brought in a prestigious New Yorker, Honourable Thomas F. O'Grady, to deliver the formal oration, and a national Trades and Labour Assembly leader also spoke. The master of ceremonies was Alexander Sullivan, noted Chicago lawyer and head of the Clan na Gael's ruling 'Triangle'. The evening's resolutions were signed by the Midwest's Clan directorate, including Sullivan and Dr Patrick Henry Cronin, a popular young physician and social singer. The same evening, 'several hundred' of the working-class South Side Irish honoured Emmet at 'Father Dorney's Hall on Forty-fifth street'. This was the parish hall of St Gabriel's in the stockyards neighbourhood of Canaryville, the home turf of Father

Maurice J. Dorney, beloved as the 'King of the Yards' and a national officer of Clan na Gael. Also on 4 March, Chicago's West Side Irish met under the aegis of 'a secret Irish organisation known as the "ARL"' at the West Twelfth Street Turner Hall. Here were songs in English ('I Dreamt that I Dwelt in Marble Halls') and Irish ('Cushla Gal Machree'); an oration titled 'Half an Hour with Emmet'; recitations of a piece 'Anne Devlin' and 'a most dramatic poem, entitled "Shaun's Head"' by a man 'in the costume of an ancient Gallowglass'; and performance of *Robert Emmet*, 'a drama, written for the occasion', with 'ARL' members playing Emmet, Anne Devlin, Sarah Curran, Miles Dolan, and William Dowdall. 'The drama was well rendered', the report concludes, 'and the celebration closed with a ball'.[71]

Eleven years later this tradition was still going strong, as the 4 March 1895 Emmet Celebration of the 'Irish Nationalists of Chicago' at the Auditorium on Michigan Avenue attracted an audience of 10,000. Thousands more were turned away, according to Finerty's *Citizen*, which declared this to be the largest Irish-American gathering in Chicago since Parnell's visit in 1880. Here, though, was a salient ulterior motive for the crush. The oration was given by Alexander Sullivan, and the event marked his return to public life after the notoriety of his implication in the May 1889 murder of Dr Cronin, whose public accusations that Sullivan had embezzled Clan funds had led to his death.[72] These larger meetings are only part of the story, however. For example, in Chicago from 4 to 17 March in 1903, the Emmet anniversary blended towards St Patrick's Day in neighbourhood events scheduled for at least thirteen parish halls and secular venues scattered all through the city.[73]

The centennial of Emmet's death in September 1903 was also a huge affirming event for Irish-American nationalism. In Philadelphia, 5,000 packed the Grand Opera House on Broad Street and another 5,000 were turned away. In Columbus, Ohio, an estimated 40,000 people from all over the state gathered for a day and evening of activities, including a big parade, three hours of oratory, and a programme of songs during which 'the audience burst into wild demonstrations'.[74] In Boston, the commemoration took place over three days. The *Boston Globe* reported that 'Nearly every club or society whose members believe in mild moral suasion or physical force respecting Ireland and whose meetings fall on Saturday, Sunday, or Monday next, will have a celebration to mark the 100th anniversary of the execution of Robert Emmet.' The two largest gatherings represented the poles of the nationalist debate. Boston's Celtic Club ('advocates of physical force') met at Clan na Gael Hall in South Boston, and the United Irish League met outdoors at the Apollo Garden in Roxbury, where several speakers denounced the Clan and its most visible leader, John Devoy. The United Irish League meeting also featured a speech by Galway MP Charles Devlin, who urged 'every Irish man and every Irish woman to join the league. We fight in the open and we have nothing to conceal, neither in our object nor in our methods.' He cited the recently passed Wyndham Land Purchase Act as evidence of the success of parliamentary means. A third meeting drew an audience of 1,200 to Monument Hall in Charlestown under the auspices of the Ancient Order of Hibernians and the John Boyle O'Reilly Literary Association. At all three of these major gatherings, Irish veterans on the Boer side of the just-ended South African War also spoke.[75]

Moreover, during a ten-day period in late September, the United Irish League orchestrated a series of commemorative parades and observances all over New England. The *Chicago Citizen* reported that 'Boston, Lowell, Pawtucket, Pittsfield, Providence, Worcester, Holyoke and other centers of Irish thought were well to the front in the observance of the centennial', and the Boston papers also mentioned events in Brighton, Somerville, Watertown, Newton, Lynn, Woburn, and Haverhill. Large turnouts were the order of the day. The Quincy meeting was 'packed to the doors'. At the far western corner of Massachusetts in Pittsfield, 1,000 people came, and 2,000 attended in Pawtucket, Rhode Island. Many of these gatherings reflected the American dimension of the ongoing Irish language revival with bi-lingual performances. At the old Franklin School building in the heart of Irish Roxbury, the Boston 'Gaelic School' promised that 'Emmet's speech will be read in Gaelic, and a great many of the best known Fenian songs will be sung in both languages'.[76]

Elsewhere in American cities, the Emmet execution centennial was similarly of great and visible import for the Irish communities. The occasion in Chicago and New York prompts my final example of mixed motives. In Chicago, the United Irish Societies met on Sunday evening, 20 September 1903, at the vast First Regiment Armoury on Michigan Avenue. The major speaker was General Nelson A. Miles, an inexplicably lionised leader of US forces during the 1898 Spanish-American War. Though amazingly bungled, the so-called 'splendid little war' in the Caribbean had lasted less than a month. It was hilarious satire thereof that brought Finley Peter Dunne's 'Mr Dooley' columns to national attention. (For those who may not know him, Dunne wrote weekly columns for the *Chicago Evening Post*, beginning at age 26 in 1893, in the dialect voice of Mr Martin Dooley, an ageing immigrant bartender from the city's South Side.)[77] General Miles had been one of Mr Dooley's favourite targets. He had designed his own uniforms – which puts me in mind of the flight suit worn by US President George Bush when he announced the end of major hostilities in Iraq in May 2003. Miles's uniforms sported considerably more gold braid than the standard issue, and Mr Dooley remarked that they had been shipped down to Florida 'in specyal steel-protected bullyon trains fr'm the mine . . . As soon as he can have his pitchers took, he will cr-rush th' Spanish with wan blow.'[78] On the evening of 20 September 1903, General Miles entered the First Regiment Armoury to great applause and the strains of 'The Star-Spangled Banner', which had been designated the American national anthem one week earlier. His presence and his speech made the connection between the recent 'liberation' of Cuba and the cause of Irish freedom. Tickets were a not inconsiderable 50 cents, and 3,000 attended.[79]

On the same evening in New York City, 6,000 gathered at Carnegie Hall. Here again the Cuban connection was enforced, with an appearance by Tomas Estrada Palma, Jr, the son of the puppet president of Cuba, who had been installed by virtue of a new constitution, dictated by the US government. Palma offered 'my sympathy and that of the Cuban people to the Irish nation in its oppression. I hope some day that Ireland will take its place among the independent nations of the world, along with my own beloved country . . . We hope you will reach the goal we have reached.' Thus was registered among some of the most prominent Irish-American nationalists the first foray of American imperialism outside the continental United States.[80]

CONTEMPORARY CRITIQUES AND CONCLUSION

From within nineteenth-century Irish America came a healthy critique of the misappropriation of the memory of Robert Emmet. This can be verified in literature. In the newly self-critical, proto-realistic fiction that appeared towards the century's end, references to Emmet and other heroes of Irish nationalism are used as satiric counterpoint to American political bravado and venality. An 1888 short story by George Jessop contains this description of a meeting of Irish-American nationalists in San Francisco: 'By 10 o'clock the bottles were almost empty and the cigar smoke had grown so dense that the mild features of Robert Emmet, who stood in all the glory of green uniform and waved a feathered hat exultantly from an engraving above Mr Foley's head, could scarcely be distinguished.'[81] Similarly, in an 1898 novel by William A. McDermott, political and social climber James Fortune founds 'The Shamrock Club', in order 'to discuss the best means of freeing Ireland – and at the same time of holding a grip on New York'.

> This club in a few months became so large that a hall was rented, and despite the protests of James Fortune, their president, who wished to call the hall 'The Sarsfield', was named Fortune Hall. The president graciously submitted, claiming as his privilege the right to decorate the interior in a suitable manner, which was done to their taste. The decorations consisted of green flags, green ribbons, framed pictures of Saint Patrick banishing snakes, Brian Boru in his tent, Sarsfield in battle array, Emmet in a reverie, O'Connell on Tara's hill, framed sentiments, mostly warnings to 'cruel England', that the day of retribution was near at hand, and if she valued her safety she would relax her grip on green Erin.[82]

At the novel's end, James Fortune has capped his political rise (and moral fall) by becoming a congressman with a mansion on Fifth Avenue. He promptly resigns all of his Irish memberships, declares his 'Scotch-Irishness' by joining the St Andrew's Society, and has his son baptised 'Chichester Hartley Fortune' in the Episcopal Church.

The palm in satiric exposure of base elements in the alloy that was Irish-American nationalism goes to the Chicago journalist Finley Peter Dunne. In this, as in so many things about his culture, Mr Dooley was directly on target. Connected here, and similarly refreshing, are his opinions about the immigrant generation's move towards middle-class status. When the drive for respectability comes at the expense of one's neighbours, Mr Dooley exposes it as a creeping disease, one fatal to community. Hypocrisy and pretension were Dunne's meat and potatoes, especially in the 1890s when he was just starting out. Here are examples of Mr Dooley's perspective on some of the ways that his fellow Irish Americans misused Robert Emmet in oratory, the given name, and public events.

Dunne poked gentle fun at the appropriation of Emmet's speech as a Catholic school piece when Mr Dooley relates to a patron in July 1895 that 'I wint up las' night to th' school hall to see Hinnissy's youngest gradjooate'.

> Th' first number on th' program was th' speech that Robert Immitt made whin they was goin' to hang him. 'Tis a warm speech an' Grogan's boy had to say it. He come out lookin' red an' nervous, an' old man Grogan had a front seat an' begun to applaud most uproaryous. That rattled Micky all th' more an' his voice sounded like wan ye'll hear over a tiliphone whin he said, 'Oh, dear an' vinrated shades iv me departed fathers'. He thrun his hands in th' air an' begun snappin' his fingers. 'Mike', whispers Grogan fr'm th' front seat. 'Ye'er mitts', he says. 'Drop ye'er mitts. Mike', he says louder, 'ye'er mitts', he says. 'Drop thim', he says. 'Stop snappin' ye'er fingers', he says. Thin raisin' his voice he bawls, 'Mike, what in th' name iv goodness d'ye think ye'er doin' – defindin' Ireland or shootin' craps?' Th' boy was overcome with emotion an' Mrs Grogan wint home.[83]

There are lots of people in Mr Dooley's Chicago whose parents have named them after Robert Emmet. None lives up to the name, and that is the point. 'Robert Immitt Grogan' starts a fight at a genealogy lecture in the parish hall over whose ancestors were kings and whose were only dukes.[84] 'Robert Immitt Prindygast' becomes an actor and sends word home that he is playing 'Julius Cayzar with Sarrah Bernhardt', but when his company reaches Chicago their venue is a dime museum and Robert 'done th' bearded woman up-stairs an' wan iv th' bloodhounds in "Uncle Tom's Cabin" downstairs'.[85] Dunne satirises the use of heroic Irish names for the purpose of putting on American airs in the memorable Dooley column about the naming of the tenth Hogan baby. 'Be hivins', says Mr Dooley, 'Hogan have growed gray haired an' bald thryin' f'r to inthrodjooce th' name iv Michael or Bridget [his parents] in th' family . . . Th' first wan was a boy an' afther Mrs Hogan had th' polis in 'twas called Sarsfield.' The next eight names are Lucy, Honoria, Veronica, Arthur, Charles Stewart Parnell ('bor-rn durin' the land lague'), Paul, Madge, William Joyce (a South-side Chicago politician), and Aloysius. After a protracted discussion about the merits of Hogan's ancestral line, the tenth child is christened – Augustus.[86]

In many pieces, Dunne's target was the hypocrisy of blowhard Irish nationalists working for selfish American ends. In such cases, his satire turns hard and biting. Two of his best epigrammatic judgments can represent his take on events like the Emmet anniversary commemorations: 'Did ye iver see a man that wanted to free Ireland th' day afther to-morrah that didn't run f'r aldherman soon or late? Most iv th' great pathriotic orators iv th' da-ay is railroad lawyers . . . Most iv th' rale pathriots wurruks f'r th' railroads too – tampin' th' thracks.'[87] And again,

> Be hivins, if Ireland cud be freed be a picnic, it'd not on'y be free to-day, but an impire, begorra, with Tim Haley, th' Banthry man, evictin' Lord Salisb'ry fr'm his houldin'... Whin we wants to smash th' Sassenach an' restore th' land iv th' birth iv some iv us to her thrue place among th' nations, we gives a picnic. 'Tis a dam sight aisier thin goin' over with a slug of joynt powder an' blowin' up a polis station with no wan in it. It costs less; an', whin 'tis done, a man can lep aboord a Clyburn Avnoo ca-ar, an' come to his family an' sleep it off.[88]

The parody of nationalist oratory is pointed when Dorgan, 'the sanyor guarjeen in the Wolfe Tone Lithry Society' exhorts his audience at the annual 15 August picnic of Chicago's United Irish Societies: 'Ar-re ye men, or ar're ye slaves. Will ye set idly by while th' Sassenach has th' counthry iv Immitt an' O'Connell an' Jawn Im Smith undher his heel?'[89] Smith gets into the litany because he was a wealthy Chicago furniture dealer with significant clout.[90] Ultimately, Mr Dooley also marked the centenary of 1798 with pronounced scepticism:

> An' 'twill be th' gran' thing to see all th' good la-ads marchin' down Sackville sthreet singin' 'Who fears to speak iv ninety-eight, who blushes at th' name?' No wan, an' that's th' throuble. If they were afeerd to speak iv it, 'twud be dangerous, an' I'm thinkin' th' more public it is th' less it amounts to.[91]

It is clear that there was plenty to criticise in the long parade of Irish Americans who tried to use ideas of Robert Emmet for their own ends – elitist pseudo-Celticists, social climbers, shameless politicos bellying up to the public trough, mercenary melodramatists. But I do believe that for every one of these there were a hundred Old Ned McDermotts standing before the portrait in the kitchen with their children and grandchildren. I also believe that learning Emmet's speech from the dock put schoolchildren in touch with something thrillingly heroic and larger than their own lives; and that most who named their sons 'Robert Emmet' were giving something they considered solemn and priceless; and that writing a poem about Emmet was an extraordinary, enriching act for a grocer; and that overall, the impact of the plays was an antidote to the music-hall, slapstick comic Irishman; and that most who attended Emmet observances in the parish halls of working-class neighbourhoods saw themselves as bearing witness to a thoroughly ennobling ideal.

The power of the memory of the dead young patriot to instil pride in immigrant generations that had had their share of troubles was in the end unassailable. On balance, I would say of the American idea of Robert Emmet what Marcellus declared of the ghost of Hamlet's father:

> We do it wrong, being so majestical,
> To offer it the show of violence;
> For it is, as the air, invulnerable,
> And our vain blows malicious mockery.

Notes

1 Edward McSorley, *Our Own Kind* (New York, 1946), p. 5.

2 Ibid., pp. 7–8.

3 Ibid., pp. 182–3.

4 Ibid., p. 84.

5 Patrick M. Geoghegan, *Robert Emmet: A Life* (Dublin, 2002), p. 269; George Potter, *To the Golden Door, The Story of the Irish in Ireland and America* (Boston, 1960), p. 216.

6 John E. Fitzgerald, 'Irish oratory: its part in the struggle for freedom', *Boston Evening Record*, 'Irish Number', 28 Jan. 1888, p. 8.

7 George F. O'Dwyer, *The Irish Catholic Genesis of Lowell* (Lowell, 1920), pp. 33–9.

8 Charles Fanning (ed.), *Studs Lonigan: A Trilogy* (Urbana and Chicago, 1993), p. 24.

9 The poem, 'My Work', parodies self-promoting literary blurbs. It appears in *The Drift of Things* (Great Barrington, Mass., 2001), pp. 16–18. Here is the final stanza:

> There is a higher reality at play in my work.
> Sacred memories resonate with perceptual
> knowledge of the body as primal text. Yet
> my work is never subservient to the dominant
> ideology. It circulates warmly and freely
> through all available channels. My work
> is like the furniture you so much want to

sink into, but must wait as it wends its way
from distant points in a giant moving truck
screeching across the country
to your new home.

10 John Brendan Flannery, *The Irish Texans* (San Antonio, 1980), p. 108.

11 The pamphlet, *Speech of Mr Emmet, the Celebrated Irish Patriot, in Defence of Liberty and his Country*, is listed in the *National Union Catalogue of Pre-1956 Imprints* as 'New York [180–?]. 12 pp. Portrait'. The *NUC* is my source for the bibliographic material in this section.

12 The pamphlet with facing page translation was published in New York by Lynch, Cole & Meehan in 1879. See also Kenneth Nilson, 'The Irish language in New York, 1850–1900', in Ronald Bayor and Timothy Meagher (eds), *The New York Irish* (Baltimore and London, 1996), p. 637 n. 43.

13 Charles Phillips, *The Speeches of Charles Phillips*, 5th edn (Saratoga Springs, NY, 1820).

14 T. D., A. M. and D. B. Sullivan (eds), *Speeches from the Dock, or Protests of Irish Patriotism* (Dublin, 1868). 'Twenty-third Dublin edition and First American edition' (Providence, RI, 1878).

15 Solon Nourse and Mrs A. L. Rutor Dufour, *Emmet's Last Words: When Erin Shall Stand 'mid the Isles of the Sea* (New York, 1853).

16 James Jeffrey Roche, *Life of John Boyle O'Reilly Together with His Complete Poems and Speeches* (New York, 1891), pp. 183–4. The Catholic literati who composed poems about Emmet also included Denis A. McCarthy of the *Sacred Heart Review* and several members of Boston's *Pilot* circle, among them Katherine Eleanor Conway and Louise Imogen Guiney.

17 Roche, *Life of John Boyle O'Reilly*, pp. 549–52. Among the secular writers who composed poems about Emmet were Charles Graham Halpine, creator of Civil War comic figure Private Miles O'Reilly and Augustine J. H. Duganne, a colourful, mid-century potboiler novelist who wrote ghost stories, romance novels, poetry, and political tracts in mid-century New York. He was also elected to a term in the New York State Assembly as a Know-Nothing! See Charles Fanning, *The Irish Voice in America*, 2nd edn (Lexington, 2000), pp. 78–9.

18 McNeill's 'Robert Emmet' was in the *Boston Globe*, 19 Sept. 1903. The educated but not literary occasional poets also included New York Judge John Jerome Rooney, who published the poem, 'Robert Emmet. On seeing John Mulvany's portrait of the Irish patriot, now in the possession of Dr. Thomas Addis Emmet', which ends: 'See, how he smites the tyrant's ermined fraud/ With words that crash like volley-thundering ships!' *Catholic World*, 66 (Oct. 1897), pp. 92–3.

19 Pendergast's poem was in his self-published volume of *Selected Gems* (Norwood, MA, 1917), p. 46. Many poems and songs are collected on the very useful 'Robert Emmet Website': www.emmet1803.com. Also, the nineteenth-century anthologies were often organised thematically. See, for example, the sections on 'Patriotism' and 'Heroism' in Daniel Connolly (ed.), *The Household Library of Ireland's Poets, with Full and Choice Selections from the Irish-American Poets* (New York, 1887). For the Irish-American songs, the best source is Robert L. Wright (ed.), *Irish Emigrant Ballads and Songs* (Ohio, 1975).

20 *Forensic Eloquence, Sketches of Trials in Ireland for High Treason, etc.* (Baltimore, 1804). *The History of the Late Grand Insurrection; or, Struggle for Liberty in Ireland, . . . To which Is Added, a Short Account of the Insurrection by Emmet, with His Famous Speech Made to the Court Before Judgment* (Carlisle, 1805).

21 John Doherty, *Life, Trial, and Conversation and Times of Robert Emmet* (New York, 1845, 2nd edn, 1850); R. R. Madden, *Life and Times of Robert Emmet* (New York, 1856, 1857, 1880); Doherty, *Life, Trial, and Conversation* (Boston, 1852); Madden, *Life and Times* (New York, nd). Though I have not seen it and know nothing about the author, the biography published in Charleston may have been the earliest written by an American: John W. Burke, *Life of Robert Emmet, the Celebrated Irish Patriot and Orator, With his Speeches &c.* (Charleston, 1852). The book had at least three editions and also appeared in Philadelphia published by Thomas, Cowperthwaite & Co. in 1852.

22 Dennis O'Sullivan, *Robert Emmet, or True Irish Hearts* (New York, 1880); Varina Anne Davis, *An Irish Knight of the Nineteenth Century* (New York, 1888); Greg Morehead, *Robert Emmet the Irish Patriot, The Romance of His Life* (New York, 1902); Louise Imogene Guiney, *Robert Emmet, A Survey of His Rebellion and of His Romance* (London, 1904).

23 John V. Kelleher, 'Matthew Arnold and the Celtic Revival', in Charles Fanning (ed.), *Selected Writings of John V. Kelleher on Ireland and Irish America* (Carbondale, 2002), pp. 3–23.

24 Fanning, *Irish Voice in America*, pp. 166–7.

25 Despite the appropriateness for the centennial of Emmet's death, the *Atlantic*, bastion of Boston Brahmin taste, had rejected Guiney's Emmet material in essay form in August 1903 There is evidence that even in Oxford the rejection hurt. In one letter, Guiney suggests that she wrote her *Robert Emmet* specifically as a two-part piece for the *Atlantic*, and in another, she deplores her mother's having told friends that 'my orphaned article on Emmet' was causing dismay: 'I have no notion of being quite so helpless as all that! I have the old thing back now, and as soon as I can get time to attend to it, will shoot it at another target.' Guiney to Fred Holland Day, 30 July and 2 Nov. 1903, Grace Guiney (ed.), *Letters of Louise Imogen Guiney* (New York, 1926).

26 Louise Imogene Guiney, *Robert Emmet: A Survey of His Rebellion and of His Romance* (London, 1904), p. 23.

27 Ibid., p. 25.

28 Ibid., p. 92.

29 Ibid., pp. 26–8.

30 Ibid., p. 31.

31 Ibid., p. 55.

32 Ibid., p. 73.

33 Ibid., p. 13.

34 Ibid., pp. 13–14.

35 Ibid., p. 66.

36 Ibid., p. 88.

37 Ibid., p. 11.

38 Ibid., pp. 97–9.

39 Ibid., pp. 100–1.

40 Ibid., pp. 100–2.

41 Fanning, *Irish Voice in America*, p. 167.

42 Yeats gave a famous speech on Robert Emmet in New York City in February 1904 at the end of his first American tour. See R. F. Foster, *W. B. Yeats: A Life, I: The Apprentice Mage 1865–1914* (Oxford and New York, 1997), pp. 312–14.

43 In conversation with me, June 2003.

44 Colin Simkin (ed.), *Currier and Ives' America* (New York, 1952), pp. 2–9.

45 *Currier & Ives, A Catalogue Raisonné* (Detroit, 1984), II, p. 578; I, p. 194.

46 The Gies and Kirwan images can be seen in the Prints and Photographs Division at the Library of Congress. The lantern slides and cigar box can be seen at the 'Robert Emmet Website'. On the Fenian bonds, see Carl Wittke, *The Irish in America* (Baton Rouge, 1956), p. 155. A $20 bond dated 1866 and one of the 1880 plates were in the Robert Emmet Bicentennial Exhibition at Kilmainham Jail in September 2003.

47 The Emmetsburg statue can be seen at www.eyeoniowa.com/stpats/archives.

48 Potter, *To the Golden Door*, p. 216.

49 Alice McDermott, *Child of My Heart* (New York, 2002), pp. 28–9.

50 Michael Glazier (ed.), *The Encyclopedia of the Irish in America* (Notre Dame, IN, 1999), p. 414.

51 Leo R. Ward, *Holding Up the Hills* (New York, 1941).

52 Michael F. Funchion (ed.), *Irish American Voluntary Organizations* (Westport, Conn., 1983), pp. 101–5.

53 Lawrence J. McCaffrey, 'Preserving the Union', in Ellen Skerrett (ed.), *At the Crossroads, Old Saint Patrick's and the Chicago Irish* (Chicago, 1997), p. 56. Emmet's name was popular throughout the century in Chicago. From its first division of 300 members on the West Side in 1872, Chicago's Ancient Order of Hibernians had grown to 7,000 members just ten years later, with a division in every Irish parish in the city. The AOH celebrated its expansion by building a central meeting place, Robert Emmet Memorial Hall, at Ogden and Leavitt Streets. *Diamond Jubilee Book* (Chicago, 1942), pp. 789–90.

54 Wittke, *The Irish in America*, p. 117.

55 David M. Emmons, *The Butte Irish* (Urbana and Chicago, 1989), pp. 17, 21, 108–10, 406–7.

56 The earliest published version I have seen is listed as 'Spencer's Boston Theatre, No. CXXIII' (Boston, 1857). This edition contains the casts for four productions of the play: New York (1853), Philadelphia (1854), New York (1854), and Boston (1856). My thanks to Joyce Flynn for sending me this book. The Townsend revision appears as *Robert Emmet, The Martyr of Irish Liberty, A Historical Drama in Three Acts*, by James Pilgrim, revised by Charles Townsend (New York, 1903). An earlier condensation by the Reverend Louis Griffa was published in Oswego, New York, in 1879, with a second edition in 1882.

57 Allardyce Nicoll and F. Theodore Cloak (eds), *Forbidden Fruit and Other Plays* by Dion Boucicault (Princeton, 1940), pp. 263–4. An early essay on the Boucicault play and the twentieth-century Irish Emmet plays of Conal O'Riordan, Lenox Robinson, and Denis Johnston is Harold Ferrar, 'Robert Emmet in Irish drama', *Eire-Ireland* I: 2 (1966), pp. 19–28.

58 Joseph I. C. Clarke, *Robert Emmet, A Tragedy of Irish History* (New York and London, 1888).

59 B. M. O'Boylan, *The Rebels; or, The Irish Insurgent Chiefs of 1803, An Historical Drama in Five Acts* (Newark, Ohio, 1894). A second edition appeared in 1907.

60 The Sherman Collection consists of 4,000 play scripts, the holdings of the Chicago Manuscript Company, a printing business that sold and rented scripts to theatre companies in the United States in the late nineteenth century.

61 In his preface, Clarke thanks 'Dr Thomas Addis Emmet, of this city, a grand-nephew of Robert Emmet, for the kindness with which he allowed a thorough examination of the rare collection of family documents, illustrations, and priceless relics which he has gathered and which he treasures with such loving care', p. vi.

62 O'Boylan, 'Preface', p. 3.

63 The song ends:

> For the spirit of Justice and Truth shall inspire
> The hearts and the minds lit by Liberty's fire;
> And although for a season enthralled they may be
> Still, still shall they break every chain and be free! (p. 48)

Not only is there dancing in this play, but, in keeping with his stated aim of refuting the stage-Irish stereotype, O'Boylan also includes instruction that 'This dance is to be conducted with merriment, but with that modesty and decorum that are always to be found among the cheerful and modest peasants of Ireland. The vulgar Irishman, as he is represented too often on the stage, has no existence among the peasants of Ireland, and, I trust, he will never be introduced into this play on any stage'. Furthermore, 'Statistics prove that Ireland stands to-day at the head of the list in Europe for morality, and in point of education it has a larger percentage of pupils attending school than any branch of the English speaking people. See US statistics for 1887–88' (pp. 15–16). This last date suggests that O'Boylan's play may have been performed well before its publication in 1894.

64 In the Chicago premiere the part was played by Dion Boucicault, Jr, whose last words led to a freeze-frame 'Tableau': 'I ax your pardon for dyin' like this, and thrubblin' you all. Kiss me, Mike! I believe I – am goin' now! 'Tis asier than I thought! [Dies]'.

65 The reviewer concludes that 'The author has fitted himself with a role which can never be very popular because Michael Dwyer's cold-blooded killing of the traitor, although justifiable, is in no degree inspiring'. *Chicago Tribune*, 9 Nov. 1884, p. 11.

66 Finerty calls on Irish Americans to demand more honest dramatic representation: 'The Kippeen and the bottle, the tattered coat, the caubeen and the dudeen must be banished from the stage as national characteristics. Hiss the actor that vulgarly and ignorantly presents either . . . The traditional and conventional stage Irishman must be driven from the stage, if it takes murder to do it'. *Chicago Citizen*, 8 Mar. 1884, p. 4. See also Finerty's later denunciation of Boucicault, *Chicago Citizen*, 12 Nov. 1887, p. 4.

67 *Chicago Citizen*, 13 June 1903. The Emmet play *Sherman B* discussed earlier may be a pirated version of Tynan's play, as both contain a character called 'Noonan' who is the traitor.

68 Small group productions included the following: *Robert Emmet*, performed by the Thalian Dramatic Combination Company in Wilmington, North Carolina, in July 1875. *Robert Emmet, an historical, spectacular, musical, military and allegorical drama* in three acts, by T. H. O'Brien with music by J. G. Rampone, performed in Troy, New York, in 1877. An Emmet play performed for St Patrick's Day of 1877 and again in 1878 at the University of Notre Dame in Indiana. John C. Monaghan's *Emmet, or the Hero of 1803* in Providence, Rhode Island, in 1879. Jessie Adele Cole's *Robert Emmet*, performed in Denver, Colorado, in 1884. Also that year, an Emmet play in German by Carl von Heckel in Milwaukee. *Robert Emmet, the Last of the United Irishmen*, by W. J. McKiernan in Newark, New Jersey, in 1902. An Emmet play in repertory from June through October of 1904 at the Burbank Theatre Stock Company near Los Angeles. Another by Harry Davis's Stock Company in Pittsburgh, Pennsylvania, in November 1904. One by Philadelphia's Forepaugh Stock Company and one by Jessie Shirley's Stock Company in Spokane, Washington, during the 1905–6 season. See *Dramatic Compositions Copyrighted in the United States, 1870–1916* (Washington, 1918), II, pp. 1995–6, *passim*, and Weldon B. Durham (ed.), *American Theatre Companies, 1888 1930* (New York, 1987), pp. 70, 110,177, 410. Some also are listed under 'Dramas' on the 'Robert Emmet Website'.

69 St Louis *Post-Dispatch*, 26 Nov. 1905. See Margaret Sullivan, 'The Irish in St Louis' (PhD thesis, St Louis University, 1968), p. 104.

70 Sullivan, 'The Irish in St Louis', *passim.* Chicago's John Finerty reported having spoken at March 1893 Emmet birthday celebrations in Lowell and Lynn, Massachusetts, and Pawtucket, Rhode Island. *Chicago Citizen*, 4 Mar. 1893. San Francisco Mayor James Duval Phelan had his 1899 speech published as *Robert Emmet's Birthday: Address Delivered at Metropolitan Temple, March 4th, 1899 Under the Auspices of the Knights of the Red Branch, in Aid of the Wolfe Tone Monument Fund* (San Francisco, 1899).

71 Thomas N. Brown, *Irish-American Nationalism, 1870–1890* (Philadelphia, 1966), pp. 155–6. *Chicago Citizen*, 8 Mar. 1884, p. 5.

72 *Chicago Citizen*, 9 Mar. 1895. On the Cronin case, see Charles Fanning, *Finley Peter Dunne and Mr Dooley, The Chicago Years* (Lexington, 1978), pp. 152–4.

73 Among these were church halls at Holy Cross, St Rose of Lima, Holy Name, St Stephen's, and St Columkill's parishes, as well as meeting rooms at 37th and Halsted, 40th and Cottage Grove, 12th and Kedzie, 12th and Blue Island, Taylor and Robie, Clybourn and South Park, the Stockyards district, and South Chicago. *Chicago Citizen*, 28 Feb. 1903, p. 1.

74 *Chicago Citizen*, 3 Oct. 1903. Wittke, *The Irish in America*, p. 198.

75 *Boston Globe*, 17, 19, 20, 21, Sept. 1903.

76 *Chicago Citizen*, 3 Oct. 1903. *Boston Globe*, 17, 19, 20, 21, Sept. 1903.

77 See Charles Fanning, *Finley Peter Dunne and Mr Dooley* and Fanning (ed.), *Mr Dooley and the Chicago Irish: The Autobiography of a Nineteenth-Century Ethnic Group* (Washington, 1987).

78 From a Dooley piece of 4 June 1898, quoted in Fanning, *Finley Peter Dunne and Mr Dooley*, p. 198. Miles's previous claim to fame had been his capture of Apache chief Geronimo in 1885. When Miles took over this mission, decreeing a 'hunt and destroy' policy, there were only 33 hostile Apaches left in Geronimo's band, and 13 of them were women. It took Miles's 2,000

soldiers five months to find them and negotiate a surrender. See James L. Roark, et al., *The American Promise: A History of the United States*, 2nd edn (Boston, 2002), II, p. 595.

79 *Chicago Citizen*, 12, 26, Sept. 1903.

80 This meeting had been organised by the United Irish League. True to form, the Clan na Gael ran a competing event on the same evening at the Academy of Music on 14th Street. The following year, the same Clan leaders persuaded W. B. Yeats to deliver his famous New York speech on Robert Emmet. Again the venue was the Academy of Music. *New York Tribune*, 21 Sept. 1903. *Chicago Tribune*, 21 Sept. 1903.

81 George H. Jessop, 'The rise and fall of the Irish aigle', *Century Magazine* 15; (Dec. 1888). Reprinted in Charles Fanning (ed.), *The Exiles of Erin: Nineteenth-Century Irish-American Fiction*, 2nd edn (Chester Springs, PA, 1997), p. 192.

82 William A. McDermott, *Père Monnier's Ward. A Novel* (New York and Cincinnati, 1898), in Fanning (ed.), *The Exiles of Erin*, pp. 225–6.

83 In Fanning (ed.), *Mr Dooley and the Chicago Irish*, pp. 50–1. Hereinafter cited in the text.

84 Ibid., pp. 60–1.

85 Ibid., p. 279.

86 Ibid., pp. 137–9.

87 Not anthologised, the column in which this quotation appears was in the *Chicago Evening Post*, 17 Aug. 1895.

88 In Fanning (ed.), *Mr Dooley and the Chicago Irish*, p. 286.

89 Ibid., p. 287.

90 Similarly, Mr Dooley quotes a speech from Clan na Gael member McGuire, 'th' mos'rarin', tarin' dinnymiter that iver lived', as follows: 'Will ye sit idly here with ye'er hands in ye'er pockets while th' craven flag iv th' Sassenach floats o'er th' green land, . . . Or will ye ray-mimber O'Donnell an' O'Neill iv th' r-red hand, an' Sarsfield an' Immit an' Meagher an' Wolf Tone an' John Mitchel an' sthrike wan blow f'r freedom?' Ibid., p. 266. The column ends with McGuire refusing to pay an assessment of five dollars to help the cause. He quits the Clan and joins 'th' peace movement'.

91 Ibid., p. 323.

CHAPTER 8

Prophecy and posterity

Robert Emmet in America

Patrick M. Geoghegan

The novelist William Dean Howells once asserted that 'what the American public always wants is a tragedy with a happy ending'.[1] The story of Robert Emmet, like many other struggles in Irish history, was a tragedy with an unhappy ending, and thus seemed unsuited to remembrance in the United States. And yet, the way in which the story was reinvented and reimagined in the late-nineteenth and twentieth centuries transformed it into an acceptable American legend. Emmet's rebellion was a failure, but his heroic death and sacrifice enabled the creation of a mythology which allowed for its own happy ending. Central to this was the belief that Emmet had triumphed through the transformative powers of death. For example, when speaking in 1903 at the commemorative dinner for Emmet's birthday (it was also the centenary of his death), John W. Goff insisted that 'Emmet did not die in vain. He was more powerful in death than in life. The principle for which he gave his young life has been handed down to us in all its purity.'[2] But when it came to defining this principle there was a notable disconnection between the different interpretations presented in the United States. Many people, from Oscar Wilde to Woodrow Wilson, were happy to speak about Emmet, but the principles they honoured were often unrecognisable. People were quick to appropriate Emmet for their own agenda: using 'the memory of a past innocency to project a future of higher virtue'.[3] What the interpretations shared was an understanding that Emmet's lasting victory was the spirit he bequeathed to the Irish nation and the world. As Goff explained when discussing the speech from the dock, 'the scene of his action became the arena of human conduct for human liberty. His voice was prophecy, his audience posterity. His tones were not sad with lamentations, but vibrant with hope'.[4]

OSCAR WILDE AND THE DAUGHTER OF THE CONFEDERACY

The way in which Robert Emmet was remembered in the United States often reflected the political certainties of the day. Emmet's birthday, 4 March, was celebrated annually and it served as a kind of rehearsal for St Patrick's Day by Irish-American groups, as well as an opportunity to champion current political beliefs. But the fact that Emmet had failed made things awkward, and a recurring theme was to challenge the definition of success. Twenty cities in the United States held Emmet events in 1882, the year Oscar Wilde was visiting on his speaking tour. In Racine, Wisconsin, the oration was delivered by William Kennedy of Appleton who directly addressed the question of whether Emmet was a failure. He explained to his audience that 'Success in life has a double meaning, and in its higher and nobler and better sense, Emmet's life was a pre-eminent success.'[5] The next day, Oscar Wilde arrived at the capital of Wisconsin, and expressed his disappointment that he had missed the Emmet event. Indeed, he revealed to reporters that he would have cancelled his own lecture in Racine – which in any case had been an embarrassing flop – to have attended the commemoration.[6] He also noted with pride that when he had spoken in Cincinnati he had taken the time to visit a kinsman of Robert Emmet.[7] To a certain extent Wilde was playing to his audience, he regularly overdid the flattery on his American tour, and was mocked for it in a popular song which included the lines 'Oscar dear, how utterly, flutterly, utter you are.'[8] But there was also a genuine element to his focus on Emmet. Wilde found failure fascinating – it was considerably more entertaining than success – and Emmet fitted neatly into his mission on his American tour, which was to champion the cause of failure. As he later explained in New Orleans, 'The head must approve the success of the winners, but the heart is sure to be with the fallen.'[9] When touring the south he consistently expressed his admiration for the defeated Confederacy, drawing parallels between its struggle and Irish history. To much applause he declared in New Orleans that: 'the case of the South in the Civil War was to my mind much like that of Ireland today. It was a struggle for autonomy, self-government for a people.'[10] He also proclaimed that the only man he wanted to meet on his travels was Jefferson Davis. He finally got his wish, when he was invited to Beauvoir, Mississippi, on 27 June 1882 to meet the former Confederate president. It was, as one newspaper reported, 'like a butterfly making a formal visit to an eagle'.[11] Apparently the meeting did not go well. Jefferson Davis pleaded a slight illness and went to bed early; it was later reported that he had found 'something "indefinably objectionable" about Wilde's personality'.[12] But Wilde did make an impression on Davis's youngest daughter, Varina Anne, known as 'Winnie', who would later be heralded as 'the Daughter of the Confederacy'. The 18-year-old Winnie was enchanted by the visitor, and was charmed 'beyond words' by his powers as a conversationalist. The talk, almost inevitably, turned to Irish history. The next day Wilde left a signed photograph of himself for his host, inscribed 'To Jefferson Davis in all loyal admiration from Oscar Wilde'. According to one source, Davis merely grunted 'I did not like the man' but refused to elaborate.[13] Wilde returned to his tour, and continued with his theme of linking the Confederacy to the cause of Ireland. He declared that it had been a great pleasure to meet 'the leader of such a great cause. Because although there may be a failure in fact, in idea there is no failure possible. The principles for which Mr Davis and the south went to war cannot suffer defeat.'[14] In private Wilde was more revealing in his comments, and he slyly noted 'how fascinating all failures are!'[15]

Perhaps influenced by Wilde, Winnie began to see the story of Ireland through the prism of the defeated Confederacy. And she believed that the figure who most epitomised the principles of heroic struggle and tragic glory was Robert Emmet. This interest developed into a paper on Emmet, which was published in 1888 as *An Irish Knight of the Nineteenth Century*. It sold for 25 cents and ran to three editions, making Winnie $300 in royalties. Bought by many of the Irish societies, it is credited with reviving interest in Emmet.[16] It may seem strange that the youngest daughter of the Confederate president should choose to write a biography of Emmet, but in many ways it was an obvious choice. Emmet's life was perfectly suited to reinvention; and just as Wilde had linked Ireland and the Confederacy, in her mind too the causes were inextricably connected. There was also a family interest. Her maternal great grandfather, James Kempe, had taken part in the rebellion of 1803 and claimed to have known Emmet personally. Winnie would soon become a shining symbol of the Lost Cause, the mythology adopted by the south after the end of the Civil War, as it struggled to come to terms with the trauma of defeat. Put simply, the Lost Cause allowed the southerners to 'cope with the cultural implications' of failure.[17] This thinking coloured Oscar Wilde's perceptions of the defeated south, and it also defined how Winnie Davis viewed the defeated Emmet.

It is very easy to dismiss the book out of hand. There are numerous factual errors and the introductory section on Irish history is laughable. Davis does not even give Emmet's date of birth correctly: she is out by four years.[18] But the book has some value as evidence of the attempts to create a Lost Cause mythology for Ireland, following Wilde's lead in linking the two together. Printed in New York by the John W. Lovell Company, the book began with a note from the publisher informing the reader that Robert Emmet's story 'was also the history of Ireland'. After providing an overview of this history, Davis sketched the early life of Emmet, a 'strange, knightly child, who met the probability of death with the same utter fearlessness which formed so marked a characteristic of his after life'.[19] Davis failed miserably to understand Emmet's character, but she did succeed in providing the rebellion of 1803 with an elegant epitaph: 'So ended the rebellion of July, born of a patriot's brain, nursed in a patriot's heart, and baptised in patriot blood.'[20]

As a child, Winnie had grown up with stories of the heroism of the Confederate cause. At the age of 15, while at school in Germany, she received a letter from her mother about the publication of the first volume of Jefferson Davis's *The Rise and Fall of the Confederate Government*, a canonical text in the Lost Cause mythology. Her mother explained that it was 'a splendid but heartbreaking record of cherished hopes now blasted, brave warriors bleeding and dying, and noble men living, yet dead, in that they are hopeless'.[21] This was powerful language, and very similar to the imagery and sentiments that her daughter would use in her biography of Emmet. Winnie ended her account discussing how 'Ireland's true knight' sunk into the 'grave clothed in all the bright promise of his youth . . . never to feel the hopelessness of those who live to see the principles for which they have suffered trampled and forgotten by the onward march of new interests and new men'.[22] Central to the Lost Cause was the concept of heroic sacrifice, of one man suffering Christ-like for the sake of his people. This was how Winnie viewed her father, the hero who had been 'manacled for us' according to the post-war Confederate propaganda. It also shaped how she viewed Robert Emmet. In her conclusion she made a statement on the course of every revolution in which she speculated that perhaps there must always be 'some sacrifice to fill the ravenous jaws of watchful tyranny before the new liberated people can march forward to the fruition of their hopes'.[23] For the Confederacy this figure was her father, for Ireland this figure was Emmet.[24] Winnie even ended the book with a verse about causes lost:

> Oh not for idle hatred, not for honour, fame, nor self-applause,
> But for the glory of the cause
> You did what will not be forgot.[25]

The success of Davis's book proved Wilde's dictum that the Americans were great hero-worshippers, even though Wilde had insisted that all their heroes were drawn from the criminal classes.[26]

ROBERT EMMET IN AMERICA

It soon became evident that the problem with Robert Emmet in America was not that he would be forgotten, but that there was no agreement about how he should be remembered. Too often his principles were hijacked by politicians attempting to make their own point. At the New York Emmet commemoration in 1884, former American senator, Thomas C. E. Eccleston, urged the

Irish-American community to bring about a war between the United States and Britain 'as soon as possible'. A year later, in 1885, the key speaker at the event was the Rev. George W. Pepper who urged the creation of an Irish republic with Parnell as its president, but crucially one not ruled by the Catholics. He explained that 'Emmet was an Episcopalian; Parnell is an Episcopalian, and John Bull is a (word deleted) hyena.'

The links with American history were often made explicit. General D. F. Burke delivered the oration at the 125th anniversary of Emmet's birth and declaimed that, 'the two greatest martyrs to civil liberty of the nineteenth century were Emmet in Ireland and Abraham Lincoln in America'. The happy ending to Emmet's tragedy was provided by the fact that 'his judicial murder was but the handwriting on the wall, a notice to the government under which he was executed that the liberty and justice he sought for his country would be ultimately won'. The outbreak of the Boer War created a wave of sympathy among the Irish-American community. The Emmet commemorations in 1900 and 1901 were notable for the decorations on stage of flags from the Transvaal and Orange Free State alongside those of the United States and Ireland. The meeting in 1900 also saw expressions of support for Cuba, which had been liberated from Spanish rule after the war of 1898. The chairman of the commemoration committee, John W. Goff, explained that liberty was the creed of Emmet, and it was also the creed of the United States. The main speaker was W. Bourke Cockran, the so-called 'Demosthenes' of the Irish-American community, who insisted that 'Emmet's life was a struggle for freedom, and freedom is justice'. In 1903, for the centenary of Emmet's death, Cockran refused to speak at an event in Carnegie Hall because of the prominence being given to Irish politicians who supported Home Rule. Instead he attended the rival event, organised by Clan na Gael, at the Academy of Music. Occasionally, Emmet's name was enlisted for incendiary causes. In 1901 the Limerick mayor, John Daly, spoke in New York where he said that the 'only hope for Ireland is the burning of London'. Although he declined to take on the job himself, because 'it is too big a one', he said he would not try to stop someone who attempted it.[27]

Perhaps the nationalist most anxious to incorporate Emmet's image into his own agenda was John Devoy, the leader of Clan na Gael. Every March his newspaper, the *Gaelic American*, gave extensive coverage to the Emmet commemorations nationally, and sometimes even dedicated entire issues in his honour. But for all of the energy that Devoy expended in commemorating Emmet, it was quite clear that he was interested only in Emmet as a symbol. His speeches rarely touched on the historical figure, preferring to interpret his legacy for a modern audience. Devoy believed that Emmet was the 'political patron saint' of the Irish diaspora, and he championed the speech from the dock for it was 'Emmet's last will and testament' to the Irish people.[28] The annual celebration of Emmet's birthday was taken by Devoy as a statement of support for republican principles and a promise to 'carry out the terms of his legacy'. For Devoy this legacy was a commitment to establish an independent Ireland, with anything less than this (like Home Rule for example) a 'desecration of his memory'. Devoy had little interest in the details of Emmet's life, but was keen to use Emmet as the vehicle for his own ambitions. Nor did he like to dwell on the fact that Emmet had failed; he preferred to look to the future and how his cause might triumph, and he admitted that otherwise celebrating his life would 'be meaningless and without significance'.[29]

At the Emmet commemoration in New York in 1915 the German flag flew alongside the Irish and American flags, and 'Deutschland über Alles' was played.[30] The use of Emmet to express support for Germany in the war reached its climax in March 1916. Jeremiah O'Leary delivered a thundering address in Philadelphia in which he proclaimed his pride in his American citizenship, and insisted that Rousseau was an American, Lord Byron was an American, Christ was an American, and Robert Emmet was an American.[31] Ironically he excluded from American citizenship the only genuine American on his list, J. P. Morgan, because he was a capitalist – he 'places the dollar before the man'. But this was not the extent of O'Leary's extravagant claims. He insisted that Germany's U-boat campaign should be attributed to Emmet, because 'the submarine is an American idea perfected by an Irishman inspired by Robert Emmet to destroy the naval power of England'.

The most damaging episode in Anglo-American relations during the war occurred shortly after with the execution of the Easter 1916 leaders, and in particular the sentencing to death of Roger Casement. Irish-American opinion had been divided about the merits of the 1916 Rising but, as in Ireland, the letting of blood changed everything.[32] Anxious about the effect on American public opinion, the British foreign secretary, Sir Edward Grey, urged placing Casement in a lunatic asylum, otherwise he would be hailed as the 'new Robert Emmet'. This was not the first time Casement and Emmet had been compared. In 1914 when Casement visited Philadephia he was greeted by a deputation which christened him 'Robert Emmet'. He was stunned to find that 'The Irish here would make me into a demi-God if I let them . . . they are mad for a Protestant leader.'[33] On 4 March 1916, while waiting in Germany to sail for Ireland, Casement was sent a copy of the speech from the dock. 'Alas', he said, 'I know it far too well.'[34] The execution of Casement fractured President Woodrow Wilson's relationship with the Irish-American community in a difficult election year. And although Wilson won re-election in the autumn of 1916 he never forgave the Irish-American community for what he perceived (incorrectly) as their desertion in the election. Attempts were made to mend the relationship in 1917 and 1918, and the symbol who was enlisted in this cause was none other than Robert Emmet.

WOODROW WILSON AND THE APOTHEOSIS OF PRINCIPLE

On 28 June 1917 Wilson attended the dedication of a Robert Emmet statue at the New National Museum (the Smithsonian) in Washington DC.[35] The statue, which was draped in an American flag and an 'ancient Gaelic' flag, was presented by Judge Victor Dowling of New York who made a poignant speech in which he praised America, 'the land from which Emmet took his inspiration'.[36] This was also a time for propaganda. Dowling declared that if Emmet were alive today he would be supporting the United States in the war it had entered 'to make the world safe for democracy'. And he called upon all those who revered the memory of Emmet to do their duty and cherish 'the principles for which he died'. To conclude the ceremony, the Irish tenor, John McCormack, sang 'She is far from the land', 'Oh breathe not his name', and the American national anthem.

A monument to Robert Emmet in the United States was something that had been long desired by Irish-Americans, and a couple of months after the unveiling in August 1917, John Denis Joseph Moore, the secretary of the Friends of Irish Freedom, wrote to Wilson commending him for his wartime leadership of the United States, and especially his support for the 'rights of small nations'. Referring to his presence at the dedication of the Emmet statue, Moore declared that it was 'an act on your part that we feel indicates your devotion to Emmett's [*sic*] principles and your sympathy for the revolutionary effort he made to establish them'.[37] Moore then drew parallels between Roger Casement and Patrick Pearse in the pantheon of Irish heroes, and George Washington 'and the patriots of "76"'. This was an attempt to mend Wilson's relationship with the Irish-American community which had become fractured in 1916, an election year, first by his perceived unwillingness to act on behalf of Casement, and then by his constant attacks on the hyphenates, those Americans who 'need hyphens in their names, because only part of them has come over'.[38] As the election drew near, on 29 September 1916 Jeremiah O'Leary even sent Wilson a telegram in which he accused him of 'truckling to the British empire'.[39] Enraged, Wilson sent an intemperate reply without consulting any of his advisers, expressing his delight that O'Leary would not be voting for him and asking him to convey this message to all the 'many disloyal Americans', as O'Leary had access to them and he had not. John Devoy's newspaper, the *Gaelic American*, promptly declared that this message was 'an expression of hatred for the Irish'. In the event, on polling-day Irish-Americans voted for Wilson in great numbers,[40] and it seems that ultimately Irish-Americans 'responded to American issues and not those of Ireland'.[41] But because Wilson did not win a single state that contained a large Irish-American population, he never forgave the community for its perceived desertion and blamed it for the narrowness of his victory. In reality, only certain sections of the Irish-American leadership had defected, while the rank-and-file, by-and-large, had remained loyal. But neither Wilson, nor these Irish-American leaders, recognised this. At the time of the Versailles negotiations, Devoy was impudent enough to run an editorial in which he declared that if Wilson left Ireland out of the settlement, 'he will never live long enough to live it down'.[42] Perhaps it is no wonder that Wilson later acknowledged that by raising the hopes of millions without understanding the complexities of the matter, he had created a 'great metaphysical tragedy'.[43]

It is interesting, given Wilson's open hostility to hyphenates in the 1916 general election, that the publicity for the Emmet statue in 1917 consistently emphasised how unambiguously American it was. Even though the sculptor, Jerome Connor, was Irish born, it was noted explicitly that he was an American citizen, and that the replica and original statue had been 'cast from American standard bronze at the Washington Navy Yard, and all material and labour on the finished product are of American origin and citizenry'.[44]

Wilson did not speak at the unveiling of the statue, much to the disappointment of John Devoy who had urged him to take it upon himself to 'direct the writing' of Emmet's epitaph.[45] But seven months later, Wilson was presented with a small bronze replica of the statue at a special presentation in the White House, and when he was called upon to speak he delivered an important oration on the Irish patriot. Wilson was not unfamiliar with the story of Robert Emmet. He had listened to speeches about him in 1909, at a time when he was developing his ideas on the question of American identity. On 17 March 1909, in his final year as president of Princeton University, Wilson was the guest of honour at the annual dinner of the Society of the Friendly Sons of St Patrick, held at Delmonico's restaurant in New York.[46] The president of the society was William Temple Emmet, a prominent lawyer and grandson of Thomas Addis Emmet. There were seven speeches during the evening, and the ghost of Robert Emmet was regularly saluted as one of the 'great self-sacrificing Irishmen' who had a claim on being remembered.[47] Archbishop Glennon of St Louis delivered one of the key orations and he spoke eloquently about Emmet as one of those 'dreamers who offered up his young life upon the altar of liberty' so that Ireland might be free.[48] During the evening Wilson was in jovial form, and in his after-dinner remarks he began by declaring that he was 'happy to believe that there runs in my veins a very considerable strain of Irish blood'.[49] He then added, to much laughter, that he could not 'prove it from documents' but that he had 'internal evidence'. Wilson's father, a Presbyterian minister, had emigrated from Ulster, and Wilson had inherited many of his attitudes from him.

Despite his Irish background, Wilson visited Ireland only once. This was in the summer of 1899, when he was 42 years old and a professor of jurisprudence and political economy in Princeton. It had not been an unqualified success and he considered the Dublin part of his Irish adventure 'a great fiasco'.[50] He had arrived in Dublin just in time for the annual horse show, which he was told was 'the greatest horse show in the world'. But unfortunately all the hotel rooms were booked and instead he boarded a train for Drogheda, even though he admitted he did not 'yet know exactly where Drogheda is!' Before he left the capital he did a quick tour of the most important locations, including Dublin Castle, the old parliament buildings, and everything that he 'could think of as worth seeing'. As a university man, he was particularly excited to visit Trinity College. It was a Sunday and the gates were open, and he spent a half an hour wandering around the grounds with his 'thoughts full of Burke'.[51] Wilson was always a difficult man to please and he was not impressed with the buildings which he considered 'dignified and spacious', but not 'beautiful'. The problem was that he associated them with the formal style of Sir Christopher Wren, 'Greek, pseudo-Greek, or whatever it is'. However, he was struck by 'the magnitude of the college', and was particularly impressed with the 'striking' statues of Burke and Goldsmith at the front, and also the 'open space which the college faces . . . [where] there is an uncommonly fine statue of Grattan'. Apart from these delights, the city held little joy for Wilson. In fact, he thought Dublin was 'singularly unattractive, plebeian, without distinction, except', he was quick to add, that it must also be, from what he had seen, 'one of the dirtiest cities in the world'.[52]

Ten years later, Wilson put his memory of the visit to good use in his St Patrick's Day speech. Wisely avoiding any negative comment on the capital city, he moved quickly to address the question of race and identity. The genesis of Wilsonism was also contained in the speech. To much applause he argued that the time had come 'to think in terms of the world, and not in terms of America'.[53] This did not involve showing the world 'the way to material success'. Rather, it involved discovering the means 'for translating our material force into moral force' so that the people might 'recover the traditions and the glories of American history'. In his peroration, Wilson linked his vision of America's role in the world with the Irish heroes who were being celebrated that night. He asked: 'what sort of men ought we to be if America is to be a country in which subsequent generations will remember us in the way in which we are remembering great self-sacrificing Irishmen tonight?'[54] For, he said, even though the Irishmen who were being celebrated had been defeated, 'yet there was a triumph in their defeat which makes them great in our eyes'. And the image of Robert Emmet was included in his follow-up remark that certain 'men went down to their graves in sorrow to be resurrected in the hearts of their fellow-countrymen on evenings like this'. The previous speeches had touched upon Emmet's sacrifice and Wilson neatly combined this to telling effect in his final comments:

> The dreams that we have heard tonight were not dreams of personal success; they were dreams of the apotheosis of principle; they were the dreams of men who were willing themselves to be forgotten provided the great ideals which they had sought to embody in their lives might inform the minds and invigorate the generations that followed them.

This powerful tribute to the 'apotheosis of principle' drew great applause from the gathering. And more than any other figure from the Irish past, Emmet epitomised this spirit, and provided 'the great ideals'. As president, Wilson never wavered in his attitude about what it meant to be 'a true citizen of America'. Nor did he lose his determination to lead America on to 'a stage of international responsibility'.[55] But on the subject of the 'great ideals' of noble Irishmen which would never forgotten, in the White House Wilson fell victim to a form of amnesia. In 1909 he had proudly declared the necessity of celebrating not the 'victories of the mind, but the victories of the heart'.[56] He had even claimed that certain great men would prefer to be forgotten, once their ideals were remembered. But, after the entry of the United States on the side of Britain in the First World War, Wilson was less inclined to resurrect these principles when it came to Irish rebels, and he preferred to remember the person and not the ideals. This was particularly evident in 1918 when he was called upon to deliver his speech about Robert Emmet.

The occasion was the presentation of a small bronze replica of the Emmet statue to Wilson by some Irish-American supporters.[57] On 10 January 1918 a special ceremony took place in the White House where Wilson was presented with the replica of the Emmet statue.[58] Judge Dowling had intended to give the speech but he was unavoidably delayed. In his place, Irish-American Senator James Phelan made the presentation, but his lack of preparation proved disastrous and in a relatively short speech he made a number of ill-judged comments about Ireland securing her independence. Phelan began well, with an arresting opening sentence: 'Robert Emmet was a poor potter, and he died for his country.'[59] But his speech went all downhill from there, as he made the extravagant claim that he was not just presenting the president with the 'image of an Irish rebel', rather he was presenting him with 'the representative of a nation, in rebellion against the oppression which has been put upon them for centuries'. The very next sentence contained the most offence. In his naïveté, Phelan declared that he did not think it was 'inappropriate here to say, from my knowledge of history, that no greater indignity, no more atrocious acts, have ever been committed against a people as have been committed against the people of Ireland'. This was stirring stuff, and although Phelan admitted that 'this is all back in the past', he did so only in the certainty that the future would be different for Ireland.

Horrifed by these comments, Wilson could barely conceal his anger, and was afterwards shaking with rage. At a cabinet meeting the next day he was still furious and said that he had been 'so mad he could hardly restrain himself'. He believed that 'at this time, with England fighting with us, such talk [was] almost treasonable'.[60] The speech offended all of Wilson's sensibilities, especially his idea of what constituted 'good taste'. Masking his anger at Phelan's speech, Wilson graciously accepted the gift and made a short reply. It was his major statement on Robert Emmet, and is revealing not just for what it says about his attitude to Ireland but also for his attitude to the legacy of history.

He began by skilfully side-stepping the issue of Ireland in the present day, while also directing a pointed comment to Phelan, by suggesting that 'it would not be in good taste for me to say anything about the particular Irish cause'.[61] He explained that, 'at the same time', he was at liberty to say that not only did he appreciate the gift 'as a work of art' which he would always value, but also that it made him reflect on the legacy of history. Wilson was now able to disengage from any debate about Emmet's relevance for the present day, by situating him clearly as a figure from the past. For, as he looked at the statue, he said that the thing that impressed him most was 'that it is in the costume of a past age. And I believe that this is not without its significance.' This statement was certainly significant. Wilson was challenging the relevance of Emmet, for Ireland or the United States, in the twentieth century. As he explained:

> What Robert Emmet did in his time would not be necessary to do in our time, and we can, all of us, appreciate, without any partisanship of any kind, the spirit of a man like that – the spirit of self-forgetfulness, the spirit of devotion, the spirit of idealism, the spirit which leads a man to go to the full length of sacrifice for the purpose that he holds most dear.

In a single stroke Wilson had succeeded in paying an elegant tribute to Emmet, while also denying that he had any relevance to the modern world. It was a diplomatic solution to an otherwise difficult problem. Wilson could praise the historical rebel, while refusing to support any more recent rebellions. Thus he could say with a clear conscience that 'in that sense, if not in order, Robert Emmet represents some of the finest traits of human nature'. And this allowed him to turn the remainder of the speech into a justification for America's war effort on the side of Britain and the allies.[62] Wilson had neatly moved the debate away from the historical injustices of Britain to the more pressing reality of the present-day injustices of Germany. Once again dead Irish patriots, and specifically Robert Emmet, were being reinvented as disciples of Wilsonism.

The most important phrase in Wilson's speech is the reference to Emmet's 'spirit of self-forgetfulness'. In the most obvious reading he meant that Emmet had been so devoted to the principle of Irish independence that he had ignored his own concerns and interests. He had forgotten about the risk to his own life, and had gambled everything in the attempt to achieve a republic. This allowed Wilson to praise his devotion, his idealism, and his sacrifice. But there was also a second level to Wilson's application of the phrase. For someone who was a trained historian, indeed the first president of the United States to hold an earned doctorate (as well as being a former lecturer and president at Princeton University), Wilson was very distrustful of history. Whenever he was faced with confronting a difficult subject from the past that had implications for the present, whether it was the American Civil War or the fight for Irish independence, he always adopted a formula of words that invoked the spirit of forgetfulness. In this speech Wilson was making it clear that not only was Emmet's quarrel with Britain long over, perhaps it was better if everyone chose to forget about the quarrel altogether. Where Phelan had drawn a consistent line between Emmet's aspirations in 1803 and the aspirations of the Irish nationalists in 1918, Wilson preferred to leave all historical abstractions in the past. The quarrel was over, and should be forgotten: 'what Robert Emmet did in his time would not be necessary to do in our time'. Therefore, he was urging his listeners to forget about the rights and wrongs of his actions and rather 'appreciate, without any partisanship of any kind, the mind of a man like that'.[63] Wilson wanted Emmet to be remembered for his character, not for his conflict, and this is what he consistently emphasised in his oration.

This dilemma epitomised Wilson's approach to the past. Applying a politician's eye to historical events, he preferred to see the past as something to be forgotten, or else adapted to suit the concerns of the present. So Robert Emmet was deliberately reinvented, to suit the demands of a United States at war. It was uncomfortable dealing with the specifics of Ireland's conflict with Britain in 1803; after all, that conflict had never really gone away, and had re-erupted in 1916. Instead it was easier to repackage Robert Emmet as 'an interesting and spirited figure', and not a representative of a nation still in rebellion, as Phelan had attempted. It marked the completion of Emmet's transformation into an acceptable American legend.

As a symbol, Robert Emmet was a mirage, and the more people tried to incorporate him into their own agenda, the more he faded away. Emmet remained as elusive and enigmatic in death as he had been in life. In the United States the symbol of Emmet was used to support the Home Rule movement as well as the demands for complete Irish independence. It was used to campaign for the Boers, Cuban independence, and even the struggle of the Confederacy. It was enlisted on the side of the allies in the First World

War, while also representing those who would have preferred a war with Britain. It even found time to represent the German U-boat campaign. After the entry of the United States into the First World War Woodrow Wilson reinvented Emmet as a symbol whose ideals should be remembered, but the quarrel forgotten. For Winnie Davis, on the other hand, Emmet was the symbol of the quarrel remembered. Because of the romance and tragedy of his life, because essentially very little was known about his real personality, it was easy for different groups to over-write their own ambitions and aspirations on to his story. As Wilson had shrewdly noted, Emmet represented 'the dreams of the apotheosis of principle'. His life was therefore ready made for anyone with a message that involved idealism, heroism, or sacrifice. Emmet became more powerful in death than he had ever been alive. He represented not only the tragedy of Irish history, but also the triumph of faith, hope and redemption. His story had at last become a tragedy with a happy ending.

Notes

1 See David Brion David, 'The terrible cost of reconciliation', *New York Review of Books* 49: 12 (18 July 2002). Howells made the observation to Edith Wharton after the failure of a staged performance of *The House of Mirth*.

2 *Gaelic American*, Mar. 1903.

3 To borrow Reinhold Niebuhr's phrase in *Faith and History* (New York, 1949).

4 *Gaelic American*, Mar. 1903.

5 *The Irish World and American Industrial Liberator*, 18 Mar. 1882.

6 Lloyd Lewis and Henry Justin Smith, *Oscar Wilde Discovers America [1882]* (New York, 1936), p. 215.

7 Ibid., p. 201.

8 Ibid., p. 375.

9 Ibid., p. 366.

10 Eileen Kott, William Warren Rogers and Roger David Ward, 'Oscar Wilde in Vicksburg, at Beauvoir, and other Southern stops', *Journal of Mississippi History* 59 (1997), p. 201.

11 Ibid., p. 204.

12 Ibid.

13 Ibid., pp. 204–5. The authors of the article, however, have challenged the popular account that Davis objected to Wilde (fn. 73, p. 205).

14 Ibid., p. 206.

15 Oscar Wilde to Julia Ward Howe, 6 July 1882, Merlin Holland and Rupert Hart-Davies (eds), *The Complete Letters of Oscar Wilde* (New York, 2000), pp. 175–6.

16 Tommie Phillips LaCavera (ed.), *Varina Anne 'Winnie' Davis: 'The Daughter of the Confederacy'* (Athens, Georgia, 1994), p. 75.

17 Gaines M. Foster, *Ghosts of the Confederacy* (New York, 1987), p. 8.

18 Varina Anne Davis, *An Irish Knight of the Nineteenth Century: Sketch of the Life of Robert Emmet* (New York, 1888), p. 19.

19 Ibid., p. 22.

20 Ibid., p. 84.

21 Varina Howell Davis to Varina Anne Davis, 25 Apr. 1880, Hudson Strode (ed.), *Jefferson Davis: Private Letters, 1823–1889* (New York, 1966), p. 500.

22 Davis, *An Irish Knight*, p. 89.

23 Ibid., pp 89–90.

24 The lines resonated with advice her father had once given her, that every important 'duty demands self-sacrifice'. LaCavera (ed.), *Varina Anne 'Winnie' Davis*, p. 11.

25 Ibid., p. 91.

26 Holland and Hart-Davis (eds), *The Complete Letters of Oscar Wilde*, p. 164.

27 *New York Times*, Mar. 1901.

28 *Gaelic American*, 6 Mar. 1909.

29 Ibid., 18 Mar. 1916.

30 Ibid., 13 Mar. 1915.

31 Ibid., 18 Mar. 1916.

32 See Edward Cuddy, 'Irish-Americans and the 1916 election: an episode in immigrant adjustment', *American Quarterly* 21: 2 (Summer 1969): 228–43, at p. 230.

33 New York Public Library, MCIHP, Box 1.

34 Ibid.

35 See Arthur S. Link (ed.), *The Papers of Woodrow Wilson*, 69 vols (Princeton, 1966–94), XLIII, p. 510.

36 *Washington Post*, 29 June 1917.

37 John Denis Joseph Moore to Woodrow Wilson, 17 Aug. 1917, Link (ed.), *Wilson Papers*, XLIII, p. 509.

38 Cuddy, 'Irish-Americans and the 1916 election', p. 233. The speech was a dedication to naval hero John Barry.

39 William M. Leary, Jr, 'Woodrow Wilson, Irish Americans, and the election of 1916', *Journal of American History* 54 (1967): 57–72.

40 Cuddy, 'Irish-Americans and the 1916 election', p. 236.

41 Leary, Jr, 'Woodrow Wilson, Irish Americans', p. 72.

42 *Gaelic American*, 21 Dec. 1918, quoted in John B. Duff, 'The Versailles treaty and the Irish-Americans', *Journal of American History* 55: 3 (Dec. 1968), pp. 582–98, at p. 586.

43 Duff, 'The Versailles treaty', p. 596. Wilson was talking to the Irish diplomatic representative Frank P. Walsh.

44 *New York Times*, 29 and 30 June 1917.

45 Letter to President, 25 June 1917, quoted in *Gaelic American*.

46 See *New York Herald Tribune*, 18 Mar. 1909.

47 Link (ed.), *Wilson Papers*, XIX, p. 108.

48 *Gaelic American*, 27 Mar. 1909.

49 Link (ed.), *Wilson Papers*, XIX, p. 103.

50 Wilson to his wife, 20 Aug. 1899, Link (ed.), *Wilson Papers*, XI, p. 234.

51 Ibid., p. 235.

52 Ibid. XIX, p. 107

53 Ibid., p. 107.

54 Ibid., pp. 107–8.

55 Ibid., p. 107.

56 Ibid.

57 See report in the *Washington Post*, 11 Jan. 1918.

58 Link (ed.), *Wilson Papers*, XLV, p. 561, fn. 1. For a good overview of Wilson's policies see David Steigerwald, 'The synthetic politics of Woodrow Wilson', *Journal of the History of Ideas* 50 (1989), pp. 465–84.

59 An address and a reply, Link (ed.), *Wilson Papers*, XLV, p. 560.

60 From the diary of Josephus Daniels, Link (ed.), *Wilson Papers*, XLV, p. 573.

61 Ibid.

62 Ibid., p. 561.

63 10 Jan. 1918, ibid., p. 560.

CHAPTER 9

Saying 'No' to Robert Emmet

Norman Vance

With Emmet, as with other iconic figures in Irish history such as William of Orange, the passage of time and the tricks of selective historical memory can make it difficult to realise how strategically constructed the familiar image actually is, and what a complex and controversial tradition lies behind it. Northern Orangemen have their own reasons for continuing to insist on the glorious, pious and immortal memory of King William III, or rather an ideologically conditioned and tendentious memory of what he could be made to stand for. There is an equal and opposite cult of remembering Robert Emmet, of patriotic affirmation which now seems so natural that one needs to be reminded that it was once possible to dissent. The glorious and immortal – and frequently also rather pious – memory of Emmet was politically useful to the Young Ireland rebels of 1848, to the Fenians twenty years later and to Irish-American poets such as John Boyle O'Reilly, editor of the *Boston Pilot*, who in 1878 celebrated the centenary of Emmet's birth by praising at rather embarrassing length 'The young heart laid on the altar, as a nation's sacrifice.'[1] In the National Museum of Ireland in Dublin there is a Fenian flag on display, captured at the battle of Tallaght in County Dublin in March 1867. It is boldly inscribed 'God and Country – Remember Emmet'. Patrick Pearse certainly remembered Emmet almost half a century later, identifying him as a kind of protomartyr for the cause of Irish nationhood whose example he had every intention of following. In the 1970s Sinn Féin and other enthusiasts for the continuing armed struggle in Northern Ireland were still invoking Emmet and reading republished (if textually unreliable) versions of the speech from the dock.

So much for saying 'yes' to Emmet. How and why did people once say 'no'? When the Old Lady (Lady Gregory) said 'no' to Denis Johnston in 1929 she was rejecting his ambitiously expressionist Emmet play (later retitled *The Old Lady Says No)*. Johnston's strategic fragmentations of Emmet's rhetoric and stage presence were a kind of sceptical interrogation of the Emmet legend. Lady Gregory, in the grip of the legend, was saying no to that interrogation rather than saying no to Emmet himself. She had indeed put Emmet into her own dramatic poem about rebellion, *The Old Woman Remembers*, some years previously, in 1923. This *contretemps* between Johnston and Lady Gregory signals a continuing tension which has never been fully acknowledged or explored. The tradition in literature and in politics of more or less romantic and patriotic endorsement of the Emmet legend, extending from the poets Thomas Moore, and Percy Bysshe Shelley in 1812, by way of Young Ireland and Fenianism to Pearse and beyond, needs to be balanced by considering a less radiantly luminous tradition of saying no, of rejecting or being equivocal about the man, or the mystique, or the message. By the time of the Emmet Centenary of 1903 this could mean distancing oneself not so much from Emmet himself as from the Emmet legend.

One could say this equivocal distancing began with John Philpot Curran, the celebrated barrister who might have become his father-in-law. Curran seems to have been uncomfortable with his daughter Sarah's attachment to Emmet when he found out about it. Despite Emmet's fairly unhopeful request, he said no to defending him, though he defended some of his followers and had famously defended several of the United Irishmen in the 1790s. Curran is obviously a special case, and probably placed in an impossible position legally, but what about those recently retired English radicals Southey and Coleridge?

Southey's poem on Emmet, written in the calm of Keswick in 1803 soon after Emmet's execution, begins 'Emmet, no!' Southey, equivocal rather than downright hostile, was not repudiating Emmet so much as deliberately flouting his famous injunction 'Let no man write my epitaph'. Writing the epitaph is precisely what the poem proceeds to do, much more explicitly than Moore's poetry ever did. But the disregard of Emmet's wishes, however generously intended, signals aloofness from, indeed disdain for his patriotic project. Some years later, from 1817 onwards, the radical London publishers such as the Carliles and John Cleave, who hoped to taunt and embarrass the increasingly conservative Southey, now Poet Laureate, by constantly republishing that revolutionary play of his youth *Wat Tyler*, were also among those who contributed to the Emmet legend by republishing Emmet's speech from the dock. But in 1803 Southey was less hostile to Emmet than they might have expected, if less positive than they might have wished.

There is an element of English national self-congratulation, which makes the praise fainter, in Southey's convoluted tribute:

Here, here in this free Isle,
To which in thy young virtue's erring zeal
Thou wert so perilous an enemy,
Here in free England shall an English hand
Build thy imperishable monument.

But the justice of his death by execution is not unquestioned, and there is a poignant sense of loss:

> If she in truth be Justice who drives on,
> Bloody and blind, the chariot wheels of death.
>
> So young, so glowing for the general good,
> Oh what a lovely manhood had been thine,
> When all the violent workings of thy youth
> Had pass'd away, hadst thou been wisely spared . . .

All too clearly Southey could see in Emmet a less fortunate version of his earlier radical and idealistic self. But if Emmet had succeeded he would have lived to mourn his 'disastrous triumph', which, Southey claims, would have led to sectarianism and spite and so increased rather than expelled tyranny and oppression, with

> Wild Ignorance
> Let loose, and frantic Vengeance, and dark Zeal,
> And all bad passions tyrannous, and the fires
> Of Persecution once again ablaze.
> How had it sunk into thy soul to see,
> Last curse of all, the ruffian slaves of France
> In thy dear native country lording it![2]

Coleridge, also in Keswick at the time, professed himself 'extremely affected by the death of young Emmett – just 24!' At that age, he assured Sir George Beaumont, his own political involvement was already ebbing because he was 'disgusted beyond measure by the manners & morals of the Democrats, & fully awake to the inconsistency of my practice with my speculative Principles'. Whether the dreamy Coleridge was ever fully awake to inconsistency, or indeed anything else, is of course another question. More hostile and less ambivalent than Southey, more interested in himself than in Emmet, Coleridge used the occasion to bury his own radical past as deeply as possible by distancing himself from 'the poor young Enthusiast', this 'most mistaken & bewildered young Man'. A dreamer who had bad dreams, he elaborated, in even more extreme terms than Southey, with unacknowledged help from Milton's *Paradise Lost*, a nightmare vision of what might have happened,

> a Vision of all the Massacres, the furious Passions, the Blasphemies, Sensualities, Superstitions, the bloody Persecutions, and mutual Cannibalism of Atheist & Papist, that would have rushed in, like a Torrent of Sulphur & burning Chaos, at the Breach which thou thyself hadst made.[3]

Although the excesses of the Reign of Terror are the proximate source of denunciations of 'the merciless Gaul' and 'a mob of Fiends in Anarchy', this anti-Catholic vision of horror and persecution, like Southey's, goes back to the fires of Smithfield and the Massacre of St Bartholomew where in Ireland it would have been folk memory of the atrocities associated with the 1641 rebellion.

Precisely because of the legendary 'memory' of 1641, one might have expected horrified responses from Irish Protestants, particularly perhaps those involved in upholding British colonial hegemony. But such emotions seem to have been largely exhausted by the experiences of 1798 and outside the courtroom were apparently little in evidence in 1803.

Perhaps the brief duration and manifest futility of the rebellion left space for milder reactions, less strident than those of Southey or Coleridge, involving formal disapproval tempered with regret and even fugitive sympathy. Lady Anne Barnard, Scots-born daughter-in-law of a Church of Ireland Bishop of Limerick, wife of the Secretary of Cape Colony (1795–1802), deplored the harshness of Dutch colonialism and was in general compassionately conservative in outlook, with a Burkean distrust of revolutionary France. Unlike Coleridge, she had no radical past to bury in bluster. In 1803 her sense of horror was partly on Emmet's behalf. As she wrote in a letter from Ireland on 10 September:

> such solemn scenes are going forwards to freeze the blood and sometimes awaken pity for youth and talents so perverted! – yet when one recollects *what* the *aim* of the rebel one was pitying went to, it stops it short, or *ought* to stop it.[4]

This attitude, in which the writer almost has to remind herself to repudiate what Emmet stood for, contrasts interestingly with that of the Catholic Daniel O'Connell, radical but constitutionally-minded even in youth. O'Connell said no to Emmet for rather different reasons, and was harsher in his condemnation than Southey or Coleridge or Lady Anne, an 'Ascendancy' Protestant by marriage. Writing to his wife Mary on 28 August 1803, after Emmet's arrest but before his trial and execution, he insists that Emmet

> merits and will suffer the severest punishment. For my part I think pity would be almost thrown away upon the contriver of the affair of the 23rd of July. A man who could coolly prepare so much bloodshed, so many murders – and such horrors of every kind has ceased to be an object of compassion.[5]

In view of this attitude it comes as something of a surprise that the broadly O'Connellite *Dublin and London Magazine* ran a series on 'Robert Emmet and His Contemporaries' from its second to its tenth number in 1825, telling the story in lightly fictionalised form. But, if not precisely saying no, this version of Emmet, pre-Young Ireland and pre-Fenian, stops well short of full endorsement. The narrative was designed to keep violence at a distance, as much as possible, and to reinvent Emmet as a politically enlightened contemporary – rather like O'Connell, in fact. The journal, effectively Catholic-nationalist and cultural-nationalist *avant la lettre*, prided itself on representing – and re-presenting – the reformist but constitutional spirit of Curran and Grattan, and was particularly associated with O'Connell's campaign for Catholic emancipation. It ran a series on 'Catholic orators' and carried a long and extremely hostile review of 'Mr Blanco White's evidence against the Catholics' in September 1825. But it was cautious, anxious not to invite government interference or even suppression. So far from overtly espousing republican separatism it artfully quoted on its title page Curran's quasi-unionist declaration that 'As the advocate of society, of peace, of domestic liberty, and the lasting union of the two countries' he saw a free press as indispensable to 'the security of the crown'.

The first-person narrative of 'Robert Emmet and his Contemporaries' purports to be by one Godfrey K-n, a contemporary of Emmet's. It is in fact by the editor of the magazine, M. J. Whitty, later chief constable of Liverpool, who was only eight years old at the time of the Rebellion in 1803. Whitty's fictional narrator meets Emmet and is drawn into long conversations with him on 'The political capacity of Catholics' and 'Impediments to emancipation' – these are actual headings in the magazine serial – which anachronistically address the agenda of the 1820s rather more than that of Emmet himself. The sense of distance from violent rebellion is emphasised in that, while the narrator stands by Emmet on the fatal day, he has few illusions as he notes the 'expressive countenances of the desperate and infatuated men around me'. There is no mention of the murder of Lord Kilwarden in the course of the rising and Emmet is represented as a restraining influence determined to save the lives of his fellow-countrymen by 'preventing the revolt of last night from assuming the form of rebellion'. Despite being pro-Catholic rather than anti-Catholic the general attitude is in fact similar to that of Southey, balancing sympathetic respect for Emmet's fire and zeal and burning sense of injustice with the perception that he was sincere but sincerely mistaken. At the end of the narrative, when all is over, the senior figure of the 'the Exile', who speaks with an authority not challenged in the narrative, pronounces the obituary that Emmet had not wanted and buries him, rather awkwardly, in fustian:

> Mistaken youth! Thy death has been ignominious; but in thy fate there has been . . . much that challenges attention and excites regret . . . Thy views were doubtless erroneous, but thy intentions I believe were honest; at all events thy short career warrants the supposition, and let us not uncharitably conclude otherwise.[6]

More or less anachronistic appropriation of Emmet has characterised the later tradition. Nearly half a century later Whitty reappropriated him for changed times when he revisited and substantially revised his own early narrative, publishing it as a book in 1870 in the aftermath of the Fenian movement. By 1870 Emmet was sufficiently a figure of myth and legend on both sides of the Atlantic for the violence of the familiar tale, easily trumped by later episodes in the national story, not to matter too much. In Whitty's revised and expanded version space is found for mention of the murder of Lord Kilwarden, and the praise of Emmet is less qualified, more mythopoeic, although the summary verdict is still cautious: 'His mind, though misled, had in it all the assured elements of greatness.'[7]

Other popular invocations of the story were so vague and sentimental, like the ballad of 'Bold Robert Emmet', or so anachronistic and histrionic that they served in the end to discredit the legend. But it has to be said that there was a strong element of the histrionic, of theatre, present from the beginning. It seems that, like his contemporary and elegist Thomas Moore, Emmet had attended Samuel Whyte's school in Dublin (though the evidence for this is inconclusive), and Whyte, a friend of the Sheridans, had strongly promoted spoken English and school plays. The spectacle and rhetoric of theatre, probably familiar from schooldays, influenced Emmet as leader and as heroic defendant in court. The famous green coat, white breeches and Hessian boots that Emmet wore were an already theatrical costume, faithfully stipulated in stage directions in the various Emmet plays produced in the course of the nineteenth and twentieth centuries, even if they were right about nothing else. The court scene and the speech from the dock, with or without the savage interruptions of Lord Norbury, played very well on the boards and the hustings. As late as 1965, in Sam Thompson's posthumous television drama *Cemented with Love*, the cynical election agent tells the fledgling nationalist candidate for Drumtory to 'give 'em Emmet from the dock'.

But Thompson's intention is to laugh at a politics and a tradition which, like traditional Unionism, has become tired and threadbare. There were symptoms of fatigue much earlier, saying 'yes, yes, yes' if not exactly saying 'no'. In *Ulysses*, set in 1904, soon after the 1903 centenary celebrations, Joyce sardonically makes Leopold Bloom break the rhythm of the over-familiar speech from the dock as he breaks wind, reflecting

> *When my country takes her place among.*
> Prrprr.
> Must be the bur.
> Fff. Oo. Rrpr.
> *Nations of the earth.* No-one behind. She's passed. *Then and not till then.* Tram. Kran, kran, kran . . . *let my epitaph be.* Karaaaaaaa. *Written.*[8]

The New Yorker James Pilgrim must have been tired already from his catchpenny adaptations of Lady Morgan's *The Wild Irish Girl* (1850) and John Boyce's *Shandy Maguire: or the Bould Boy of the Mountain* (after 1848), not to mention original gems such as *Paddy Miles, the Limerick Boy. A Farce* (1836) and *Eveleen Wilson, the Flower of Erin*. But, undeterred, he wrote and acted in *Robert Emmet, the Martyr of Irish Liberty: An Historical Drama in Three Acts*, produced, apparently with some success, in New York, Boston and Philadelphia (1853–6). The green coat is carefully specified, 'collar and cuffs embroidered with small scrolls of shamrock in gold'. To liven things up a little Emmet is given a wife called Maria and a stage-Irish sidekick called Darby O'Gaff, 'a Sprig of the Emerald Isle', played by Pilgrim himself. There seems to be a little confusion in the published text as to whether the action takes place in 1798 or later, but this may be due to editorial incompetence rather than to the author. Emmet dies in the third act to the strains of Judy O'Dougherty singing 'The harp that once through Tara's halls', a remarkable achievement since in 1803 Moore had not yet written it.[9]

Moore also contributes to the otherwise much better play by the American Joseph Clarke, *Robert Emmet: A Tragedy of Irish History* (1888). In the second act a harper plays a few bars of Moore's 'Let Erin remember the days of old'. But even here the dark tale is further darkened by anachronistic shadows as Emmet's value-added rhetoric prophetically includes the insistent calling to arms of Ireland's 'famine-dead, in ghostly myriads, [who] wave maledictions upon those who'd lag behind'.[10]

Anachronism can of course be viewed and excused as merely superficial, indirect evidence of essential timelessness. My own early article on Emmet was delayed in the press for several years because, as the editor genially pointed out, it was 'in the best sense timeless'.[11] By the time of the 1798 centenary celebrations, Emmet and his green coat were timelessly or anachronistically part of a nationalist legend which did not pedantically distinguish between 1798 and 1803, or 1848 or 1867, and indeed prints of Emmet and Parnell might be hung side by side on the wall, doomed co-workers in the timeless struggle. The artist Jack Butler Yeats found two such prints in an hotel sitting-room in Claremorris in 1905, and he executed two Emmet sketches derived from old prints. In 1898 he had gone to see the laying of the foundation stone for the Bartholomew Teeling statue on the road between Ballysodare and Collooney in Sligo. There was a 'Magnificent Demonstration', as described in the *Sligo Champion*, and he found plenty for his sketchbook, including the leader of the Tobercurry Band, dressed in Emmet green with tricorne hat and sword. It is this leader of the band, not images of Emmet himself, that lies behind Yeats's sketch entitled 'Robert Emmet'. As Yeats wrote to Ernie O'Malley many years later, he was dressed not in 'cloth of gold but cloth of billiard table'.[12] Yeats was not saying no to

Emmet himself, but his response was aesthetic rather than political, amused rather than reverent.

Willie Yeats, more complicated than his brother, sufficiently influenced by John O'Leary and Fenian tradition to lament Emmet and Lord Edward Fitzgerald in verse, had been with some difficulty persuaded to give the audience more or less what it wanted at the New York Emmet commemoration in 1903, but by early 1916 he was rather disenchanted, bored and irritated with Emmet and with Patrick Pearse, which was perhaps much the same thing. Ezra Pound represented him as saying that Pearse was 'half-cracked and wanting to be hanged – has Emmet delusions same as other lunatics think they are Napoleon or God'.[13]

But Yeats, like Emmet and like Coleridge, understood the power of dreams and knew that in dreams begin responsibility. Lennox Robinson's well-made Emmet play *The Dreamers* (1915), dedicated to Yeats, is really a play about dreams, which he describes as 'the only permanent things in life, the only heritage that can be hoarded or spent and yet handed down with interest from generation to generation'. Its epigraph from Lionel Johnson seems absolutely right for Emmet:

> Brief life and hapless? Nay:
> Through death, life grew sublime.
> *Speak after sentence?* Yea:
> And to the end of time.[14]

This actually comes from Johnson's poem 'By the statue of King Charles at Charing Cross': the legendary figure in the dock is not Emmet but Charles I. Royalist or nationalist, English or Irish, dreams are detachable from context and from the prosaic realities which they so often serve to challenge, not always successfully.

Unsuccessful dreams and defeated heroes are usually more effective theatrically than politically, but they can still embody political challenge. Two one-act plays by Conal O'Riordan (who wrote as F. Norreys Connell) explore repudiations of Emmet and what he stood for in ways intended to shame those who said no. For patriots and nationalists, subsequent political failure or apparent failure such as the downfall of Parnell in 1890 had only enhanced the dramatic power and poignancy of doomed personal witness and short-lived, seemingly futile gesture. There was support for such a position from within traditional Catholic teaching. As Canon Sheehan's popular religious novel *The Triumph of Failure* (1901) had reminded pious readers, lack of success in worldly or material terms was no barrier to significant witness and ultimate moral triumph.

O'Riordan's *The Piper; an Unended Argument*, first performed at the Abbey on 13 February 1908, does not explicitly refer to Emmet but it was almost certainly influenced by the Emmet centenary celebrations of 1903, a year before it was first drafted. The theme of this uncomfortable problem-play was described as 'the history not only of Ireland but of democracy in arms'. The uncompromising hero, Black Mike, is described in the author's preface as the 'type of noble fools, who for their country suffered ignoble deaths . . . [thinking] that no death could be so ignominious as the life of slaves'.[15] Emmet is of course a founding father of this tradition of noble fools in Ireland, though there are also suggestions of Parnell in Black Mike's practical realism and his unpopularity with Father Hanrihan, who denounces him as a renegade for not making his Easter duty. Set 'an hundred years ago and more', which could be at the time of Emmet's rising in 1803 but is more likely to be during the United Irishmen's rebellion of 1798, the play uses snatches of 'The Shan Van Vocht', that famous ballad of 1798, as a kind of leitmotif. It opens with canon and musketry and a cause already lost. But Black Mike's brothers in arms, Tim the Trimmer and the grandiloquent 'General' Larry the Talker, unlike Mike, are too stupid to realise it. Larry lacks the rudimentary common sense even to post sentries. By the end of the play they have melted away, Black Mike has been killed and the honour of the cause has been maintained only by the humble Piper who continues to sing 'The Shan Van Vocht' and wave the flag until he too is killed. The only tribute to the Piper's courage is offered by the English officer Captain Talbot, a prisoner of the rebels, who arranges for him to be buried in the patriot flag he has spread over the body.

The audience did not like the play, but Yeats read them a curtain-lecture from the stage on 15 February 1908, vigorously defending it and perhaps over-interpreting it (certainly the author thought so) as a specifically Parnellite allegory which attacked all those who had earlier failed Robert Emmet, a play which celebrated 'the ceaseless heroic aspirations of the Irish people'.[16]

Emmet features more directly in a lighter and later piece by O'Riordan invoking Walter Savage Landor's *Imaginary Conversations* with its title *An Imaginary Conversation* (1909). Set in 1797 in the home of Emmet's friend the poet Thomas Moore, with Moore seated at the piano, it is not completely imaginary. The fiery Emmet wants the cautious Moore to play and sing the *Marseillaise*, but Moore is evasive and uncomfortable, saying his mother would not like it. Emmet retorts 'I had no mother to keep me from loving Liberty.' He then taunts Moore into playing his song of Irish liberty 'Let Erin remember the days of old' to the stirring and very ancient tune of 'The Red Fox', later published (as 'The Little Bold Fox') by Edward Bunting.[17] Emmet's response is historically documented in Moore's *Memoirs*:[18] 'O, that I were at the head of twenty thousand men marching to that!' But Moore, scared, says in the play 'I think that'll do for today'. The Moore who effectively said no to Emmet's patriotic fire, for all that he discreetly celebrated it in verse in later years, is condemned with all like him in a scathing endnote which observes that when Emmet was hanged on 20 September 1803 Moore was sailing for the Bermudas, to an 'office of emolument under the Crown'.[19]

The harshest form of saying no to Emmet, of repudiating the passionate idealism and the dream which even Southey had saluted, is described in Brinsley MacNamara's bleak novel *The Clanking of Chains* (1919). Set in the very recent Irish past, to take in gun-running and the Volunteers and Easter 1916, its Ibsenite defeated hero Michael Dempsey, son of a loyal Parnellite, is described ironically as 'An Enemy of the People'. He is a passionately serious Robert Emmet in the Ballycullen amateur dramatic production of an Emmet play, and in love with the actress who plays Sarah Curran, to complete the identification. But the small-minded audience have no wish to look beyond the familiar image on the stage and the moth-eaten legend retailed by 'drunken ballad-singers'.[20] Spiritually dead, insensitive to the real power and significance of the dream, they repudiate Dempsey and his vision of better things as they had repudiated Parnell himself.

Saying no to Robert Emmet might be a mark of political caution, as it had been with Coleridge and Daniel O'Connell, or of boredom and sophisticated disillusionment, as it had been with Joyce and Denis Johnston and the later Yeats, but it could also be a way of rebuking the narrowness, superficiality and facile sentimentality of Ballycullen and the windy rhetoric of Larry the Talker and his brethren and appealing to the real Robert Emmet, the self-sacrificing best self of Irish nationalism embodying the ultimate triumph of failure.

Notes

1 John Boyle O'Reilly, 'The patriot's grave' (read at the Emmet Centennial, Boston, 4th March 1878), reprinted in James Jeffrey Roche, *Life of John Boyle O'Reilly Together with his Complete Poems and Speeches* (London, 1891), pp. 549–52. The poem is prefaced by a complete text of the speech from the dock.

2 Robert Southey, 'Written immediately after reading the speech of Robert Emmet, on his trial and conviction for high treason, Sept. 1803', *Poetical Works*, 10 vols (London: 1837), II, pp. 245–7.

3 Coleridge to Sir George and Lady Beaumont, 1 Oct. 1803, E. L. Griggs (ed.), *Collected Letters of Samuel Taylor Coleridge*, 6 vols (Oxford, 1956–71), II, pp. 999, 1001.

4 A. M. L. Robinson (ed.), *The Letters of Lady Anne Barnard to Henry Dundas from the Cape and Elsewhere, 1793–1803* (Cape Town, 1973), p.288, quoted by David Johnson, to whom I am indebted for the reference, in his 'Talking about revolution: Lady Anne Barnard in France, Ireland, and the Cape Colony', in Glenn Hooper and Colin Graham (eds), *Irish and Postcolonial Writing: History, Theory, Practice* (Basingstoke, 2002), p. 165.

5 O'Connell to Mary O'Connell, 28 Aug. 1803, quoted in Oliver MacDonagh, *The Hereditary Bondsman: Daniel O'Connell 1775–1829* (London, 1988), p. 94.

6 'Emmet and his contemporaries', *Dublin and London Magazine* (Dec. 1825), p. 436.

7 [M. J. Whitty], *Robert Emmet* (London, 1870), p. 251.

8 James Joyce, *Ulysses* (1922) (London, 1968), Sirens episode, pp. 289f.

9 James Pilgrim, *Robert Emmet, the Martyr of Irish Liberty: An Historical Drama in Three Acts* (New York, [1868?]), p. 27.

10 Joseph I. C. Clarke, *Robert Emmet: A Tragedy of Irish History* (New York and London, 1888), p. 52.

11 R. N. C. Vance, 'Text and tradition: Robert Emmet's speech from the dock' *Studies* 71 (Summer 1982), pp. 185–91.

12 Bruce Arnold, *Jack Yeats* (New Haven and London, 1998), pp. 144, 78f. There is a reproduction of the watercolour *Robert Emmet* (1898) in James White, *Jack B. Yeats: Drawings and Paintings* (London, 1971), p. 29.

13 R. F. Foster, *W. B. Yeats: A Life, Volume 1: The Apprentice Mage, 1865–1914* (Oxford, 1997), pp. 312f; R. F. Foster, *W. B. Yeats: A Life, Volume 2: The Arch Poet, 1915–1939* (Oxford, 2003), pp. 46, 49; R. F. Foster, *The Irish Story: Telling Tales and Making it up in Ireland* (London, 2001), p. 62.

14 Lennox Robinson, *The Dreamers: A Play in Three Acts* (London and Dublin, 1915), preface.

15 Conal O'Riordan, *Shakespeare's End and Other Irish Plays* (London, 1912), pp. 9, 11.

16 Foster, *W.B. Yeats: A Life*, 1, p. 378; discussed in Ben Levitas, *The Theatre of Nation: Irish Drama and Cultural Nationalism 1890–1916* (Oxford, 2002), p. 149.

17 Edward Bunting, *The Ancient Music of Ireland* (Dublin, 1840), p. 98, no. 129. Bunting, closely associated with the famous Belfast Harp Festival of July 1792, gives his source as the antiquarian George Petrie.

18 O'Riordan, *Shakespeare's End*, pp. 64–5, 82, 83, 84.

19 Discussed in Terence de Vere White, *Tom Moore: The Irish Poet* (London, 1977), p. 15.

20 Brinsley MacNamara, *The Clanking of Chains* (1919) (Dublin and London, 1920), p. 10.

CHAPTER 10

'It might be just as well, perhaps, to forget about poor Emmet'

Anne Dolan

Schoolchildren are often herded around the corridors and rooms of Leinster House. They are supposed to soak up democracy through the ether or something like that. On one occasion Godfrey Timmons, deputy for Wicklow, shepherded a flock of teenagers from a school in his constituency. Mindful of keeping the potential future voters entertained he decided to liven matters up when he reached the ante-room of the Upper Chamber. He showed the teenagers two portraits in the room but made them guess the names of their subjects. Typically, Timmons got a little more than he bargained for. 'I asked one girl to identify one of the portraits and I was amazed when she gave me the name of a continental dictator who was partly responsible for the Second World War.'[1] The correct answer was Robert Emmet.

But ignorance was not the preserve of the schoolchildren of County Wicklow, or of the late 1960s when Timmons rounded up his unsuspecting flock. In 1930 Frank Fahy admitted to the Dáil that

> I myself know of some pupils in the sixth standard in a pretty large Dublin school being asked questions on recent Irish history, and displaying abysmal ignorance. A question was answered by the best informed of ten pupils as to what leaders were executed in Easter Week. His answer was Pearse, Connolly and Robert Emmet.[2]

And this boy was the only one who knew anything about it at all.

Looking at the sixth standard and the Wicklow teenagers may be all very well, but there was similar ignorance in loftier circles too. Bill Cashin pointed out in the Seanad that 'when the President of the United States visited the country and this House. The taoiseach described a statue in the Green Hall as that of Robert Emmet when, in fact, it was that of "The Liberator", Daniel O'Connell.'[3] There are some in Fianna Fáil who might not be surprised by Deputy Bruton's alleged lack of knowledge of the pantheon of Irish nationalist heroes, but that would be to open a whole different can of worms. I have given this example not to belittle the then taoiseach: he may have been nervous in the presence of American greatness; he may have made an honest mistake. In the same way it seems cruel to mock a child's answer to a question over 70 years later in order to make a cheap shot in this chapter. He was only doing his best and most people would probably cringe if their childhood essays came back to haunt them. And perhaps the girl in Godfrey Timmons's tour was just fed up with him, was just trying to be a bit smart; and perhaps Maurice McGonigal's portrait leaves a little to be desired. Either way, these examples are not attempts to blame a taoiseach or to load all of the responsibility of history on to the shoulders of the nation's schoolchildren. Successive governments had already overburdened them with the weight of preserving the national language for any more to be heaped on top. The point of these examples lies more in the contemporary responses to them. On the one level they demonstrate that from the 1930s to the 1990s there was a great deal of ignorance about Robert Emmet. But there is something more telling in the motivation for raising the matters and the responses that they aroused in the Dáil and Seanad. Cashin asked for a label to be placed on O'Connell's statue. As he said 'the Kerryman should have his full rights'.[4] Timmons, too, wanted labels on the portraits; Fahy just asked for better school books. In the taoiseach's case his error went unremarked. There was simply a snide reference to 'The Liberator' and Deputy Bruton's alter ego.[5] No one seemed to care that Robert Emmet had been lost somewhere along the way.

It may seem odd in the light of recent conferences, in the context of the five books that have been published in the course of a few months in 2003, and the government's enthusiastic sponsorship of the bicentenary, to allege that Robert Emmet has been lost.[6] Indeed, I went to the archives and libraries expecting to be overcome by references to the great Robert Emmet. How could it be otherwise? I was reading about Emmet as 'the spirit' of the country,[7] that in some sort of imagined top ten of Irish nationalist icons he was 'the best loved'.[8] I kept finding references to his picture on the walls of Irish cottages, that this was a register of his popularity, that for at least one senator this even proved that Irish Catholics were not the intolerant brood that some wanted them to seem, that 'the humblest cot in the countryside' displayed their pluralism with their portrait of 'the young Irish Protestant patriot'.[9] W. B. Yeats, after all, had said Emmet's picture was there, though how often he visited 'the thousands of Irish cottages' that he claimed had the portrait I do not know.[10] And Emmet was on the walls of emigrant kitchens too, nestled however nervously between St Patrick and John F. Kennedy, the other Irish martyrs, and Jesus Christ.[11] He was there for all to see, there even if the clashing portraits gave Ernie O'Malley another reason to sneer at the bad taste of the Irish peasant whom he had sworn in his great act of sanctimonious magnanimity to liberate. It was all very well to contemplate in the refined air of an artist's colony in New Mexico (where O'Malley wrote a large portion of his memoirs with Hart Crane correcting his drafts over his shoulder), and to wonder what the portraits of Emmet and Daniel O'Connell would say to each other if they could speak.[12] For O'Malley they may have rested uneasily together. To the people in the cottage whose food he ate and whose lives he endangered by his presence, there was no distinction. Both men had done what they could for Ireland; republican purism be damned.

I knew O'Malley's attitude was not necessarily typical, and for this reason I expected to find plenty of documents to contradict him, to prove him wrong, to confirm the instincts of all the people who bought the cheap portraits for their walls. Because a brief chapter would never allow me to trace the extent of Emmet's popularity after independence, I went looking instead for the role of Irish governments in the maintenance of the Emmet myth. This myth has been stringently assessed and reconsidered in the course of the bicentenary; by virtue of the books and conferences, there is an inherent assumption that it is as healthy as ever. But in the archives of the Irish state I found no reason to believe that Emmet was anything other than lost.

Sir John Simon, the former British Home Secretary, arguably got things off to a bad start. On the signing of the Treaty he announced to the press that

> Ireland is rich in her store of poetry and history, but the chief of her possessions and the greatest of her gifts to the world is the Irish epic that stretches from Robert Emmet, through Butt, Parnell, and Redmond, to the Irish Delegates. 'Let no man write my epitaph', cried Robert Emmet, in the dock. 'When my country takes her place among the nations of the earth then, and not till then, let my epitaph be written'. It would be a fine gesture if Sinn Féin wrote it now.[13]

While Michael Collins and Erskine Childers may have found it difficult enough to be cast in the same mould as Isaac Butt and John Redmond, there was no sense, no matter what one's position on the Treaty after its signing on 6 December 1921, that the agreement was worthy of Emmet's definition of nationhood. At best it was a compromise, a start, the freedom to achieve freedom, and there would be no epitaph written until then. The suggestion that it should be came only from the sympathetic Irish abroad, those in other dominions who perhaps thought dominion status should be good enough. One such letter was written to W. T. Cosgrave in November 1923. It came from Reverend T. J. Cahill, who preferred to sign himself 'a New Zealand Priest'. Congratulating Cosgrave on his victory in civil war and passing on some tips from Benito Mussolini, he announced:

> It is unfortunate that there are, it appears, many people in Ireland who do not seem to be able to appreciate the fact that Ireland is a 'Nation once again' – an

> equal with England, Canada, Australia, New Zealand, in the Commonwealth of British Nations of the world – and that Ireland's nationality is sure to develop under orderly government and goodwill towards Ulster and England.

He wanted to ask Cosgrave

> and the Free State Government to make a great appeal to her children everywhere to honour Eire's Nationality – Eire, a Nation – by contributing to a great national fund for the erection of a monument and writing an epitaph to that young noble Protestant patriot ROBERT EMMETT who has been the soul and symbol of Patriotism to the sons and daughters of Eire all those years.

Whether with a statue or a College of Arts to encourage music and oratory, he felt, as he said, in his own humble opinion, that the time had come to write Emmet's epitaph. His good wishes were accompanied by £50 'for the Emmett Epitaph Fund'.[14] Three months later Cosgrave replied.

> I have given careful thought to your suggestion that the time is ripe to undertake the erection of a monument worthy of the heroic soul and lofty patriotism of Robert Emmett [*sic*] . . . I feel, however, and my colleagues whom I have consulted agree, that so long as a minority of our fellow-countrymen, professing in great part the faith of Emmett, are sundered from us by an unnatural partition of our common country, it would not be in accord with Emmett's dying wish that we should proceed to write his epitaph.

The cheque was returned with the hope that it would not be long before 'the tribute of Emmett's memory can be offered by a united people'.[15] There was no need to disillusion the far away Irish priest. However misguided, he had meant well. There was no need to tell him about the last letter from Liam Mellows to his mother, in which he told her that he was about to receive 'the greatest human honour that can be paid to an Irishman or Irishwoman, [that] I go to join Tone and Emmet, the Fenians, Tom Clarke, Connolly, Pearse, Kevin Barry and Childers';[16] that the government had executed him as a reprisal for another's actions; that amongst other things he claimed to be that bit more like Robert Emmet than they were. Emmet was lost to them as Cumann na mBan and the remnants of various republican groups sang Moore's melodies and denounced the Free State government in his name. That they did so on the anniversary of every other Irish nationalist made no difference. Emmet would not accept an epitaph until there was a nation – he would brook no compromise. The most extreme realms of republicanism proceeded to claim him for their own. So much so that Desmond FitzGerald feared that the mention of his name in the wilds of Leitrim might inspire the county's young men with impassioned thoughts of revolution; so much so that the Bishop of Galway who asked 'What did Emmet do? He led a rabble through the streets of Dublin', denounced him from the pulpit along with all the other greats, the 'so-called heroes . . . who never were of any benefit to the country'.[17] Like all the other names, Emmet had to be watched when he fell into potentially dangerous hands. This may explain why the Free State government feared the arrival of the body of Thomas Addis Emmet in 1922; why there was a scramble for the corpse in case the republicans in burying him were vindicated by the association with the Emmet name. This may be what prompted Kevin Whelan to claim that the Emmet family were kept out of Ireland by the Free State government in the 1920s. This was, however, one conspiracy theory too many.[18] There were no attempts to exclude the family; if anything, the government was keen to see the return of the Emmets, welcoming the endorsement that their return seemed to imply.

The Free State government may have shared the green-tinted vision of a united Ireland, but an army mutiny, and the ignominy of the boundary commission crisis, made 'She is Far from the land' rather more difficult for them to sing. Two years after Arthur Griffith's death the government had not even paid the £5 10*s* 0*d* it had taken to bury him; when it did, departments quibbled over which should bear the pitiable cost.[19] A Cenotaph rotted on Leinster Lawn because the government was too mean and too nervous to commemorate its first president and commander-in-chief. For Robert Emmet there was little hope. He could only make their failure seem worse. Marianne Elliott argues that 'despite the coyness about public memorials, a large portrait of Emmet had hung in the Irish government's Council (Cabinet) Chamber since 1926'.[20] Of course it had: the government had got it for free and the government liked getting things for free. The only reason Michael Collins had a cross at Béalnabláth was because an anonymous woman had donated it. The picture was in the Dáil because the donors wanted it there. And it would have been rude not to display it. The presence of the portrait might also give the impression that the Emmet family approved of the Free State, and given their position in the United States, there was no harm in that.

In 1931 the government was faced with the offer to purchase a statuette of Emmet by Jerome Connor. Oliver St John Gogarty thought that the state should buy this smaller version of the statue that would eventually stand on the side of St Stephen's Green. According to Thomas Bodkin, the Director of the National Gallery, whom the government had sent to inspect the statuette, its only virtue was that it seemed to look 'exceedingly like General Mulcahy'.[21] On hearing this, Joseph McGrath with all his sweepstakes millions came to mind. It was thought 'he might be inclined to purchase' especially when W. T. Cosgrave told him that Robert Emmet had once lived in the house that McGrath had just bought.[22] McGrath was to bankroll many of the commemorative endeavours of the Free State government and more latterly Fine Gael. He was a soft touch when it was anything to do with Michael Collins. Cosgrave and his colleagues assumed that £50 for a statuette of Robert Emmet was not too much to ask. In 1932 Emmet appeared on the stained glass window in the University College Dublin Earlsfort Terrace building, placed to commemorate Kevin Barry. But the UCD students had paid for that; selected the images and courted all the associations.

In 1938 a plaque was placed on Emmet Bridge. But like the renaming of the bridge itself, it came at the dictate of the Old IRA. Albert Power had been commissioned to produce the plaque as he had for many of the Old IRA monuments that were beginning to be seen throughout the country. For Seán Dowling, a veteran of the 4th battalion of the Dublin Brigade, the plaque was just another chance to say that England's difficulty was still Ireland's opportunity.[23] The epitaph was still to be written; the change of government had made no difference. There had been no recasting of the border and IRA men were soon to be imprisoned and executed by a Fianna Fáil government. Fianna Fáil were now confirmed as traitors too.

In the closing days of 1938 a letter arrived from New South Wales. In death Thomas Gilmartin, another exile, had bequeathed £10 10*s* to the Irish nation for the erection of a monument to Robert Emmet.[24] Two letters later it was found there was 'no information at the moment as to any movement for [the] purpose mentioned'.[25] This was no surprise: Emmet had not even merited a line in the history section of the *Saorstát Éireann Official Handbook*, published in 1932.[26] There was no real reason to think he merited anything more in 1938.

There was of course the question, 'To what extent if any was [the Easter Rising] inspired by that of Robert Emmet?', in the questionnaire of the Bureau of Military History.[27] Much has been made of the association of the Easter Rising with Emmet's rebellion. As the last Dublin-based rebellion before 1916 the question made some sense. But more importantly it has to be seen for what it was – merely one question among 209 others that asked about everything from clergymen to cooking during Easter Week.

A question to the head of the inter-party government in November 1949 just brought more evasion. Would the government consider erecting a memorial to Emmet and Lord Edward Fitzgerald in Leinster House? John A. Costello replied it was not a government matter; it should be taken up with the committee of procedure and privileges.[28] By June 1950 the questioner, Joseph P. Brennan, and a cross party alliance of Seán Dunne, Cormac Breathnach and Senator Patrick Woulfe, met with a view to planning a memorial for the two men. The committee met with indifference and disappeared.[29]

The 150th anniversary of Emmet's death brought a stamp. Appropriately Emmet was only honoured in this way a year after Thomas Moore. Moore had made the myth after all.[30] The stamp may have been popular as the extra staff in the GPO proved; but in the Dáil it was another matter. Dan Desmond greeted the announcement with: 'The government will shortly produce Robert Emmet on a postage stamp but they are not producing any schemes to combat unemployment.'[31] Earlier in the year the *Evening Mail* had reacted in a much more forceful manner to the proposition of an Emmet stamp.

> It might be just as well, perhaps, to forget about poor Emmett [*sic*] as far as postage stamps are concerned. For one thing, his insurrection was a miserable affair, a tragic farce that was squashed in a matter of hours and is remembered only because he himself was a pathetic and glamorous figure and the composer of an immortal speech from the dock; but he belongs rather to romantic letters than to the story of Ireland, upon which he exerted no influence.[32]

Within two weeks of this article Bob Briscoe asked the taoiseach in the Dáil 'whether he will take steps, if necessary by the introduction of proposals for legislation, to prevent anti-national attacks such as this on Irish patriots'; whether the taoiseach was aware of the paper's 'wide circulation mainly amongst our young people and can influence wrongly the minds of people in matters of this kind?'[33] The answer was one that had been used when a similar attack had been made on Roger Casement: 'The reputation of Robert Emmet, like that of any other patriots who gave their lives in efforts to secure the freedom of our country, is safe in the affections of the people'. When General Mulcahy began to chime in with complaints about newspaper attacks on the memories of Griffith and Collins the Ceann Comhairle wisely intervened.[34] The *Evening Mail* was entitled to its opinion of Emmet: in many ways there was a lot of truth in what it said. But while the government could be commended for its refusal to capitulate to Briscoe's wish to censor the press, there was more truth in its simple statement than the government possibly realised. Emmet's reputation may have been safe in the people's affections. It had to be; no one else was going to do much about it otherwise. When a Dr T. Woulfe wrote to suggest that the 150th anniversary should be marked by the government he was given a polite but rather curt reply.[35] The taoiseach was grateful for his suggestion that the Irish people be addressed by the descendants of Emmet and Tone but 'It would be impossible in the time available to organise a worthy commemoration of the kind suggested. In any event, as the unity of the country has not yet been achieved, many would feel that the time for such a commemoration has not yet arrived.'[36] It made no difference which party was in power; it made no difference whether it was 1923 or 1953, nothing could or would be done.

It was left to the Americans to do it all; maybe appropriately, the Emmet name seemed to mean infinitely more in the country that had held Emmet's brother in such high esteem. It was forgotten that an Emmet had been treasurer of the American Irish Defence Association, a group founded to encourage the Irish to enter the Second World War; that the Association was run by the British Special Operations Executive.[37] Emmet's seal was donated in 1958. It was given to the National Museum together with Roger Casement's match box.[38] According to the Irish ambassador to Washington, John Hearne, the presentation

> symbolizes, as no other event could the closeness of the resemblance of the Irish and American struggles for liberty . . . It symbolizes also the character of the long friendship between the Irish Nation and the great American people and their common devotion to the imperishable ideals of faith and freedom. This relic of the origins of Irish and American liberties will be honoured and treasured in Ireland in all the generations to come of the free united Ireland for which Emmet fought and fell. And the names of its donors will live in Irish memories beside that of their deathless ancestor . . .[39]

Without being facetious the Irish Ambassador was perhaps over egging the pudding. The names of Rear Admiral Robert Emmett and Herman Le Roy Emmet have not quite stayed the course. The Emmet seal is not one of the most renowned treasures of our national museum.

It would not be fair to say the same about the American donation of the Jerome Connor statue of Robert Emmet. It was promised in 1923, but it took the Americans 43 years to bring it across the Atlantic Ocean. Years of indifference were punctuated with squabbles and thwarted attempts. Senators toyed with it periodically, especially when they were seeking re-election in states with a strong Irish vote.[40] By April 1965 it was finally agreed that it would be presented by a group of Congressmen of 'Irish' descent.[41] William Fay, the new Irish Ambassador to Washington, suggested that the donation should be postponed for a year until it could form part of the 1966 celebration of the Easter Rising. By now the Department of External Affairs was writing with a degree of exasperation to its man in Washington:

> As this matter has been dragging on for some considerable time and as there are many other projects under consideration for the fiftieth anniversary of the Easter Rising, the Minister considers that it would be just as well not to pursue the suggestion that the donation of the statue be postponed until 1966.[42]

By then it was too late. The congressmen of 'Irish' descent were taken with the idea of paying homage during the Easter Rising anniversary. That way there was double the appeal to the Irish-American vote and so it proceeded just as the Americans wanted. The statue arrived on 13 April 1966. It was handed into the care of the President and left in Iveagh House.[43] Consideration of where to site it would have to be made at a later date. Seán Dowling, because of his involvement with the American project in the 1930s and his prominence in the Kilmainham Jail restoration committee, became adamant that the statue should be placed in the jail. He argued that it was a place associated with the Emmet myth and that it would be safe there from any possibility of defacement.[44] Frank Aiken had been initially in favour of the Kilmainham idea, but a committee made up of members from the departments of an Taoiseach, External Affairs and the Office of Public Works, chose the west side of St Stephen's Green, just opposite Emmet's place of birth. Trinity College was mooted as a possible site but it 'was eliminated on the ground that an institution which expelled Emmet could scarcely be held to have a good claim to his statue'.[45] It seems the government had forgotten that Trinity was among the few to mark the 150th anniversary of Emmet's death 15 years before. The statue eventually reached St Stephen's Green on 20 January 1968.

When asked if he cared to unveil it, de Valera replied

> that as he attended at the ceremony in Iveagh House last year when the statue was presented to the state, another ceremony is unnecessary for the siting of the gift and in the event of a ceremony, he would not consider that he would be the appropriate person to officiate. The Parliamentary Secretary to the M/Finance or, at the highest, the Minister would be the appropriate person to perform this 'unveiling'.[46]

Although Frank Aiken was to officiate at a rather low-key affair, the Office of Public Works had recommended that 'there should be no formal "unveiling" of the statue on its present site' at all.[47] They saw no need: there was nothing to be gained; the Americans had had their day in 1966 and now it would just cost money to stage. Emmet had his statue, what more did his memory want?

While successive governments did not overburden themselves in their efforts to commemorate Emmet, buying Maurice McGonigal's portrait of him in 1958 did not tax them too unduly either. Both government and opposition were happy to use his name whenever a debate in the Dáil, or for that matter, the Seanad, was not quite going their way.[48] Like every other nationalist icon he seemed to come and go at practicality's command. Seán Dunne astutely observed the tendency in 1952 during a debate on social welfare: 'some deputies, notably Government Deputies, spent a good deal of time talking about the civil war as usual, as if it had any connection with this Bill. Other Deputies showed evidence of going back to Wolfe Tone and Robert Emmet if they got a chance.'[49] Indeed, there was a great deal of truth in what he said. Thaddeus Lynch seemed to resort to quoting Emmet whenever he was confronted with any trace of Irish progress: Ireland had taken her place among the nations on a number of occasions, and he seemed most convinced of this point when the Olympic Games were televised from Rome.[50] But perhaps Lynch was merely following an international trend. The Greek representative at the Council of Europe had, after all, evoked the names of 'Emmet and Pearse' as two of 'the great liberators of mankind' in 1956.[51] Others in the Dáil were not so easily impressed, however. For and against, Emmet was paraded out in debates on, amongst other things, the Citizenship Bill, the External Relations Bill, the Republic of Ireland Bill, joining the European Union and Ireland's role in the United Nations.[52] And there were other periodic lapses. A budget worthy of Emmet himself was produced in 1950.[53] To the threat of a Gaelic-speaking Ireland some deputies reminded the Dáil that Emmet knew no Irish and was perhaps a better patriot for it.[54] Emmet seemed to approve and disapprove regardless of policy, party or issue. With not so much known of him, he could be called upon to approve of everything; he could easily be claimed by all. Gearóid Ó Suilleabháin raised a rational voice in the wilderness in October 1927, but it was not often heard again. Beginning as an attack on Fianna Fáil's tactics, it can be read as a plague on both your houses.

> All the gods of Irish-Ireland, of nationality, were called on and were adored and claimed by one Party in this House – Tone, Davis, Emmet, and Patrick Pearse, and I suppose Michael Collins, had he died before the Treaty, would also have been claimed. Appeals like that to gods do not lend towards alleviating and lessening the difficulties that exist.[55]

Ó Suilleabháin's words of wisdom did not seem to apply to his own party. Cosgrave claimed that the Treaty 'represents work that has been done in five years, [work] greater than was accomplished by Emmet, O'Connell, Mitchell [*sic*], Davis, Smith-O'Brien, and Parnell, down even to Mr Redmond with a united country behind him'.[56] Seán MacEntee could not let him away with that and retorted the next day with 'When did the achievement of our nation's unification cease to be one of our national aspirations? Was it when Tone and MacCracken, Emmet and Russell died for Irish Union?'[57] Six years later Seán T. O'Kelly taunted Cosgrave again with his conceit, asking how any erstwhile follower of Tone and Davis and Emmet and Pearse could claim in an Irish assembly that the Treaty was 'one of the greatest victories in Irish history'.[58]

Predictably Eamon de Valera's use of Emmet was a little more selective and astute. In response to the Public Safety Bill in 1927 he argued

> I have no doubt there are men in this House who would call Padraig Pearse a traitor and who agree with Lord Norbury when he called Emmet a traitor. Treason, as defined in law, has never been accepted as true treason by those who believe in Irish Nationality and whose ideas of treason are prompted by their feelings.[59]

He was not so sympathetic towards the sincerity of nationalist feeling when he started executing IRA men 13 years later. But perhaps in 1927 it was the clever thing to say. It was emotive and effective, and his purpose had been served. James Dillon may have meant to insult de Valera when he called him 'a Robert Emmet . . . type' in 1935; but it merely showed how little Dillon knew about popular politics at this point. De Valera was more than happy to accept an insult like that.[60] In radio broadcasts to America de Valera used Emmet much more blatantly, in ways he perhaps could not afford to use at home, in ways that kept American dollars rolling in. In December 1937 he announced across the airwaves that 'the day that this Constitution becomes effective over the whole of the National territory, that day Emmet's epitaph may be written'.[61] The Treaty may be all very well, but de Valera's constitution defined the nation just as Robert Emmet had said it should. While Conor Cruise O'Brien and F. S. L. Lyons may have been suspicious of this type of rhetoric, Roy Foster took a particular dislike to 'the disingenuous litany of Protestant names invoked in the extremist nationalist tradition – Tone, Emmet, Mitchel, Parnell and Childers'.[62] He continued:

> It was an argument used ad nauseum by de Valera, and still adverted to. The implication triumphantly drawn from it is that present-day Protestants have, therefore, nothing to fear from Irish nationalism. This is hardly logical, since all the figures in the extremist-nationalist-Protestant pantheon reacted diametrically against the general Protestant background; they are exceptions, not representatives of a latent syndrome.

He ends by remarking that no one notes the treatment of Protestants during the War of Independence and Civil War. What Foster fails to take account of, even within 11 years of this victimisation in 1919–23, was the fact that de Valera's Protestant contemporaries in the Dáil and Seanad were happy to play de Valera and indeed, all the other invokers of the 'disingenuous litany' at their own game. Trinity College, whether in the context of Dáil constituency realignment or university funding, happily forgot that it had expelled Robert Emmet and most of its other 'patriots' after 1798, and revelled in the fact that it had moulded the boy genius and given the country its foremost martyr.[63] Far from being offended, Trinity's eminent professors seemed more than happy to chime in with the allegedly disingenuous chorus. But if the invocation of the litany was disingenuous, it was no more insulting than Yeats's tirade in the Seanad debate on divorce. Emmet was among the names he spat out in contempt: Swift, Emmet, Burke, Grattan, Parnell, the names that had created 'the best of its [Ireland's] political intelligence'.[64] In his tantrum he may have done well to remember that for most of the periods in question there were no Catholics in parliament for it to be otherwise.

It would be foolish to assume that Emmet's memory suffered more at the hands of Irish governments than the memory of others. He may perhaps have embarrassed them more than most, and embarrassed them equally across party political lines. They may all have claimed him, but apart perhaps from Sinn Féin, Emmet, or at least his absent epitaph, retains the capacity to discomfort them all. The official treatment of Griffith, Collins, indeed Pearse and the men of 1916, who had after all eclipsed Emmet in terms of self-sacrifice for the generation after independence, was no better. It never would be. Lip service was something that could be cheaply paid to them all, as TDs and Senators stumbled to recite as many patriots' names as possible in one breath. After the Civil War, heroes were an awkward luxury that could be done without. Emmet survived because his was a good story, with a touch of romance and a tragic ending. Even so, an Emmet Society was needed in 1963 'because . . . his character had been tarnished by neglect'.[65] His speech from the dock may have turned Countess Markievicz's head; it may have been Michael Collins's party piece: Collins may have sat at the block on which Emmet was beheaded for the film to publicise the Dáil bonds, but Emmet's rebellion was abhorred by Collins; the plumed and parading national foresters were nothing more than a joke.[66] 'I am no Robert Emmet' was all one of Collins's 'Squad' needed to say when he was asked and refused to carry out a doomed operation.[67] It was fine to recite the speech, but to these men and the type of war they fought, Emmet could mean nothing more.

In all the government files there were only three calls to write his epitaph: two were from abroad, and one of those perhaps appropriately from a dead man. It was perhaps Emmet's bad luck that successive governments had always confused or equated commemoration with the epitaph; but then there was so little else for them to commemorate. It is probably the work of another chapter and maybe another book to discover why one perhaps so unworthy of the fuss has clung so long to the popular memory of the nation. We have another nine years to wait for the centenary of Pearse's death, 18 for the 50th anniversary of de Valera's, another 15 for Michael Collins, another 40 for the bicentenary of Daniel O'Connell's demise. It is perhaps unfair but it should at least be interesting to see how the celebration of Emmet will compare to the commemoration of men who made a more discernable difference to Irish lives.

Notes

1 *Dáil Debates*, vol. CCLXVI, col. 1279, 27 June 1973.

2 Ibid., vol. XXXIV, col. 2150, 21 May 1930.

3 *Seanad Debates*, vol. CLXVI, col. 15, 31 Jan. 1996.

4 Ibid.

5 Ibid.

6 Patrick M. Geoghegan, *Robert Emmet: A Life* (Dublin, 2002); Ruan O'Donnell, *Robert Emmet and the Rebellion of 1798* (Dublin, 2003); Ruan O'Donnell, *Robert Emmet and the Rising of 1803* (Dublin, 2003); Ruan O'Donnell, *Remember Emmet: Images of the Life and Legacy of Robert Emmet* (Dublin, 2003); Marianne Elliott, *Robert Emmet: The Making of a Legend* (London, 2003).

7 Geoghegan, *Robert Emmet*, p. xiii.

8 Brian O'Higgins quoted in Elliott, *Robert Emmet*, p. 219.

9 Patrick Baxter, *Seanad Debates*, vol. XXXVI, col. 146, 10 Dec. 1948.

10 Geoghegan, *Robert Emmet*, p. xii.

11 Roy Foster, *Modern Ireland 1600–1972* (London, 1988), p. 370.

12 Richard English, *Ernie O'Malley: IRA Intellectual* (Oxford, 1998), p. 75.

13 Quoted in Frank Pakenham, *Peace by Ordeal: The Negotiation of the Anglo-Irish Treaty of 1921* (London, 1992 edn), pp. 261–2.

14 'A New Zealand Priest' [Rev. T. J. Cahill] to W. T. Cosgrave, 12 Nov. 1923 (NAI, DT s2460a).

15 W. T. Cosgrave to Rev. T. J. Cahill, 16 Feb. 1924, ibid.

16 Liam Mellows to his mother, 8 Dec. 1922.

17 *Dáil Debates*, vol. XL, cols. 70–2, 14 Oct. 1931; J. H. Whyte, *Church and State in Modern Ireland 1923–1979* (Dublin, 1980, 2nd edn), p. 90.

18 *Irish Times*, 6 Sept. 2003.

19 The Department of Finance questioned the appropriateness of the army paying for the burial. Unsigned Finance memo, 18 Aug. 1924 (NAI, DF s004/0013/24).

20 Elliott, *Robert Emmet*, p. 214.

21 Thomas Bodkin to Diarmuid O'Hegarty, 6 Aug. 1931 (NAI, DT s2460a).

22 Memo by W. T. Cosgrave, undated, ibid.

23 *Irish Times*, 2 Oct. 1938.

24 F. Boland to the Secretary of the Dept. of an Taoiseach, 28 Dec. 1938 (NAI, DT s2460a).

25 Memo by Diarmuid O'Hegarty, 31 Dec. 1938, ibid.

26 *Saorstát Éireann: Irish Free State Official Handbook* (Dublin, 1932).

27 Bureau of Military History (BMH), questionnaire, Military Archives.

28 Draft question and reply, 14 and 17 Nov. 1949 (NAI, DT s2460a).

29 *Irish Press*, 7 June 1950.

30 See NAI, DT s14441b.

31 *Dáil Debates*, vol. CXLI, col. 645, 24 July 1953.

32 NAI, DT s15467; *Evening Mail*, 27 Feb. 1953.

33 *Dáil Debates*, vol. CXXXVII, col. 2, 11 Mar. 1953.

34 Ibid.

35 Dr T. Woulfe to Seán T. O'Kelly, 28 May 1953 (NAI, DT s15467a).

36 N. S. Ó Nualláin to Dr T. Woulfe, 24 June 1953, ibid.

37 Christopher T. Emmet was listed as treasurer. American Irish Defence Association (TNA, HS 8/58). My thanks to Eunan O'Halpin for this reference.

38 Department of Foreign Affairs (DFA), Washington Embassy (NAI, DFA 3/127/1 38 p110/1).

39 Speech by John J. Hearne at the acceptance of the seal on behalf of the Irish nation at the Washington Embassy, 15 Sept. 1958, ibid.

40 NAI, DFA 3/127/38.

41 W. P. Fay to Hugh McCann, 1 Apr. 1965, ibid.

42 Hugh McCann to W. P. Fay, 12 Apr. 1965, ibid.

43 The head office of the Department of Foreign Affairs.

44 NAI, DT 96/6/39 s2460b.

45 Report of the inter-departmental committee on site for statue of Robert Emmet, 29 July 1966 (NAI, DT 99/1/9 s2460b).

46 Seán Lemass to P. Ó Foghlú, 7 Nov. 1967, ibid.

47 Memo by N. S. Ó Nualláin, 7 Nov. 1967, ibid.

48 NAI, DT s13682c.

49 *Dáil Debates*, vol. CXXX, col. 1678, 8 Apr. 1952.

50 Ibid., vol. CCXIV, col. 1643, 10 Mar. 1965; see also vol. CXCIX, col. 802, 31 Jan. 1963 and vol. CCXI, col. 695, 29 Apr. 1964.

51 Quoted in Michael Kennedy and Eunan O'Halpin, *Ireland and the Council of Europe: From Isolation Towards Integration* (Strasbourg, 2000), p. 113.

52 *Dáil Debates*, vol. LIV, col. 1607, 19 Dec. 1934; vol. LXIV, cols. 1410–11, 12 Dec. 1936; vol. CCLX, col. 510, 18 Apr. 1972; vol. CLXX, col. 2097, 19 Dec. 2002.

53 Ibid., vol. CXX, col. 2258, 11 May 1950.

54 Ibid., vol. XXVI, col. 1662, 7 Nov. 1928; vol. CCCV, col. 870, 18 Apr. 1978.

55 Ibid., vol. XXI, col. 105, 12 Oct. 1927.

56 Ibid., vol. III, col. 105, 21 Dec. 1921.

57 Ibid., col. 152, 22 Dec. 1921.

58 Ibid., vol. XXI, col. 27, 11 Oct. 1927.

59 Ibid., cols. 1269–70, 10 Nov. 1927.

60 Ibid., vol. LVIII, col. 1172, 23 July 1935. Michael Staines also accused him of being worse than Emmet in 1916. *Seanad Debates*, vol. XVIII, cols. 1376–7, 31 May 1934.

61 Eamon de Valera, broadcast to America, 29 Dec. 1937, quoted in *The Story of Fianna Fáil* (Dublin, 1960), p. 27.

62 Conor Cruise O'Brien, *States of Ireland* (London, 1972), p. 25; F. S. L. Lyons, *Ireland Since the Famine* (London, 1971), p. 232; Roy Foster, *Paddy and Mr Punch: Connections in Irish and English History* (London, 1993), p. 30.

63 See for example, *Dáil Debates*, vol. LII, col. 530, 8 May 1934; vol. LIII, col. 1513, 5 July 1934; vol. LX, col. 236, 6 Feb. 1936; *Seanad Debates*, vol. XVIII, col. 1963, 12 July 1934; vol. XX, cols. 2003–4, 12 Feb. 1936; vol. L, cols. 508–9, 11 Feb. 1959; vol. LXII, col. 409, 20 Dec. 1966. Some included Catholic members speaking in defence of the Protestant minority and its contribution to Irish nationalism.

64 *Seanad Debates*, vol. V, col. 443, 11 June 1925.

65 *Irish Press*, 5 Mar. 1966.

66 Sari Oikarinen, 'The rebel Countess: Constance Markievicz', in Philip Hannon and Jackie Gallagher (eds), *Taking the Long View: 70 Years of Fianna Fáil* (Dublin, 1998), p. 48; T. Ryle

Dwyer, *Big Fellow Long Fellow: A Joint Biography of Collins and de Valera* (Dublin, 1998), pp. 20–1; Peter Somerville-Large, *Irish Voices: An Informal History 1916–1966* (London, 2000 edn), p. 47; C. S. Andrews, *Dublin Made Me* (Dublin and Cork, 1979), p. 45.

67 Vincent Byrne, BMH, Witness Statement 423.

REFLECTIONS ON EMMET

CHAPTER 11

Pearse's Emmet

Séamas Ó Buachalla

There are obvious similarities and historical symmetries between Robert Emmet and Patrick Pearse. Both had strong-minded and principled fathers who, a century apart, influenced their sons in a similar fashion. Both were of a serious and academic cast of mind, given to poetic expression at an early age. Both succeeded by commitment and dedication in recording significant achievements in remarkably short lives, 25 and 37 years respectively. Both, of course, had fallen foul of the authoritarian discipline and anti-national sentiment of Trinity College Dublin. Both had connections with the United States, where some of Emmet's family settled and to where two of Pearse's uncles emigrated; Emmet's political ideals sprang mainly from the American War of Independence.[1] Both Emmet and Pearse had further American connections in that, in March 1914, Pearse gave two commemorative lectures on Emmet in New York, during the three months which he spent in the States seeking funds for Scoil Éanna.

Both Emmet and Pearse are romantically but inconclusively linked with two gifted young women, Sarah Curran and Evelyn Nicholls respectively, concerning both of whom colourful mythologies developed. On the political level, both Emmet and Pearse were involved in organising and leading risings against English rule; both headed a provisional government, published a manifesto and a proclamation – both documents imbued with high ideals and statements of purpose and intent. Both spent their last night in cells at Kilmainham Jail, from whence they both wrote final testamentary letters before facing execution: by hanging at St Catherine's Church in Thomas Street for Emmet, and by firing squad in the Stonebreakers' Yard in Kilmainham for Pearse. While we do have a recognised resting place at Arbour Hill for Pearse, the absence of one for Emmet led W. B. Yeats to assert that the whole country was consequently Emmet's tomb. In New York in 1904, Yeats, in a lecture entitled 'Emmet the apostle of Irish liberty', given in Brooklyn (attended by 4,000 people including three direct descendants of Thomas Addis Emmet, and the sons of John Mitchel and O'Donovan Rossa), defended Emmet from his detractors, rejecting the charge that Emmet was 'a wild, hare-brained vain young man' and presenting him as 'the leading saint of Irish nationality' whose memory is 'honoured throughout the island'.[2]

Finally in 1910, when Pearse moved his school from Cullenwood House to the Hermitage in Rathfarnham, it was to an area closely associated with Emmet, with the Curran family home situated nearby across the road at the Priory, both adjacent to Butterfield House where Emmet came to live with Anne Devlin as his housekeeper. Pearse writes that he himself, in choosing the site for St Enda's, 'Came out to Rathfarnham in the wake of Emmet, tracing him from Marshalsea Lane to Harold's Cross, from Harold's Cross to Butterfield House, from there to the Priory and the Hermitage.'[3] To this day, the long, winding, tree-covered walk to the right of the Hermitage house is known as 'Emmet's Walk', and the southern boundary of the grounds is guarded by 'Emmet's Fort'. 'Emmet's Vine' grew in the former conservatory and beyond the lake there is still a monument to a horse killed on the spot, supposedly the horse of Sarah Curran.

In Pearse's own words, 'Cúchullainn was our greatest inspiration at Cullenswood; Robert Emmet has been our greatest inspiration here.' In this context, we need to understand the use of the word 'inspiration' here by Pearse as referring to one of the central elements of his philosophy of education: for him, the two essential elements of education were *freedom* and *inspiration*. This inspiration, equivalent in its outcome to the long-term impact of the education process on the student, would be found in the ancient classics, the folk-tales of the world, in religion, in music and art taught by musicians and artists, and fundamentally from the personality and character of the teacher.[4]

Turning now to 1914 and the two lectures delivered by Pearse on Emmet in New York, on the 2nd and 9th March – straddling his birthday on the 4th – both entitled 'Robert Emmet and the Ireland of Today' (I and II). Combined with Pearse's oration on Wolfe Tone at Bodenstown on 22 June 1913, they were published under the collective title 'How does she stand' in the volume *Political Writing and Speeches* in 1922.[5] It is worth recalling that, chronologically, Pearse stands midway between us and Emmet; in the sciences of optics and astronomy there is a phenomenon or process called *parallax*, whereby the relative movement of an object and its observer are linked quantitatively. I am of the opinion that the 1914 lectures are an exercise in political or historic parallax: while ostensibly and objectively describing Emmet, they give us also a clear insight into Pearse's political thinking at the time.

The language of the New York lectures, while vehement and hortatory, full of high rhetoric and stirring phrases, is also direct and pragmatic. Disillusioned with those leaders back home who, in return for the promise of a simulacrum of liberty in Home Rule, had pledged their loyalty to the ancient enemy, Pearse asked if there were any group of true men, who could call across to Emmet in the words: 'Brother, we have kept the faith; comrade, we are ready to serve.' For Pearse, 'Patriotism is at once a faith and a service.' His analysis is based on a comparison with religious faith, reflecting the memorised orthodoxy of Butler's red-covered Catechism, which he encountered at school in Westland Row; those beyond a certain age may recognise the following from Butler: 'As the body without the spirit is dead so also faith without good works is dead.' For Pearse, patriotism needs service as the condition of its authenticity; it is not sufficient to say 'I believe' unless one can also say 'I serve.' One finds these and related sentiments throughout Pearse's writings in the years following 1912, indicating not only the evolution of his own thinking but also his wish to mould public opinion; in this case in 1914 among the New York Irish-Americans. Restating his frequently expressed opinion that the Irish revolution began on the day the Gaelic League was founded in 1893, he admits that the League could not complete the task, which was now in the hands of the newly founded Irish Volunteers. The inner significance of this new nationalist movement according to Pearse lies in the fact

> that men of every rank and class and of every shade of religious belief, have discovered that they share a common patriotism, that their faith is one and that there is one service in which they can come together at last, the service of their country in arms.[6]

Accepting that the Volunteers in their first manifestation did not have a broad membership, it does seem that Pearse overstates the position here, especially in view of the developments later in 1914, when those Volunteers who sought to serve only Ireland in arms were, in fact, the minority.

Reducing the political complexity of 1914 Ireland to a binary model, by asserting 'after all there are in Ireland but two parties, those who stand for the English connection and those who stand against it', Pearse posed the question 'where do the Irish Volunteers stand?' He answered it by stating that he could not speak for the Volunteers, but speaking personally he was of the firm conviction that the substantial task remained of achieving Irish nationhood and that could be achieved only by armed men, thus foreshadowing his decision later that year in joining the minority on the Volunteer Council. Pearse concluded by asking the audience to salute the founding of the Volunteers as an augury that Ireland would never sell her birthright of liberty for a mess of pottage.

If the first lecture was centred on patriotism and national service, the second, delivered a week later, was concerned with separatism and self-determination, and the assumed and imagined attitudes of Tone and Emmet to the Home Rill Bill of 1912. Sharing a platform with two others, Pearse began by asserting that 'we who speak here tonight, are the voice of an idea which is older than any empire and will outlast every empire'. The inheritors of that idea have been in continuous struggle with one of the most powerful empires ever built, renewing the struggle in each generation; when England seeks to purchase us with a bribe, some brave man redeems us with a sacrifice. But, according to Pearse, there can be no peace between right and wrong, between truth and falsehood, between justice and oppression, between freedom and tyranny. The Home Rule Bill, involving England holding out the hand of friendship, is regarded by Redmond as 'the final settlement between two nations'.

Pearse then poses a question: 'would Tone and Emmet have accepted the 1912 bill as the final settlement?' He replies that, if we are heirs to their principles, we cannot accept any settlement which does not, in Tone's words. 'break the connection with England, the never-failing source of all our political evils'. If we are not faithful to Tone and Emmet, how dare we go in annual pilgrimage to Bodenstown? How dare we gather here or elsewhere to commemorate the faith and sacrifice of Emmet? He asks: 'do we discharge our duty to Emmet's memory by annually according him our pity?'

He then renews his attack on the Parliamentary Party and the Redmondites, who by promising Irish loyalty to England, are wrong: they are showing that they have dallied so long at English feasts, that they have lost touch with the ancient unpurchaseable faith of Ireland, the ancient stubborn thing that forbids any loyalty from Ireland to England, any union between us and them, any surrender of one jot of our claim to freedom, even in return for all the blessings of Pax Britannica.

In Pearse's analysis, the spirit of Irish Patriotism called to Tone and Mitchel in a different manner from that in which it called to Emmet: 'In Emmet it called to a dreamer and he awoke a man of action; it called to a student and a recluse and he stood forth a leader of men; it called to one who loved the ways of peace and he became a revolutionary'. Pearse then examines the life of Emmet, whose image, he thinks, is so dominated by the memory of his death that we forget the life of which the death was only the necessary completion. Little sign there of the 'necrophilia' so recently beloved of commentators who think that Pearse located his school in the Priory, the Curran house in Rathfarnham. One expects that commentators would establish and collect the basic historical facts before ascending to the higher realms of historical psychoanalysis.

In his analysis of Emmet's life, we can discern some points of self-analysis by Pearse, in which elements of Emmet's life resonate with episodes in his own life. In Pearse's view: 'For Emmet, finely gifted though he was, was just a young man with the same limitations, the same self-questioning, the same falterings, the same kindly human emotions surging up sometimes in such strength as almost to drown a heroic purpose – as many a young man we have known.' Emmet's routine work of correspondence, committee meetings, dealing with difficulties – even the vulgar difficulty of want of funds – these are the reality of the pre-Rising period of which Pearse was also later aware. Emmet, in his time, had the same poor human material to work with: men who misunderstood, men who bungled, who talked too much, who failed at the last moment. According to Pearse, the tasks to be undertaken in 1914 were Emmet's tasks of silent unattractive work, routine correspondence, organising and planning, tasks which coloured heavily the last two years of his own life.

The historical parallax between Emmet and Pearse is evident here in the second New York lecture where, in describing the persona, 'the gentle and grave humanity of Emmet', Pearse is also revealing the contemporary dynamic tensions of his own life: the burden of supporting his family, one of whom was in prolonged need of psychiatric care; the financial problems of St Enda's; and, above all, his growing political commitment to a policy of separatism and self-determination – in a word, the abandonment of *An Claidheamh Soluis* for the Howth rifle.

SOME CONCLUDING POINTS

1 The block on which, supposedly, Emmet was beheaded was kept at St Enda's, having been purchased by Pearse from a butcher in Thomas Street, according to some of the former St Enda pupils. It was still in St Enda's in the early 1960s.[7]

2 The statue of Emmet which stands on St Stephen's Green, opposite no. 110, the house where Emmet was born on 4 March 1878, came from the Emmet family in the United States; the project of securing and erecting the statue was mainly due to the initiative of a former pupil of Pearse's, Sean Dowling, and his nephew, Piaras Mac Lochlann, who was an official in the Board of Works.

3 Pearse's 'morbidly devout Catholicism' has been adduced as a factor in relation to its relevance to the Christ-like 'blood sacrifice' and his political writings. I would beg to dissent from this view of Pearse as a pious Irish Catholic who accepted the socio-political diktats of the Catholic clergy without murmur. There is nobody else of Pearse's prominence in that first decade of the twentieth century, 1900–10, who so consistently queried, intelligently criticised, and contradicted the official church policies in print and voice. This, for example, applies to the management of national schools; the language policy of the training colleges; the Gaeltacht bishops' policy on the language; the 1907 Devolution Bill; the 1908 Irish Universities Act; and the prolonged

controversy over the dismissal of Dr Michael O'Hickey from his chair at Maynooth (this last issue was discussed in *An Claidheamh Soluis* 1 May 1909 to 5 August 1909. Pearse's Catholicism is much more German and French than Irish: had it been of the 'traditional' Irish unquestioning type, there would have been no motivation for Fr P. Dineen, SJ, to seek to remove Pearse from the editorship of *An Claidheamh Soluis* and to wish to establish a new Gaelic League more suitable for Catholics.

4 The alleged quote from Pearse in the GPO in 1916, to the effect that 'Emmet had lasted only ten minutes and we lasted a full week', seems far from authentic. The more usual scenario presented of the GPO is more akin to 'organised chaos' than to a leisurely atmosphere in which one of the leaders was engaging in trivial chatter. Furthermore, on a technical level, such a comment would have to have been made on the last day or two of the week, when the minds of those in the GPO, especially the leaders, would have been concerned with more immediate, serious matters.

Notes

1 Patrick M. Geoghegan, *Robert Emmet: A Life* (Dublin, 2002), pp. 40–8.

2 For this speech, see John P. Frayne and Colton Johnson (eds), *Uncollected Prose by W. B. Yeats*, vol. 2 (London, 1975), pp. 310–27.

3 Patrick Pearse, 'By way of comment', *An Macaomh*, II: 3 (Christmas 1910), pp. 11–12.

4 Séamas Ó Buachalla (ed.), *A Significant Irish Educationalist: The Educational Writings of P. H. Pearse* (Cork, 1980), pp. 378–80.

5 'How does she stand?', *The Collected Works of Padraic H. Pearse vol. 3: Political Writings and Speeches* (Dublin and London, 1922), pp. 64–87. First oration, pp. 64–75; second oration, pp. 76–87.

6 Ibid., pp. 72–3.

7 Observed by author, 1964.

CHAPTER 12

Robert Emmet and Roger Casement

W. J. Mc Cormack

'Do you ever remember a European question on which Ireland did not at once take the opposite side to England? – well that kills all thought & encourages the most miserable kind of mob rhetoric.'
(W. B. Yeats to George W. Russell, 5 May 1919)

In 1875, 19-year-old Sigmund Freud visited his half-brother in Manchester. During his English sojourn, he reached the shores of the Irish Sea near Liverpool, but no evidence suggests that he ever took the logical step westward. Had he done so, he could have taken part in celebrations to mark the centenary of Daniel O'Connell's birth or bought a copy of John O'Rourke's new book, *The History of the Great Irish Famine*. But had he really travelled to Ireland in 1875, Freud might more likely have looked up George Sigerson, translator of Jean-Martin Charcot's writings on neuro-psychology. Freud became Charcot's pupil.

The O'Connell business was perhaps the first major Irish exercise in centennial and semi-centennial commemoration. We have been busy ever since. Nevertheless, there is a distinct selectivity at work within the industry. In the opening pages of Francis Costello's recent book, *The Irish Revolution and its Aftermath*, the author ruefully notes the little attention given to certain occasions – the 75th anniversaries of (first) Dáil Éireann and (somewhat later) the Irish Free State.[1] In contrast, we can point to at least five books about Robert Emmet produced for or during the year of his bicentenary, not to mention stamps and conferences. Is there a discernable pattern to the business of commemoration? Perhaps the question would best be directed towards Anne Dolan whose choice of the Civil War as a focus for discussion and analysis might be described as Die Hard. Nevertheless, I hope to shed some light on the preferences and priorities underlying acts of commemoration, relative to the revolutionary period of 1798–1803 and the insurrectionary period of 1916–1923. In doing so I hope also to look at the parallel roles of Emmet and Roger Casement.

An obvious first move would be to remind Dr Costello that the commemoration business, whether official, academic or commercial, is sharply focused on individuals rather than events, institutions or other non-personal topics. The Famine is clearly an exception as was (in 1929) Catholic emancipation. The impact of the 1966 commemorations of the Easter Rising, may have discouraged similar pageant-like celebrations of the path towards independence. The Treaty, the formal inauguration of the Free State, the Constitution of 1937, the Declaration of the Republic – these have not generated extensive commemorative activities on anything like the scale of 1966.

In contrast, the heroes (with some heroines) of Irish history are regularly given the treatment. It would be helpful to know more about the way in which individual figures were and are chosen for commemoration on Irish stamps and currency notes. These have prominently featured Father Luke Wadding, Theobald Wolfe Tone, Daniel O'Connell, Charles Stewart Parnell, James Joyce, W. B. Yeats, and one or two women. Modelled on British practice, in which the monarch's head is a *sine qua non*, Irish issue has given consistent prominence to the individual portrait. I am aware that Maria Edgeworth, at one point short-listed for inclusion on the currency notes, was dropped in favour of a more religious woman. And Michael Collins was obliged to wait until 1990. But beyond a few observations on requirements of Irish birth – ignored in the case of Saint Patrick – there seems to have been no systematic analysis of this extensive body of official commemorative material.

A litany of individual names certainly informs the rituals of commemoration. In two poems – 'September 1913' and 'Easter 1916' – Yeats treats the two periods with which we are concerned here. The first is dramatised in the names of Edward Fitzgerald, Robert Emmet and Wolfe Tone, whose fate is in turn distilled into 'loneliness and pain'. The second, as everybody knows, recites the names of 'MacDonagh and MacBride,/ And Connolly and Pearse' to emphasise how, with their deaths, 'A terrible beauty is born'. These poems have often been compared, but I do not know that their common determination to convert collective group action into individual pen-portraiture has been fully noted. Yeats has little interest in the United Irishmen: he is concerned with Fitzgerald and Emmet. And, though he was supposedly a sworn member of the Irish Republican Brotherhood, he has little interest in the Citizen Army or the Volunteers as collective bodies of fighting men. His frequent invocation of the collective term, Young Ireland, however, is usually to damn or at least damage that school of Irish nationalism and especially its poets. When Yeats invokes John Mitchel, there is no association of him with Young Ireland.

Yeats did not invent this procedure of individuation. Its origins are no doubt complex and diverse, ultimately reaching back to the plethoric tradition of ten thousand Irish saints. But the Fenian practice of exploiting funerals and reinterments unquestionably concentrated rhetorical enthusiasm on the solitary deceased. The charismatic role of Charles Stewart Parnell, in leading the Irish campaign out of the doldrums and into the very processes of constructing government majorities in the House of Commons, confirmed the symbolic power of the exceptional individual, a power in no way diminished by the circumstances of his fall, his death, and his divisive legacy.

Perhaps the least recognised contributor to the Irish cult of the national hero is the enemy of these heroes – British power. As Patrick Pearse gloatingly observed, 'the fools, they have left us our Fenian dead'. But it was invariably an individual dead Fenian who served the cause, or Fenians who could be individuated by name – as in Allen, Larkin and O'Brien. The potency of naming, which Yeats acquired from popular tradition, is founded on the individual, not the collective. Here a devil's alliance may be detected. British responses to Irish nationalist clamour were for the most part channelled through due processes of law (however morally offensive the law is to some), ended in the trial of an individual, and in his conviction and punishment. The very nature of trials pitted the individual against his foes and accusers, and laid the ground for an iconography as well as a hagiography.

Consider the case of the United Irishmen, undoubtedly organisers of the most formidable challenge to the *status quo* in Ireland for a century. Their leading members included Oliver Bond, the Honourable Simon Butler, Lord Edward Fitzgerald, Henry Joy McCracken, Arthur O'Connor, the Sheares brothers, and of course Theobald Wolfe Tone. If we take Henry Boylan's *Dictionary of Irish Biography*[2] as a measure of serious popular interest in the notable figures of history, then only those who died in 1798 gain admission. These are Bond, Fitzgerald, McCracken, Henry and John Sheares, and Wolfe Tone. Though sentenced to death after a trial, Bond died in prison of natural causes. Fitzgerald died resisting arrest, Tone committed suicide in custody; McCracken and the Sheares brothers were duly executed. We might add the Reverend James Porter, hanged at Greyabbey in July 1789, though not a United Irishman.

Commemoration has chosen Tone, and I think historians are unlikely to question its decision. For a number of reasons, Tone's death was long treated as a case of unofficial murder by the authorities, a factor which in itself heightened the 'loneliness and pain' aspect of individuation. Even Tone can hardly challenge Emmet for primacy in the lists of recognisable nationalist heroes. And the remaining twenty or so rebels executed in the autumn of 1803 do not count either.

Emmet's advantages as a cultic hero can be briefly listed. He was young, he was virtually alone in his contribution to the national cause, his family situation generated sympathy, and he was tried in court and publicly executed. Additionally, he acquired in death a qualification which had distinguished Tone among the dead of 1798 – he was the author of words deemed or rendered memorable. In the creation of Emmet's cultic status – charted in Marianne Elliott's contribution to the bibliography now in flood[3] – the United Irishmen as a collective body, together with their policy and strategy in its detail, are largely forgotten. This was to prove helpful in the generation of a pedigree of Irish nationalism, for it removed awkward differences of political thinking and substituted the common name of individuated heroism. Thus Pearse's Fenian dead could by implication include Wolfe Tone, while the Mayo IRA of forty years ago felt comfortable in celebrating the Moores of Moore Hall whose house they had burnt down.

Many of the distinguishing characteristics of Emmet in relation to the United Irishmen are reproduced in the case of Roger Casement and his part in the events of 1916. Perhaps the major differences should be noted first. Whereas Emmet set about to follow up an unsuccessful rebellion with a second one, Casement strove in his last weeks to prevent a rebellion he felt could not succeed. Whereas Emmet was precociously young, Casement was in retirement. Nevertheless, the resemblances – as shaped by the cultic and commemorative processes – are more compelling. In different ways, both Emmet and Casement deplored the rebellion with which they were intimately associated. This ambiguity in relation to the consequences of rebellion assisted in generating an ethical dimension.

Like Emmet in his time, and unlike the other executed leaders of 1916, Casement faced a civil trial and an execution duly notified to the public. The execution of Emmet in 1803 and of Casement in 1916 generated complex emotional reactions among those in power, quite beyond anything to be found in the case of – say – Oliver Bond or Eamon de Valera, both sentenced to death but (for different reasons in each case) not executed. These reactions, while by no means identical, included in each case a strong element of guilty conscience. Here too we find a factor contributing to cultic status which is contributed by the hostile power.

Let us contrast these individual cases against larger historical events – the Races of Castlebar (1798), the skirmish at Tallaght (1867), and the shootings at Bachelor's Walk (1912). None of these could be regarded as decisive, yet manifestly they were occurrences involving considerable numbers of participants on both sides. I doubt if anyone (apart of course from Kevin Whelan) could name a participant killed in each of the three events. These events are remembered but they are not commemorated. They are marked off categorically or qualitatively from the deaths of Emmet and Casement, but they possess some resemblance to the deaths of those rude mechanicals of revolution executed for their part in Emmet's endeavour. Yet if one were to pick out the least known among those executed in Dublin in 1916 – let us choose Michael O'Hanrahan – is it not true that he is generally famous for being commemorated? His name on a list, together with two forgotten novels, is sufficient to establish a degree of individuation, confirmed in execution. It is unlikely that any of the first twenty people one would stop in O'Connell Street would recognise a picture of Michael O'Hanrahan any more than they could tell Oliver Bond from Henry Sheares. Yet Emmet and Casement possess a high recognition quotient at least equal to that of Tone or Pearse.

Identity in this sense is not a one-way projection. One elaborate 1803 version of Emmet's speech carried a folding portrait and a quotation from Sallust to prove the young Dubliner a reckless conspirator of the Catiline model. Nor is commemoration synonymous with celebration: one motive behind the 'Sallust' version of Emmet's speech and image may have intended a Fawkes-like perpetuation of the young man's memory.

One factor ensuring the iconic familiarity of both Emmet and Casement was the concentration provided by the processes of trial and execution – public execution in Emmet's case. At a time when the noose fell on many for crimes less grave than treason or murder, popular culture responded with a steady supply of ballads, broadsides, woodcut portraits, and 'last words'. The extensive public iconography of Robert Emmet is inextricably bound up with the complex bibliography of his last words, more correctly, his speech from the dock at the end of his trial. (There is, strangely enough, a detailed and heterodox account in the *Field Day Anthology of Irish Writing*.[4]) None of this applied in the case of the Sheares brothers, or even that of Tone.

Casement is also familiar to many who would not recognise pictures of half a dozen among those comrades of his executed in Dublin after court-martial or military tribunal. His beard was (I think) unique, but there was also a constant description of Casement as 'handsome', a term which may have allowed for a cryptic sexual reading. For that reason or others, Casement had an iconic portfolio long before he was arrested in Kerry. He had become a celebrity as early as 1904, with his report on atrocities from the Congo, and he had become an avid collector and disseminator of portrait photographs. His arraignment, trial, and appeal generated further strata of image-making, by press photographers, society artists, and personal friends. Like the rival versions of Emmet's speech, these pictures are not all tributes or endorsements. In place of the loyalist exploitation which was Emmet's initial fate after death, Casement was exposed to the ambiguity of the image itself in an age of modernity.

The famous sketch of Casement in the dock is dominated by horizontal bars which, at a literal level, encode his imprisonment but, at another, act as censor, obliterating from our view certain not-to-be aired anxieties which pertain to the viewer at least as much as to the subject. This leads me to an aspect of the comparison between Emmet and Casement which deserves more attention than it can receive here. I mean the erotics of commemoration. In the vigorous campaigns to establish the two men as heroes of their respective periods, their sexual status plays a significant role – albeit through very different vocabularies. Emmet's relationship with Sarah Curran is important in establishing its heroic virtue. He led a blameless life, we are told, and the phrase is revealing in that it seeks to eliminate precisely the element of blame. The blame is not exclusively or even primarily sexual, as Ruan O'Donnell's biography concedes in describing Emmet's conversational indiscretions.[5] Sarah Curran also functions in the heroic cult as a kind of medium through which Emmet's relationship with a different kind of politics, that of John Philpot Curran, is negotiated – at Curran's expense, of course. Thus Emmet can be invoked as a necessary heir to the old parliamentary tradition and as a proto-Fenian, a most usefully protean constituency.

The contribution of Thomas Moore to a conventional sexualisation of Emmet is evident in the Victorian reputation, and cannot have harmed the dead hero in his trans-Atlantic migration. One has also been reminded that Emmet impressed Southey and Coleridge, though perhaps 'appalled' might be the more appropriate verb. Heroes of the Romantic age were more often demonic than domestic, and the reformulation of Emmet for an emerging nationalist ideology required specialist treatment. Family is a powerful motif in the American transmission of Emmet back to his native land. This is of course augmented by a conversion to Catholicism by some members of the family – purging the legacy of excess French rationalism and any hint of a concomitant libertinism.

Casement at first looks like a very different proposition. Twice the age of Emmet at the time of execution, he is processed through a lengthy sequence of legal actions – arrest, confinement in a number of prisons (Brixton, the Tower of London, etc.) arraignment, trial, appeal, and finally execution in Pentonville. Compared to that, Emmet's end was expeditious – tried one day, dead the next. The passage of time in which Casement's fate is decided also finds him embroiled in a sexual debate through the spreading of rumours about depraved private diaries. If Emmet's speech finds its canonical text only after the various productions of rival factions have lost distinctiveness in the public memory, Casement's words become ambiguous even while he remains alive. His most tenacious defender, Eamon de Valera, suggested that the extent of Casement's sacrifice might never be known, a prospect greatly aided by Dev's refusal to take up the forensic cause. Among the biographers, Brian Inglis was inclined to see in Yeats's lines 'And what if excess of love/ Bewildered them till they died?' an anonymous reference to Casement in a poem replete with the names of Casement's colleagues.[6]

Judged in another light, Emmet and Casement converge. Each came to his role both in action and reputation from a traumatised family background in which service to the Establishment had played a part. Their commitment to Irish independence involved a high degree of overcoming, of quitting a pre-established mental context and mode of feeling, and articulating something which not only differed from, but actively opposed, their previous existence. In each case, the role of siblings was important, and one can observe in each career a form of brotherly rivalry or emulation. The Emmet brothers were, as a group, more cohesive and more equally balanced, but the death of Christopher Temple Emmet threw up a burden and a challenge which the youngest – Robert – embraced. The Casement brothers were or became borderline dysfunctional as individuals but – notably through Roger's efforts – they clung together emotionally even when scattered through three continents. It was Roger Casement's posthumous misfortune not to have Thomas Addis Emmet, but Tom Casement, as brother and advocate. And had either of the Casement brothers lived in the United States, Roger's fame might have been consolidated as a 'blameless life'.

Sigmund Freud has been patiently waiting since we left him on the shores of the Irish Sea in 1875. Perhaps he noted the Meath by-election, when a former Cambridge student who (like Emmet) never graduated won a seat in parliament. Better than either Emmet or Casement, Charles Stewart Parnell fits the model of hero later developed by Freud in what was virtually his last publication, *Moses and Monotheism* (1939).[7] Freud's scandalous discovery or proposal was that Moses had been not Jewish, but Egyptian. Alongside this particular case he developed a broader view of the modern hero, and of exceptional contributors to cultural life: he, for it was more or less a male monopoly, is frequently and crucially exceptional in coming from outside the culture which embraces him. The examples cited are now perhaps unimpressive – Napoleon, Chamisso, Disraeli, and so forth. But the theoretical basis is highly suggestive, not least for the Irish context.

Instead of hailing Grattan, Emmet, Davis, Parnell, Casement and others of that ilk as figures who, through a process of political awakening, opted to abandon the ilk for the Celt, it would be instructive to observe each through a Freudian lens, at least for a moment. Perhaps Grattan and Davis are the lesser cases, for their success occurred in a milieu where little boundary crossing was required. Grattan was always a member of the political class, with roots in Dublin's politico-administrative system. Davis was a writer and journalist at a time when those activities were becoming professionalised. It is worth noting, however, that Grattan and Davis qualify as heroes because of terminal circumstances which reshape them as glorious failures.

The other three certainly reward analysis on Freud's terms – outsiders in complex ways, unattached domestically, overcomers of the past. I would add a further characteristic to the cultic hero thus conceived: he is incomplete. Indeed, the potential for cultic development (or exploitation) depends on his incompleteness in some regard which followers can aspire to remedy. Emmet brilliantly encoded this in the speech from the dock, when he insisted on the non-writing of his epitaph. Casement, for his part, enigmatically observed that his motives might never be known. The cultic hero is not just commemorated and celebrated; he is partly or virtually invented to personify a collective of which he was, inevitably, a non-representative member. The Reverend James Porter makes for poor cultic heroism; he had not joined any collective from which an individual might be drawn up by the commemorative process.

Let me conclude with some more politically insensitive comments. A striking aspect of Emmet's cult relates to the unknown site of his burial. One could trace a motif of this kind through the posthumous sightings of Parnell at Bayreuth (of all places) and the long contention about the last resting-place of Casement's remains. Attempts to locate Emmet's grave have occasionally characterised the commemorative business, but clearly nobody's heart is in it. The grave is a necessary part of Emmet's incompleteness. Unburied in one sense, he is constantly available for resurrection: indeed, is already among us, Christ and Catiline hand in his own glove. Is it therefore entirely a coincidence that, in the month of Robert Emmet's bicentenary, the police force of an independent Irish state was digging for the grave of seventeen-year-old Columba McVeigh, deposited there by men who venerate Emmet? Is not Jean McConville the Anne Devlin of our times?

Notes

1 Francis Costello, *The Irish Revolution and its Aftermath 1916–23* (Dublin, 2002).

2 Henry Boylan, *A Dictionary of Irish Biography* (Dublin, 1978).

3 Marianne Elliott, *Robert Emmet: The Making of a Legend* (London, 2003).

4 Seamus Deane (ed.) *The Field Day Anthology of Irish Writing* (Derry, 1991), vol. 1, pp. 933–9.

5 Ruan O'Donnell, *Remember Emmet: Images of the Life and Legacy of Robert Emmet* (Bray, 2003).

6 Brian Inglis, *Roger Casement* (London, 2002), p. 397.

7 Sigmund Freud, *Moses and Monotheism*, trans. Katherine Jones (London, 1939).

CHAPTER 13

The Trial of Robert Emmet

Adrian Hardiman

I researched Robert Emmet's trial in 2003 with a view to providing a paper for the Bar Council's commemoration of the event. My emphasis was, not surprisingly in view of the intended audience, a forensic one. How did an alarmingly bad case, as Chief Secretary Wickham assessed it, turn into an unanswerable one in less than three weeks? Emmet's leading counsel, Leonard MacNally, was notoriously a Castle agent: how exactly did this affect the defence? Was Professor Marianne Elliott right in her view that, despite everything, the trial was a fair one?[1] Could anything have been done for Emmet from a legal viewpoint? Do the details of early nineteenth-century criminal trial procedure cast any light on the ongoing controversy surrounding the authenticity of the famous speech from the dock?

These issues provide the emphasis for this chapter as well. But the trial and the events immediately surrounding it have a broader interest. The trial transcript, the official and the private correspondence about it, the love letters to and from Sarah Curran and the well-recorded interrogation of Emmet before the Irish privy council are a virtual time capsule of early nineteenth-century Ireland. Various notables of the day – John Philpot Curran, Lord Norbury, MacNally himself, William Wickham and Lord Lieutenant Hardwicke – are shown in oblique and fascinating lights. Other than Curran, their very names would now scarcely be known but for their connection with Emmet. Light is also shown on such ephemera of cultural history as the notion of 'honour' shared by political opponents and the attitude that this led them to adopt to women – at once patronising and highly favourable. These things would scarcely be obtainable otherwise.

My thesis is that Emmet's was a show trial in three different senses. First and most obviously the result was rigged. Second, the trial and execution were constructed as a badly needed demonstration that the Irish administration had indeed cracked the conspiracy that had produced the alarming events of 23 July 1803. Third, the trial provided an opportunity for various ambitious men who had opposed the Union only three years before ostentatiously to change their stance and for others to affirm their loyalty. All these things are salutary to reflect on even today.

Their result was to turn the trial into a foregone conclusion. The precise way in which this was done is the principal subject of this chapter. The effect of doing it was to ensure that, in Emmet's own words, 'the sentence was already pronounced at the Castle before your jury was empanelled'.[2]

The fact that it was done enabled the government to turn the prosecution of Emmet into a show trial in two other and quite separate ways. It may help an understanding of the trial to discuss them briefly. The Irish government under Philip Yorke, Earl of Hardwicke, as lord lieutenant and William Wickham as chief secretary had been grossly embarrassed by the rebellion and the weakness and confusion of the government's response to it. Hardwicke's brother, who was a British minister, wrote privately to him telling him that letters from Ireland were feeding hysterical newspaper and parliamentary outbursts which Hardwicke had to answer immediately if his government in Ireland was to continue. The government remained under severe parliamentary attack and Hardwicke and his associates continued to construct long self-justifying accounts of their failure to predict and suppress the Rebellion.

In the immediate aftermath of 23 July, the government caused the suspension of *habeas corpus*, the passage (or rather revival) of the Insurrection Act, and they conducted mass arrests and searches. All this gave the impression of activity but the principal strategy was a policy of state trials followed by almost immediate executions in Dublin from 31 August on. This, they felt, was the best answer to their critics. Hardwicke's wife wrote to a friend at that time:

> The ignorant or angry letters from Dublin were believed in England . . . They loudly declared . . . that no jury would dare find the rebels guilty or, if they did, [no] government dare to punish them. In spite of all the violence [of the letters] they have seen that the slow but steady march of justice can overtake the offender even in this lawless country . . . The sentences being put in force the following day has struck much awe on the minds of those who talk so loud of the fear or weakness of their rulers.[3]

The principal difficulty in this strategy was that most of the prisoners tried and executed were, as Wickham himself admitted, 'miserably poor', and plainly not leader figures. When Emmet was captured the lord lieutenant said only, 'There is every reason to believe that he was deeply implicated in the affair of 23 July, but I confess that I had imagined that he had escaped.'[4] Almost immediately, however, in circumstances I shall describe, it became possible to portray Emmet as the sole leader of the rebellion, now brought to justice. This accounts for much of the hyperbole in the prosecution speeches at the trial. The government desperately needed a prominent, and Protestant, victim on whom the whole rebellion could be blamed.

Third, the trial provided the opportunity for a conspicuous display of loyalty and attachment to the government by some of those who had previously been bitter opponents. Most obvious amongst this group was William Conyngham Plunket. He had been a patriotic parliamentarian who in 1800 had promised to oppose the Union settlement with his blood. It is thus certainly true that, in the understated phrase of the chief secretary, 'He had not previously been associated with the government'. But he was instructed as the third of the seven counsel who prosecuted Emmet and he controversially exercised the crown's right of reply although the defence neither called evidence nor addressed the jury. His speech was in effect a declaration of his conversion to the government side, where it caused absolute glee. Speaking of the speech Wickham wrote to his predecessor:

> It was delivered on purpose to show his entire and unqualified renunciation of his former principles, his determination on long and mature reflection to support the Union after having been its inveterate opposer, and to stand or fall with the present administration. You may naturally suppose that this is the prelude to closer connection, and that it will be the death-blow to the anti-Union party at the bar.[5]

Before the year ended Plunket was appointed solicitor general and he went on to enjoy a remarkable political career both in Ireland and in England.

A similar though more private act of conversion occurred with John Philpot Curran whose daughter's involvement with Emmet was a cause of gross embarrassment. This, paradoxically, forced him into closer contact with the administration with results I shall shortly mention.

These men represented new supporters of the Union settlement and of the government. Their older and more reactionary supporters were typified by Lord Norbury, chief justice of the common pleas, who presided at the trial. He was the practitioner *par excellence* of the extraordinary system of jobbery which characterised the government of Ireland in the late eighteenth and early nineteenth centuries. He had held every lucrative legal office under the pre-Union parliament and his price for his services had been his own ennoblement and appointment to judicial office. Since it did not suit him to accept these rewards until after the Union had been passed, he had extracted a down payment in the form of the elevation of his wife to the peerage, in 1795. He was aptly described by Daniel O'Connell as a 'judicial bully, butcher and buffoon'.[6] A more sympathetic commentator, the former Irish Chief Secretary Charles Abbot, described him in September 1802 as 'scarcely fit for the office which he holds'.

THE CASE AGAINST EMMET

It is often thought that the case against Emmet was one of irresistible strength so that, for example, the corruption of his defence counsel, though deplorable, made no difference. For instance, the participants in an RTÉ programme broadcast on Monday 8 September 2003 mistakenly thought that Emmet had pleaded guilty so that there was 'very little role' for MacNally. Contemporary records disprove this proposition, both in terms of the evidence that was available and of the applicable law.

On 26 August 1803, the day after his arrest, Emmet was committed to Kilmainham Jail. The register of the prison shows that this was on the authority of Chief Secretary William Wickham, for the offence of high treason. But Wickham was not then confident that he could convict Emmet of this offence. On 28 August Wickham wrote to the Home Office explaining his fear that if Emmet denied having involvement in the conspiracy hc might go free. He listed the evidence then available to the crown under seven headings. Five of these were documentary, including the original draft of the proclamation of the provisional government. The other two were circumstantial – his attempted escape when arrested and his request to the owner of the house where he was staying not to put his alias on the list of persons resident in the house which, under martial law regulations, was required to be displayed on the door. Wickham's difficulty was that Emmet's handwriting could not be proved. He recorded: 'Those who know his handwriting in better days cannot say that they believe the papers of which we are in possession to be written by him.'[7] Because, in Wickham's words, 'He was very much beloved in private life', he was pessimistic about getting other witnesses as to Emmet's handwriting. Worse than that, the documents did not appear to have been written by the same person so that 'on account of the dissimilarity of the handwriting it would probably be thought more prudent not to produce them'.[8] Wickham concluded that:

> If the prosecution against him should fail, it will probably be on account of his changing frequently his manner of writing. We cannot, I fear, convict him without producing as his handwriting different papers written apparently by different persons.[9]

Furthermore, although the authorities had available to them a man who had been captured by the rebels and saved from summary execution by their leader, this person, Patrick Farrell, would not identify the leader as Emmet. In those circumstances the persons present at the prosecutor's meeting described by Wickham gave serious consideration to bringing forward what he called 'secret information'. In this context, this can only be the evidence of Leonard MacNally the radical nationalist lawyer who, from 1794 until his death in 1820, was secretly in the pay of Dublin Castle and who was to receive a special bonus for the information he supplied about Emmet. The group discussed this possibility but Wickham recorded: 'There is but one opinion on the subject . . . [I]t were a thousand times better that Emmet should escape than that we should close forever a most accurate source of information.'[10] Leonard MacNally appears to be the only source, available to the government in August 1803, who meets that description.

It thus appears that, as of the date of Wickham's letter, there was no direct evidence available to implicate Emmet in the offence of high treason. There were documents which were highly incriminating but could not be proved. This situation did not change: after the trial Wickham wrote to Hardwicke's brother Charles Yorke, who was then the British home secretary:

> Though he was educated at the college and had resided so much in Dublin there was no person to be found who could prove his handwriting in a legal manner . . . Singular as it may appear, though we were in possession of several letters and papers that were written by him, it was impossible to obtain proof of his handwriting.[11]

The other evidence available at the end of August 1803 was not believed even by Wickham himself to amount to a sufficient case of high treason: he expressly contemplated the possibility that Emmet would escape conviction.

Notwithstanding this, on the day after the trial the lord lieutenant, Hardwicke, was able to report to the home secretary that it was 'universally admitted that a more complete case of treason was never stated in a court of justice'.[12] Accordingly, the principal legal mystery of the case against Emmet is to explain how a prosecution weak almost to the point of non-existence – so weak that those in charge of it seriously considered exposing their most effective and most secret agent to shore it up – became one of irresistible strength in a period of less than three weeks.

It is noteworthy that Emmet was charged only with treason and not with the murder of Lord Kilwarden, who had been killed on Thomas Street after Emmet had withdrawn. This is particularly strange because, to the outraged loyalist community, the murder of a distinguished judge and notable moderate had caused more fear and distress than any other aspect of the rebellion. But to have charged Emmet with murder would have required explicit evidence of his participation in the crime or his ordering of it, or of the murder of government officials generally. Since the government had no evidence whatever along these lines, it adopted the much easier expedient of charging treason which could be inferred, *so the Judge directed*, from very oblique proofs.

INTERROGATION AND MUZZLING OF THE DEFENCE

On 30 August Emmet was taken from Kilmainham Jail to Dublin Castle for interrogation before the Irish Privy Council. The members present were Lord Redesdale the lord chancellor, Attorney General Standish O'Grady, Wickham, and the under secretary, Alexander Marsden. At this session the crown was presented with a solution to their dilemma, though they did not at first recognise it. Emmet confirmed his identity and stated: 'Having now answered my name I must decline answering any further questions.'[13] He declined to say whether he had been in France; when he had first heard of the insurrection; whether he had had any previous knowledge of it; whether he had been in Dublin during it; or whether he had corresponded with persons in France. He refused to say whether he was acquainted with a number of persons whose names were put to him; whether he would identify his handwriting; whether he had seen the proclamation of the provisional government in various forms. He was then asked: 'By whom are the letters written that were found on your person?' He replied 'As to the letters taken out of my possession by Major Sirr, how can I avoid this being brought forward?'[14]

This was the turning point of the interrogation and, indeed, of the whole case against Emmet. At the time of his arrest he had been in possession of unsigned letters from Sarah Curran, daughter of the famous nationalist lawyer and politician John Philpot Curran. They appeared to be love letters, though the crown did not accept them at face value. She had particularly asked him to destroy them but he had not done so. Emmet was also in possession of some locks of her hair which he, in some distracted state, thought might also lead to her identification. When the letters were referred before the Privy Council Emmet immediately began speaking volubly. He asked whether 'anything has been done in consequence of those letters being taken? May I learn what means, or what has been done to them?' On being told that this was not possible he said:

> You must, gentlemen, be sensible as to how disagreeable it would be to one of yourselves to have a delicate and virtuous female brought into notice. What means would be necessary to bring the evidence in those letters forward without bringing the name forward? Might the passages in those letters be read to me?

He eventually said, 'I would rather give up my own life than injure another person.'[15]

In this and later stages of the examination before the Privy Council Emmet sought to appeal to conventional contemporary notions of honour. The attorney general rather graciously said, 'We know before you came into the room that this would be the line you would take.'[16] Emmet then effectively prefigured the arrangement subsequently come to, saying:

> I am glad you have had that opinion of me. Have any proceedings been taken on those letters? I will mention as near as I can the line I mean to adopt. I will go so far as this: if I have assurances that nothing has been done, and nothing will be done, upon those letters I will do everything consistent with honour to prevent their production . . . I would do anything to prevent the production of those letters . . . [W]ith notions of honour in common persons may have different principles but all might be agreed as to what a person might owe to a female. Personal safety would weigh nothing if the production of those letters could be prevented.[17]

Although this seems very plain in hindsight, the extraordinary fact is that the prosecutors and Emmet were at cross purposes. The government men were firmly of the opinion that, 'The language of a love intrigue had been assumed as a means of misleading the government.'[18] They thought the letters were military communications in a cipher that had not been cracked and which had actually been penned by Emmet's sister on the instructions of some other conspirator. This appears from a note later added by the under secretary to the record of the interrogation, in order to explain the apparent obtuseness of the interrogators to the British Home Office.

The interrogators then used two techniques to turn up the pressure on Emmet. First, the attorney general said that the letters 'formed evidence against the person who wrote them'. Emmet, in what was very definitely a pre-feminist attempt to exculpate Sarah Curran, replied that

> I can only say that a woman's sentiments are only opinions and they are not reality. When a man gives opinions it is supposed that he has actions accordingly; but with a women the utmost limit is only opinion. I declare on my honour as a man that the person had only opinions.[19]

Emmet refused, however, to make any specific disclosures about the insurrection, but said that he would consider what he might do if he could have an interview with a named lawyer. This was refused. He was reminded of the disclosure made by Thomas Addis Emmet and William McNeven in 1798, but said the two cases were different. At the end of the interrogation he was asked whether he would like the author of the letters to be produced before him. He took this as an indication that Sarah Curran was already in custody and the interview ended with the lord chancellor observing that 'Mr Emmet's feelings are a good deal affected'.[20]

On 7 September Emmet was arraigned and pleaded not guilty. He nominated John Philpot Curran as his counsel and Leonard MacNally, a son of the barrister, as his solicitor. The next day, in an extraordinarily ill-advised move, he was sufficiently distracted to write a letter to Sarah Curran under her own name and at her father's address. This he entrusted to a prison warder whom he thought was trustworthy: it was immediately placed in the hands of the authorities. The result of this was a raid led by Major Sirr on the Curran household, the Priory, Rathfarnham, in the course of which Sarah seems to have suffered a sudden nervous collapse. Ironically, the principal subject of the letter was his guilt at implicating her by non-destruction of the letters. Upon the belated realisation of the identity of his correspondent, the Castle's anxieties about the trial were at an end. The letters were also regarded as remarkable in themselves, and in the identity of their writer. They were passed for private perusal to the home secretary and to the king himself. The former observed that 'Mademoiselle, seems to be a true disciple of Mary Wollstonecraft.'[21]

An immediate consequence of these things was that John Philpot Curran, in a terse and frigid letter, withdrew as Emmet's counsel. He did not refer in detail to the reasons for this but suggested 'That if those circumstances be not brought forward by the crown, which from their humanity I hope will be suppressed, it cannot be of any advantage to you to disclose them to your agent or counsel.' This, undoubtedly, was Curran attempting to protect his own position, and perhaps not unreasonably so. But it is clear from MacNally's secret dispatches that government had made him fully aware of Sarah Curran's compromised position. Curran had in fact been ordered by the lord lieutenant to withdraw as Emmet's counsel, but it must be said that he could scarcely have continued to act with propriety, since vigorous defence, such as he had often provided for other prisoners, might have led to his daughter's public exposure. Emmet wrote him a long letter in reply. Most of it was devoted to an attempt to exonerate Sarah in her father's eyes. He also, very generously, stated that he had not expected Curran to be his counsel, and 'I nominated you because not to have done so might have appeared remarkable.'[22] Responding to the tone rather than the content of Curran's note, he memorably said: 'A man with the coldness of death on him need not be made to feel any other coldness.'[23] Leonard MacNally and Peter Burrowes were nominated as alternative counsel. Having regard to other state prisoners' choice of counsel in September 1803 and for many years before that, it was entirely predictable that if Curran dropped out, MacNally would replace him.

It unfortunately appears that Curran was severely compromised, politically and professionally, by the revelation of his daughter's romance. One of MacNally's secret dispatches records that he was very unpopular in radical circles because of his refusal of Emmet's brief. He returned his other rebellion briefs. The reason for this is more than hinted at in a Dublin Castle memorandum of 2 October 1803. Speaking of a pending case which raised a point embarrassing to the government it said: 'I am very sorry to think we are likely to have this question brought forward, but there is no avoiding it in the circumstances. It is fortunate that Mr Curran is completely in our power.'[24]

When Curran's political allies unexpectedly came into power at Westminster in 1806, the Whig grandees felt that 'the transaction between Mr Curran's daughter and Robert Emmet' made his appointment to political office impossible. So untouchable was he that Henry Grattan, with grim humour, suggested that he be made an Irish bishop. He was eventually made master of the rolls in Ireland, an office which was then only quasi-judicial and had recently been held by a layman. He did not shine in it and resigned, miserably, in 1814.

Once the interception of the letter to Sarah Curran became known to him, Emmet apparently thought of nothing but how to protect her. Leonard MacNally in one of his reports to the Castle said:

> On this subject his mind seems wholly bent, and cruelly afflicted. For his own personal safety he appears not to entertain an idea. He does not intend to call a single witness, nor to trouble any witness for the Crown with a cross-examination, unless they misrepresent facts. [He will not] controvert the charge by calling a single witness.[25]

This is, of course, an extraordinary letter for a defending counsel to write to the prosecution before the trial. It is confirmed by what the other counsel involved, Peter Burrowes, told Thomas Moore thirty years later: that Emmet had 'made the most earnest entreaties to the government that if they suppressed the letters in the trial he would not say a word in his defence but go to his death in silence'.[26]

EFFECT OF THE CROWN'S BLACKMAIL

That an agreement was in fact to come along the lines suggested is evidenced by two things in particular that happened in the course of the trial. The attorney general in opening the case actually quoted a passage from one of Sarah Curran's letters in which she raised the question of whether French assistance was or was not desirable. This, however, he ascribed to 'a *brother* contributor acquainted with his schemes and participating in his crimes'.[27] He also quoted a passage suggesting the view that the Irish people were 'incapable of redress and unworthy of it', and that this accounted for the rebellion's failure.

The other revealing event occurred during the evidence of Major Sirr. He said that he had found certain letters on Emmet at the time of his arrest. The letters were produced and laid on the table of the court. Lord Norbury said: 'If the prisoner wishes to have any other part of these papers read' (other, that is, than the part already read by the attorney general) 'he may'. This appears to be a judicial intervention of the utmost fairness, but its true significance is apparent from the response of Peter Burrowes, Emmet's uncompromised defence counsel, who said: 'My Lord, the prisoner is aware of that, and throughout the trial will act under that knowledge'. Emmet was being reminded of what precisely his position was and that any attempt at defence would lead to Sarah Curran's exposure. Immediately afterwards, Burrowes attempted to address the jury but, according to what he later told Thomas Moore, Emmet stopped him from doing so, saying: 'Pray do not attempt to defend me – it is all in vain.'[28]

Just before the last-mentioned intervention the attorney general had attempted to make Sirr read from a very incriminating letter to the government allegedly found in the room where Emmet had been arrested. No objection was taken but the court intervened saying that 'nothing can be read but what is legally proved', an attitude which of course was embarrassing to the prosecution since they had no proof of handwriting. Extraordinarily, MacNally declared that no objection was being taken to the admissibility of the letter. Norbury said that the court had wanted to protect Emmet from the admission of any evidence 'which is not strictly legal' but having consulted with his colleagues after MacNally's intervention, admitted it.[29]

Any possibility that the attorney general's misrepresentation of the sex of Emmet's correspondent might have been accidental is removed by a letter from the chief secretary to the British Home Office on the day of the trial, where he said:

> Mister Yorke [the home secretary] will have observed that the attorney general when he gave in evidence such parts of the young lady's letter found upon Emmet as it was found necessary to produce, stated boldly that the letter from which the extract was made had been written by a *brother* conspirator.[30]

The word brother was underlined in the original. He went on to say that information about the true identity of the correspondent might leak out but that it was important that it should not be seen to do so from the government in either country.

It is accordingly clear that, before the trial, the government had ensured that Emmet would make no attempt to defend himself. The seeds of this arrangement, which was quite improper but which Emmet was very willing to come to, were to be found in the recorded notes of the interrogation before the Privy Council. The fruits of this arrangement are clear from the trial itself. It is probable, though the details are at this stage irrecoverable, that the arrangement was finalised by and through MacNally.

As a result of this arrangement the government were able to introduce in evidence without objection highly incriminating documents which they were admittedly unable to prove in the manner required by law. If this had not occurred, then, even on the government's own view, they were liable to lose the case.

They were also able to supplement this evidence with that of three witnesses, Fleming, Colgan and Farrell, who had been in the depot of Thomas Street, which had been Emmet's headquarters immediately before the insurrection, to identify him as having been there in a position of authority. The first of these, Fleming, had been thoroughly involved in the rebellion of his own admission. He said of Emmet: 'He was the headman of it. He gave directions to Quigley, and he to the others.' Fleming was a painfully weak witness who claimed that he had 'given himself up to the government to become a good subject'.[31] He said he had come to no arrangement with them and could not say whether or not he expected to be prosecuted. He was precisely the sort of witness who, in other trials arising from the insurrection, had been devastatingly cross-examined by advocates such as John Philpot Curran, but of whom no serious attempt was made to examine his account.

The next witness, Colgan, was a tailor who claimed that he had been drinking in a neighbouring public house and fallen asleep. He then woke up in a dark outhouse where he was forced to work for the rebels making uniforms. He put Emmet in the depot. He admitted that he would not have given evidence or information if he had not been arrested himself. At the end of his brief evidence he contradicted himself by saying to a juror who enquired, presumably struck by the incredibility of his story of having been shanghaied while in a drunken slumber, that he had actually fallen asleep not in the public house, but in the depot.

The last witness of this sort was Patrick Farrell, who genuinely had stumbled on the depot a day or two before the insurrection and had been held there against his will. It will be remembered that this was the man who, according to Chief Secretary Wickham's letter, had been unable to identify Emmet when given the opportunity to do so between 25 and 28 August. He now identified him clearly and without doubt. It seems manifest that the process of identification could have been explored and perhaps challenged, but no attempt was made to do so. Instead – incredibly – MacNally cross-examined only to establish that he had been well treated while he was held, and that he had heard no discussion of French aid amongst the rebels. He actually apologised for doing so much: 'At the express wish of my client, I shall be excused in putting such questions as he suggests to me, and which will be considered as coming directly from him.'[32]

Two prisoners were acquitted in the 1803 commission because identifying witnesses had collapsed on cross-examination. Not to cross-examine here was virtual acquiescence in a conviction.

Emmet had been known to the government since his brother's participation in the United Irishmen in 1798 and his own expulsion from Trinity College following the celebrated visitation to the College by the lord chancellor in that year. But he was not a major, publicly known agitator in the intervening period and there had been no great hue and cry for him specifically after the insurrection. He had not been identified, for example, as the gorgeously uniformed figure leading the rebels along Thomas Street. The direct evidence of his involvement was remarkably weak and came from very questionable sources. Both the opening and closing prosecution speeches heavily relied on the documents which – albeit that they were legally unproven – could be attributed to him because his counsel failed to object to them or actually invited their admission. MacNally's annual pension from the government in respect of his work as an informer amounted to £300 a year. For his actions and failures to act in the Emmet case he was paid a special bonus of £200. He died in 1820 with his activities still unrevealed: it was the extraordinary act of his family in seeking to have his pension continued after his death which alerted a later historian, W. J. Fitzpatrick, to his double life. Of his bonus £100 was paid on 14 September 1803, five days before the trial: it is tempting to link this with his conveying an absolute assurance that the trial would be a walkover.

TREASON

One of the most obvious defects in the defence of Robert Emmet was the omission to take any issue at all as to whether the activities of Emmet actually constituted treason, as alleged in the first count of the indictment. Treason had always been a controversial charge because of its peculiar constitution in English law. It was the first common law offence to obtain statutory definition, in the year 1351 under a statute of King Edward III. Ironically, this was introduced because the vagueness of the offence at common law made it a valuable and flexible weapon. Accordingly, count 1 of the indictment against Emmet charged treason in the classic form, that of 'compassing or imagining the death of the King'. This mental act was the offence: specific overt acts, as in the offence of conspiracy, were merely the evidence of it. Over the centuries, there had been a tension between a narrow interpretation requiring an actual intention physically to kill the king, and a broader approach, whether statutory or otherwise, which validated an offence of constructive treason whereby an intention to imprison, depose or restrain the king was regarded as including an intent to kill him.

The 1790s were a time of considerable radical activity in England as well as in Ireland. In 1794 there was a great state trial of persons concerned with the London Corresponding Society, a group favouring universal suffrage, annual parliaments, and, it was alleged, the overthrow of the king. In the trial for high treason of its leader, Thomas Hardy, the prosecution and defence were conducted by two luminaries of the English bar, Lord Eldon and Thomas Erskine respectively. Eldon contended that it was sufficient if the persons performing the overt acts intended 'to put the King in circumstances in which, according to the ordinary experiences of mankind, his life would be in danger'. Erskine contended for a literal construction of the Act, as requiring an intention physically to kill the king. He admitted that an intention to depose was something which entitled the jury to draw an inference that the prisoner intended to kill the king, but said that this was a matter for the jury, and that unless they did draw that inference, Hardy could not be convicted of treason even though he had, by an overt act, manifested an intention to depose the king. Chief Justice Eyre then left the issue of intention to the jury. This was not done in Emmet's case, where the jury was simply told that if they accepted the evidence of the witnesses the offence of treason was complete. This deprived Emmet of the very point on which Hardy and his colleagues were acquitted.

Immediately following their acquittals, Pitt's government introduced an act, 36 George III, Chapter VII, which extended the definition of treason from compassing the death of the king to compassing, imagining or intending his death, destruction, or any bodily harm tending to death or destruction, maiming, wounding, imprisonment, or restraining the person of the king, or levying war with him in order to change his policy, or in order to overawe either or both of the Houses of Parliament. It also criminalised conspiring with any foreigner to invade any part of the king's dominions. This would certainly have encompassed Emmet's acts as we know them. *But this Act did not apply in Ireland.*

In the Irish state trials between 1798 and 1803 a much broader definition of treason than that available at English common law was used: specifically, the question of intent to kill the king was regarded by the judges as conclusively proven by proof of an act of rebellion or an intention to depose, and never left to the jury. In his *History of the Common Law*, Sir James Fitzjames Stephens wrote: 'The doctrine against which Erskine is supposed to have prevailed in the trials of 1794 was applied to many later cases without hesitation. This occurred in the trials for the Irish Rebellion in 1798 and in particular of two brothers, Henry and John Sheares.' That is the very point: the cases in which the English decision of 1794 was ignored were all Irish cases.

The statute of 1795 also required that the overt acts of treason be proved by not less than two witnesses. In the case against the Sheares brothers there was only one relevant witness, the notorious felon setter Captain Armstrong. When this point was taken by Curran on their behalf, the Irish court held that the requirement for two witnesses arose by statute only, and in England only and not in Ireland. That is, that the act of 1795 did not apply here. Fifty years later, when the Treason Felony Act of 1848 was introduced after the rebellion of that year it was stated that 'doubts were entertained whether the provisions [of the said 1795 Act] extended to Ireland'. This is an understatement, since it is perfectly clear from the decision of Lord Carleton in the Sheares case that they had been positively held not to apply.

It should also be noted that, in relation to Irish cases, there was an additional difficulty in maintaining a constructive intention to kill the king from an act of rebellion in Ireland. King George III had never resided in or even visited Ireland. In the English state trials Lord Eldon had contended that deposing the king endangered his life 'according to the ordinary experiences of mankind'. This is, of course,much harder to maintain if the overt acts of rebellion take place on a different island. But that point, too, was ignored.

The Irish lord chancellor in 1803, Lord Redesdale, had, as Sir John Mitford, solicitor general of England, been one of the counsel for the prosecution in Hardy's case and was thus fully aware of the points taken there and of the amending legislation which he had advocated in Parliament. It is extraordinary that no attempt was made in Emmet's case to argue a point as to whether the overt tangible acts amounted to proof of treason. The procedure in such cases was to seek a respite of sentence to argue a point of law on writ of error before the king's bench, of which the Commission of Oyer and Terminer was a division. This was frequently done in the late eighteenth century in ordinary criminal cases turning on bare technicalities of law, but MacNally made no attempt whatever to do so.

Notes

1 'Contrary to legend it was a fair trial', Marianne Elliott, *Robert Emmet: The Making of a Legend* (London, 2003), p. 78.

2 Patrick M. Geoghegan, *Robert Emmet: A Life*, 2nd edn (Dublin, 2004), p. 252.

3 Elliott, *Robert Emmet*, p. 69.

4 Michael MacDonagh, *The Viceroy's Postbag* (London, 1904), p. 335.

5 Elliott, *Robert Emmet*, p. 79.

6 Maurice R. O'Connell (ed.), *The Correspondence of Daniel O'Connell*, 8 vols (Dublin, 1972–80), III, p. 323.

7 William Wickham to Pole Carew, 28 Aug. 1803, MacDonagh, *Viceroy's Postbag*, p. 339.

8 Ibid., pp. 339–40.

9 Ibid., p. 339.

10 Ibid., p. 340.

11 Ibid., p. 397.

12 Hardwicke to Charles Yorke, 20 Sept. 1803, ibid., p. 397.

13 Ibid., p. 347.

14 Ibid., pp 348–9.

15 Ibid., p. 349.

16 Ibid.

17 Ibid.

18 Ibid., p. 351.

19 Ibid., p. 350.

20 Ibid., p. 352.
21 Ibid., p. 361.
22 Robert Emmet to John Philpot Curran, 12 Sept. 1803, ibid., p. 391.
23 Ibid., p. 393.
24 Elliott, *Robert Emmet*, p. 92.
25 Report of Leonard MacNally, 12 Sept. 1803, MacDonagh, *Viceroy's Postbag*, p. 390.
26 Geoghegan, *Robert Emmet*, p. 221.
27 Ibid., p. 230.
28 Elliott, *Robert Emmet*, p. 79.
29 Geoghegan, *Robert Emmet*, p. 239.
30 MacDonagh, *Viceroy's Postbag*, p. 398.
31 William Ridgeway, *A report of the proceedings in cases of high treason at a court of oyer and terminer* (Dublin, 1803), p. 103.
32 Geoghegan, *Robert Emmet*, p. 235.
33 Ibid., introduction.
34 R. F. Foster, *Modern Ireland 1600–1972* (London, 1988), p. 286.
35 *Irish Times*, 24 July 2003.
36 Geoghegan, *Robert Emmet*, Appendix C.
37 Ibid., p. 250.
38 Ibid., p. 252.
39 Ibid.
40 Ibid., p. 253.
41 Ibid., p. 254.
42 Ibid., p. 266.
43 PRONI, T/2627/5/Z/13.
44 Robert Emmet to William Wickham, 20 Sept. 1803 (BL, Add. MSS MS35742, f. 196).
45 Ibid.
46 PRONI, T/2627/5/Z/12.
47 Geoghegan, *Robert Emmet*, p. 271.
48 PRONI, T/2627/5/Z/18.
49 William Wickham to Armstrong, 20 Nov. 1835 (PRONI, T/2627/5/Z/12).
50 Ibid.
51 See Elizabeth Sparrow, *Secret Service* (London, 1999).

Index